GRAMMAR AND BEYOND

Laurie Blass
Susan Iannuzzi
Alice Savage
Deborah Gordon
with Randi Reppen

3B

CAMBRIDGE
UNIVERSITY PRESS

CAMBRIDGE
UNIVERSITY PRESS

University Printing House, Cambridge CB2 8BS, United Kingdom

One Liberty Plaza, 20th Floor, New York, NY 10006, USA

477 Williamstown Road, Port Melbourne, VIC 3207, Australia

314–321, 3rd Floor, Plot 3, Splendor Forum, Jasola District Centre, New Delhi – 110025, India

79 Anson Road, #06–04/06, Singapore 079906

Cambridge University Press is part of the University of Cambridge.

It furthers the University's mission by disseminating knowledge in the pursuit of education, learning and research at the highest international levels of excellence.

www.cambridge.org
Information on this title: www.cambridge.org/9780521143196

First published 2012
20 19 18 17 16 15 14 13

Printed in Dubai by Oriental Press

A catalog record for this publication is available from the British Library.

ISBN 978-0-521-14298-4 Student's Book 3
ISBN 978-0-521-14315-8 Student's Book 3A
ISBN 978-0-521-14319-6 Student's Book 3B
ISBN 978-1-107-60197-0 Workbook 3
ISBN 978-1-107-60198-7 Workbook 3A
ISBN 978-1-107-60199-4 Workbook 3B
ISBN 978-1-107-68502-4 Teacher Support Resource Book with CD-ROM 3
ISBN 978-0-521-14339-4 Class Audio CD 3
ISBN 978-1-139-06187-2 Writing Skills Interactive 3

Art direction, book design, layout services, and photo research: Integra
Audio production: John Marshall Media

Contents

Introduction to *Grammar and Beyond*   vii

About the Authors   xi

Acknowledgments   xii

Tour of a Unit   xiv

PART 7 Questions and Noun Clauses

UNIT 14 Negative Questions and Tag Questions Geographic Mobility   **190**

Negative Questions   192

Tag Questions   194

Grammar for Writing: Using Negative Questions and Tag Questions in Blogs   200

UNIT 15 *That* **Clauses Cultural Values**   **202**

That Clauses   204

Agreement Between *That* Clauses and Main Clauses   207

That Clauses After Adjectives and Nouns   210

Grammar for Writing: Using *That* Clauses to State Reasons, Conclusions,
Research Results, Opinions, and Feelings   214

UNIT 16 Noun Clauses with *Wh-* **Words and** *If/Whether*

Inventions They Said Would Never Work   **216**

Noun Clauses with *Wh-* Words   217

Noun Clauses with *If/Whether*   220

Noun Clauses in Direct and Indirect Questions   223

Grammar for Writing: Using Noun Clauses with *Wh-* Words and *If/Whether*   226

PART 8 Indirect Speech

UNIT 17 Direct Speech and Indirect Speech Human Motivation   **228**

Direct Speech   230

Indirect Speech   233

Indirect Speech Without Tense Shift   236

Other Reporting Verbs   238

Grammar for Writing: Using Descriptive Reporting Verbs   242

**UNIT 18 Indirect Questions; Indirect Imperatives,
Requests, and Advice Creative Problem Solving**   **244**

Indirect Questions   245

Indirect Imperatives, Requests, and Advice   248

Grammar for Writing: Using Indirect Questions, Imperatives, Requests,
and Advice   252

PART 9 The Passive

UNIT 19 The Passive (1) **English as a Global Language**   254
    Active vs. Passive Sentences   256
    Verbs and Objects with the Passive   260
    Reasons for Using the Passive   263
    Grammar for Writing: Using the Passive to Write About the Object
              of an Action   266

UNIT 20 The Passive (2) **Food Safety**   268
    The Passive with *Be Going To* and Modals   269
    Get Passives   273
    Passive Gerunds and Infinitives   276
    Grammar for Writing: Using the Passive with Modals, Gerunds, and Infinitives 280

PART 10 Relative Clauses (Adjective Clauses)

UNIT 21 Subject Relative Clauses (Adjective Clauses with Subject
Relative Pronouns) **Alternative Energy Sources**   282
    Identifying Subject Relative Clauses   283
    Nonidentifying Subject Relative Clauses   287
    Subject Relative Clauses with *Whose*   290
    Grammar for Writing: Using Subject Relative Clauses to Avoid Repetition   294

UNIT 22 Object Relative Clauses (Adjective Clauses with Object
Relative Pronouns) **Biometrics**   296
    Identifying Object Relative Clauses   297
    Nonidentifying Object Relative Clauses   300
    Object Relative Clauses as Objects of Prepositions   302
    Grammar for Writing: Using Object Relative Clauses to Provide
              Background Information   306

UNIT 23 Relative Clauses with *Where* and *When*; Reduced
Relative Clauses **Millennials**   308
    Relative Clauses with *Where* and *When*   310
    Reduced Relative Clauses   314
    Grammar for Writing: Using Reduced Subject Relative Clauses to
              Make Ideas Clearer   320

PART 11 Conditionals

UNIT 24 Real Conditionals: Present and Future

Media in the United States	**322**
Present Real Conditionals	323
Future Real Conditionals	327
Real Conditionals with Modals, Modal-like Expressions, and Imperatives	330
Grammar for Writing: Using a Single *If* Clause with Multiple Main Clauses	334

UNIT 25 Unreal Conditionals: Present, Future, and Past

Natural Disasters	**336**
Present and Future Unreal Conditionals	337
Past Unreal Conditionals	341
Wishes About the Present, Future, and Past	345
Grammar for Writing: Using *If* Clauses to Support Ideas	348

PART 12 Connecting Ideas

UNIT 26 Conjunctions **Globalization of Food**

	350
Connecting Words and Phrases with Conjunctions	352
Connecting Sentences with Coordinating Conjunctions	356
Reducing Sentences with Similar Clauses	360
Grammar for Writing: Using Coordinating and Correlative Conjunctions to Join Words and Clauses	364

UNIT 27 Adverb Clauses and Phrases **Consumerism**

	366
Subordinators and Adverb Clauses	368
Reducing Adverb Clauses	371
Subordinators to Express Purpose	373
Grammar for Writing: Using Adverb Clauses to Give More Information About Main Clauses	376

UNIT 28 Connecting Information with Prepositions and Transitions **Technology in Entertainment**

	378
Connecting Information with Prepositions and Prepositional Phrases	379
Connecting Information with Transition Words	382
Grammar for Writing: Using Prepositions and Transition Words to Support an Argument	388

Appendices

1 Irregular Verbs   A1

2 Stative (Non-Action) Verbs   A2

3 Modals and Modal-like Expressions   A3

4 Noncount Nouns and Measurement Words to Make Noncount Nouns Countable   A5

5 Order of Adjectives Before Nouns   A6

6 Verbs That Can Be Used Reflexively   A6

7 Verbs Followed by Gerunds Only   A7

8 Verbs Followed by Infinitives Only   A7

9 Verbs Followed by Gerunds or Infinitives   A7

10 Expressions with Gerunds   A8

11 Verbs + Objects + Infinitives   A8

12 *Be* + Adjectives + Infinitives   A9

13 Verbs + Prepositions   A9

14 Adjectives + Prepositions   A10

15 Verbs and Fixed Expressions that Introduce Indirect Questions   A10

16 Tense Shifting in Indirect Speech   A11

17 Reporting Verbs   A11

18 Passive Forms   A12

19 Relative Clauses   A13

20 Conditionals   A15

21 Academic Word List (AWL) Words and Definitions   A16

22 Pronunciation Table International Phonetic Alphabet (IPA)   A24

Glossary of Grammar Terms   G1

Index   I1

Art Credits   I9

Introduction to *Grammar and Beyond*

Grammar and Beyond is a research-based and content-rich grammar series for beginning- to advanced-level students of North American English. The series focuses on the grammar structures most commonly used in North American English, with an emphasis on the application of these grammar structures to academic writing. The series practices all four skills in a variety of authentic and communicative contexts. It is designed for use both in the classroom and as a self-study learning tool.

Grammar and Beyond Is Research-Based

The grammar presented in this series is informed by years of research on the grammar of written and spoken North American English as it is used in college lectures, textbooks, academic essays, high school classrooms, and conversations between instructors and students. This research, and the analysis of over one billion words of authentic written and spoken language data known as the *Cambridge International Corpus*, has enabled the authors to:

- Present grammar rules that accurately represent how North American English is actually spoken and written
- Identify and teach differences between the grammar of written and spoken English
- Focus more attention on the structures that are commonly used, and less attention on those that are rarely used, in written and spoken North American English
- Help students avoid the most common mistakes that English language learners make
- Choose reading and writing topics that will naturally elicit examples of the target grammar structure
- Introduce important vocabulary from the Academic Word List

Grammar and Beyond Teaches Academic Writing Skills

Grammar and Beyond helps students make the transition from understanding grammar structures to applying them in their academic writing.

In the Student's Books

At Levels 1 through 3 of the series, every Student's Book unit ends with a section devoted to the hands-on application of grammar to writing. This section, called Grammar for Writing, explores how and where the target grammar structures function in writing and offers controlled practice, exposure to writing models, and a guided but open-ended writing task.

At Level 4, the most advanced level, the syllabus is organized around the academic essay types that college students write (e.g., persuasive, cause and effect) and is aimed at teaching students the grammar, vocabulary, and writing skills that they need in order to be successful at writing those kinds of essays.

Online

Grammar and Beyond also offers *Writing Skills Interactive*, an interactive online course in academic writing skills and vocabulary that correlates with the Student's Books. Each unit of the writing skills course focuses on a specific writing skill, such as avoiding sentence fragments or developing strong topic sentences.

Special Features of *Grammar and Beyond*

Realistic Grammar Presentations

Grammar is presented in clear and simple charts. The grammar points presented in these charts have been tested against real-world data from the *Cambridge International Corpus* to ensure that they are authentic representations of actual use of North American English.

Data from the Real World

Many of the grammar presentations and application sections in the Student's Book include a feature called Data from the Real World, in which concrete and useful points discovered through analysis of corpus data are presented. These points are practiced in the exercises that follow.

Avoid Common Mistakes

Each Student's Book unit features an Avoid Common Mistakes section that develops students' awareness of the most common mistakes made by English language learners and gives them an opportunity to practice detecting and correcting these errors in running text. This section helps students avoid these mistakes in their own work. The mistakes highlighted in this section are drawn from a body of authentic data on learner English known as the *Cambridge Learner Corpus*, a database of over 35 million words from student essays written by nonnative speakers of English and information from experienced classroom teachers.

Academic Vocabulary

Every unit in *Grammar and Beyond* includes words from the Academic Word List (AWL), a research-based list of words and word families that appear with high frequency in English-language academic texts. These words are introduced in the opening text of the unit, recycled in the charts and exercises, and used to support the theme throughout the unit. The same vocabulary items are reviewed and practiced in *Writing Skills Interactive*, the online writing skills course. By the time students finish each level, they will have been exposed several times to a carefully selected set of level-appropriate AWL words, as well as content words from a variety of academic disciplines.

Series Levels

The following table provides a general idea of the difficulty of the material at each level of *Grammar and Beyond*. These are not meant to be interpreted as precise correlations.

	Description	TOEFL IBT	CEFR Levels
Level 1	beginning	20 – 34	A1 – A2
Level 2	low intermediate to intermediate	35 – 54	A2 – B1
Level 3	high intermediate	55 – 74	B1 – B2
Level 4	advanced	75 – 95	B2 – C1

Components for Students

Student's Book

The Student's Books for Levels 1 through 3 teach all of the grammar points appropriate at each level in short, manageable cycles of presentation and practice organized around a high-interest unit theme. The Level 4 Student's Book focuses on the structure of the academic essay in addition to the grammar rules, conventions, and structures that students need to master in order to be successful college writers. Please see the Tour of a Unit on pages xiv–xvii for a more detailed view of the contents and structure of the Student's Book units.

Workbook

The Workbook provides additional practice of the grammar presented in each unit of the Student's Book. The exercises offer both discrete and consolidated practice of grammar points and can be used for homework or in class. Each unit also offers practice correcting the errors highlighted in the Avoid Common Mistakes section in the Student's Book to help students master these troublesome errors. Self-Assessment sections at the end of each unit allow students to test their mastery of what they have learned.

Writing Skills Interactive

This online course provides graduated instruction and practice in writing skills, while reinforcing vocabulary presented in the Student's Books. Each unit includes a vocabulary review activity, followed by a short text that builds on the theme presented in the Student's Book and provides an additional context for the vocabulary. The text is followed by an animated interactive presentation of the target writing skill of the unit, after which students have the opportunity to practice the target skill in three different activities. Each unit closes with a quiz, which allows students to assess their progress.

Teacher Resources

Teacher Support Resource Book with CD-ROM

This comprehensive book provides a range of support materials for instructors, including:

- Suggestions for applying the target grammar to all four major skill areas, helping instructors facilitate dynamic and comprehensive grammar classes
- An answer key and audio script for the Student's Book
- A CD-ROM containing:
  - Ready-made, easily scored Unit Tests
  - PowerPoint presentations to streamline lesson preparation and encourage lively heads-up interaction

Class Audio CD

The class audio CD for each level provide the Student's Book listening material for in-class use.

Teacher Support Website

www.cambridge.org/grammarandbeyond

The website for *Grammar and Beyond* contains even more resources for instructors, including:

- Unit-by-unit teaching tips, helping instructors plan their lessons
- Downloadable communicative activities to add more in-class speaking practice
- A monthly newsletter on grammar teaching, providing ongoing professional development

We hope you enjoy using this series, and we welcome your feedback! Please send any comments to the authors and editorial staff at Cambridge University Press, at grammarandbeyond@cambridge.org.

About the Authors

Laurie Blass has more than 25 years' experience teaching and creating materials for ESL students in the United States and abroad. She is currently a full-time materials developer with a special interest in ESL for academic success and educational technology. Laurie is co-author of *Writers at Work: From Sentence to Paragraph*, published by Cambridge University Press, among many other titles.

Susan Iannuzzi has been teaching ESL for more than 20 years. She has trained English teachers on five continents and consulted on the national English curricula for countries in Africa, Asia, and the Middle East. She has authored or co-authored more than 10 English courses in use today. *Grammar and Beyond* is her first publication with Cambridge University Press.

Alice Savage is an English Language Teacher and Materials Writer. She attended the School for International Training in Vermont and is an author on the *Read This!* series, published by Cambridge University Press. She lives in Houston, Texas with her husband and two children.

Deborah Gordon, creator of the Grammar for Writing sections, has more than 25 years' experience teaching ESL students and training ESL teachers in the United States and abroad. She is currently an ESL instructor at Santa Barbara City College and a TESOL Certificate instructor at the University of California, Santa Barbara Extension. Deborah is coauthor of *Writers at Work: From Sentence to Paragraph*, published by Cambridge University Press, among many other titles.

 Randi Reppen is Professor of Applied Linguistics and TESL at Northern Arizona University (NAU) in Flagstaff, Arizona. She has over 20 years' experience teaching ESL students and training ESL teachers, including 11 years as the Director of NAU's Program in Intensive English. Randi's research interests focus on the use of corpora for language teaching and materials development. In addition to numerous academic articles and books, she is the author of *Using Corpora in the Language Classroom* and a co-author of *Basic Vocabulary in Use*, 2nd edition, both published by Cambridge University Press.

Advisory Panel

The ESL advisory panel has helped to guide the development of this series and provided invaluable information about the needs of ESL students and teachers in high schools, colleges, universities, and private language schools throughout North America.

Neta Simpkins Cahill, Skagit Valley College, Mount Vernon, WA

Shelly Hedstrom, Palm Beach State College, Lake Worth, FL

Richard Morasci, Foothill College, Los Altos Hills, CA

Stacey Russo, East Hampton High School, East Hampton, NY

Alice Savage, North Harris College, Houston, TX

Acknowledgments

The publisher and authors would like to thank these reviewers and consultants for their insights and participation:

Marty Attiyeh, The College of DuPage, Glen Ellyn, IL

Shannon Bailey, Austin Community College, Austin, TX

Jamila Barton, North Seattle Community College, Seattle, WA

Kim Bayer, Hunter College IELI, New York, NY

Linda Berendsen, Oakton Community College, Skokie, IL

Anita Biber, Tarrant County College Northwest, Fort Worth, TX

Jane Breaux, Community College of Aurora, Aurora, CO

Anna Budzinski, San Antonio College, San Antonio, TX

Britta Burton, Mission College, Santa Clara, CA

Jean Carroll, Fresno City College, Fresno, CA

Chris Cashman, Oak Park High School and Elmwood Park High School, Chicago, IL

Annette M. Charron, Bakersfield College, Bakersfield, CA

Patrick Colabucci, ALI at San Diego State University, San Diego, CA

Lin Cui, Harper College, Palatine, IL

Jennifer Duclos, Boston University CELOP, Boston, MA

Joy Durighello, San Francisco City College, San Francisco, CA

Kathleen Flynn, Glendale Community College, Glendale, CA

Raquel Fundora, Miami Dade College, Miami, FL

Patricia Gillie, New Trier Township High School District, Winnetka, IL

Laurie Gluck, LaGuardia Community College, Long Island City, NY

Kathleen Golata, Galileo Academy of Science & Technology, San Francisco, CA

Ellen Goldman, Mission College, Santa Clara, CA

Ekaterina Goussakova, Seminole Community College, Sanford, FL

Marianne Grayston, Prince George's Community College, Largo, MD

Mary Greiss Shipley, Georgia Gwinnett College, Lawrenceville, GA

Sudeepa Gulati, Long Beach City College, Long Beach, CA

Nicole Hammond Carrasquel, University of Central Florida, Orlando, FL

Vicki Hendricks, Broward College, Fort Lauderdale, FL

Kelly Hernandez, Miami Dade College, Miami, FL

Ann Johnston, Tidewater Community College, Virginia Beach, VA

Julia Karet, Chaffey College, Claremont, CA

Jeanne Lachowski, English Language Institute, University of Utah, Salt Lake City, UT

Noga Laor, Rennert, New York, NY

Min Lu, Central Florida Community College, Ocala, FL

Michael Luchuk, Kaplan International Centers, New York, NY

Craig Machado, Norwalk Community College, Norwalk, CT

Denise Maduli-Williams, City College of San Francisco, San Francisco, CA

Diane Mahin, University of Miami, Coral Gables, FL

Melanie Majeski, Naugatuck Valley Community College, Waterbury, CT

Jeanne Malcolm, University of North Carolina at Charlotte, Charlotte, NC

Lourdes Marx, Palm Beach State College, Boca Raton, FL

Susan G. McFalls, Maryville College, Maryville, TN

Nancy McKay, Cuyahoga Community College, Cleveland, OH

Dominika McPartland, Long Island Business Institute, Flushing, NY

Amy Metcalf, UNR/Intensive English Language Center, University of Nevada, Reno, NV

Robert Miller, EF International Language School San Francisco – Mills, San Francisco, CA

Marcie Pachino, Jordan High School, Durham, NC

Myshie Pagel, El Paso Community College, El Paso, TX

Bernadette Pedagno, University of San Francisco, San Francisco, CA

Tam Q Pham, Dallas Theological Seminary, Fort Smith, AR

Mary Beth Pickett, Global-LT, Rochester, MI

Maria Reamore, Baltimore City Public Schools, Baltimore, MD

Alison M. Rice, Hunter College IELI, New York, NY

Sydney Rice, Imperial Valley College, Imperial, CA

Kathleen Romstedt, Ohio State University, Columbus, OH

Alexandra Rowe, University of South Carolina, Columbia, SC

Irma Sanders, Baldwin Park Adult and Community Education, Baldwin Park, CA

Caren Shoup, Lone Star College – CyFair, Cypress, TX

Karen Sid, Mission College, Foothill College, De Anza College, Santa Clara, CA

Michelle Thomas, Miami Dade College, Miami, FL

Sharon Van Houte, Lorain County Community College, Elyria, OH

Margi Wald, UC Berkeley, Berkeley, CA

Walli Weitz, Riverside County Office of Ed., Indio, CA

Bart Weyand, University of Southern Maine, Portland, ME

Donna Weyrich, Columbus State Community College, Columbus, OH

Marilyn Whitehorse, Santa Barbara City College, Ojai, CA

Jessica Wilson, Rutgers University – Newark, Newark, NJ

Sue Wilson, San Jose City College, San Jose, CA

Margaret Wilster, Mid-Florida Tech, Orlando, FL

Anne York-Herjeczki, Santa Monica College, Santa Monica, CA

Hoda Zaki, Camden County College, Camden, NJ

We would also like to thank these teachers and programs for allowing us to visit:

Richard Appelbaum, Broward College, Fort Lauderdale, FL

Carmela Arnoldt, Glendale Community College, Glendale, AZ

JaNae Barrow, Desert Vista High School, Phoenix, AZ

Ted Christensen, Mesa Community College, Mesa, AZ

Richard Ciriello, Lower East Side Preparatory High School, New York, NY

Virginia Edwards, Chandler-Gilbert Community College, Chandler, AZ

Nusia Frankel, Miami Dade College, Miami, FL

Raquel Fundora, Miami Dade College, Miami, FL

Vicki Hendricks, Broward College, Fort Lauderdale, FL

Kelly Hernandez, Miami Dade College, Miami, FL

Stephen Johnson, Miami Dade College, Miami, FL

Barbara Jordan, Mesa Community College, Mesa, AZ

Nancy Kersten, GateWay Community College, Phoenix, AZ

Lewis Levine, Hostos Community College, Bronx, NY

John Liffiton, Scottsdale Community College, Scottsdale, AZ

Cheryl Lira-Layne, Gilbert Public School District, Gilbert, AZ

Mary Livingston, Arizona State University, Tempe, AZ

Elizabeth Macdonald, Thunderbird School of Global Management, Glendale, AZ

Terri Martinez, Mesa Community College, Mesa, AZ

Lourdes Marx, Palm Beach State College, Boca Raton, FL

Paul Kei Matsuda, Arizona State University, Tempe, AZ

David Miller, Glendale Community College, Glendale, AZ

Martha Polin, Lower East Side Preparatory High School, New York, NY

Patricia Pullenza, Mesa Community College, Mesa, AZ

Victoria Rasinskaya, Lower East Side Preparatory High School, New York, NY

Vanda Salls, Tempe Union High School District, Tempe, AZ

Kim Sanabria, Hostos Community College, Bronx, NY

Cynthia Schuemann, Miami Dade College, Miami, FL

Michelle Thomas, Miami Dade College, Miami, FL

Dongmei Zeng, Borough of Manhattan Community College, New York, NY

Tour of a Unit

Grammar in the Real World presents the unit's grammar in a **realistic** context using **contemporary** texts.

Notice activities draw students' attention to the **structure**, guiding their own **analysis** of form, meaning, and use.

U N I T

4
Past Perfect and Past Perfect Progressive
Nature vs. Nurture

1 Grammar in the Real World

A Have you ever reconnected with someone from your past? Read the web article about twins who lived apart for many years. What surprised the twins when they reconnected?

The Science of Twins

Twins, especially identical[1] twins, have always fascinated scientists. Identical twins develop from one egg, have identical DNA,[2] and are usually very similar in appearance
5 and behavior. There have been many studies of identical twins raised in the same family. There have also been a number of studies of identical twins separated at birth and raised in separate families. These studies have provided
10 interesting information about the impact of *nature* (genetics) and *nurture* (the environment) on the development of the individual. However, some of the studies have been controversial.[3]

Take the case of Elyse Schein and Paula Bernstein. Elyse and Paula were identical twins separated at birth. Both girls knew that their parents **had adopted** them as infants, but
15 neither girl knew about her twin. When Elyse grew up, she longed to meet her biological mother, so she contacted the agency that **had arranged** the adoption. She **had been doing** research on her birth mother when she made a surprising discovery. She had an identical twin. Even more surprising, she learned that she **had been** part of a secret scientific study. At the time of the adoption, the agency **had allowed** different families to
20 adopt each twin. The agency **had told** the families that their child was part of a scientific study. However, it **had** never **told** the families the goal of the study: for scientists to investigate nature versus nurture.

[1]**identical:** exactly the same | [2]**DNA:** the abbreviation for deoxyribonucleic acid, a chemical that controls the structure and purpose of every cell | [3]**controversial:** causing or likely to cause disagreement

When Elyse and Paula finally met as adults, they were amazed. They had many similarities. They looked almost identical. They **had** both **studied** film. They both loved
25 to write. Together, the twins discovered that the researchers **had stopped** the study before the end because the public strongly disapproved of this type of research.

Although that study ended early, many scientists today make a strong case for the dominant[4] role of nature. Schein and Bernstein agree that genetics explains many of their similarities. However, recent research suggests that nurture is equally important. It
30 is clear that the nature versus nurture debate will occupy scientists for years to come.

[4]**dominant:** more important, strong, or noticeable

B *Comprehension Check* Answer the questions.

1. What was surprising about the twins' adoption?
2. What characteristics and interests did Elyse and Paula have in common?
3. What is the nature versus nurture debate?

C *Notice* Underline the verbs in each sentence.

1. Both girls knew that their parents had adopted them as infants.
2. She had been doing research on her birth mother when she made a surprising discovery.
3. Even more surprising, she learned that she had been part of a secret scientific study.

Which event happened first in each sentence? What event followed? Write the verbs. What do you notice about the form of the verbs?

1. First: _____ Then: _____
2. First: _____ Then: _____
3. First: _____ Then: _____

2 Past Perfect

▶ **Grammar Presentation**

The past perfect is used to describe a completed event that happened before another event in the past.	*Elyse finally met her sister, Paula. Paula **had been** married for several years.* (First, Paula got married; Elyse met Paula at a later time.)

The *Grammar Presentation* begins with an **overview** that describes the grammar in an **easy-to-understand** summary.

Charts provide clear guidance on the form, meaning, and use of the target grammar, for **ease of instruction and reference**.

Data from the Real World, a feature **unique** to this series, takes students **beyond traditional information** and teaches them how the unit's grammar is used in authentic situations, including differences between spoken and written use.

2.1 Forming Past Perfect

Form the past perfect with *had* + the past participle of the main verb. Form the negative by adding *not* after *had*. The form is the same for all subjects.

Elyse and Paula did not grow up together. They **had lived** *with different families.*
They were available for adoption because their birthmother **had given** *them up.*
*"**Had** she* **talked** *about the study to anyone at the time?"*
"No, she **hadn't**."
"What **had** *you* **heard** *about this study before that time?"*
*"**I'd heard** very little about it."*

⏴ Irregular Verbs: See page A1.

2.2 Using Past Perfect with Simple Past

a. Use the past perfect to describe an event in a time period that leads up to another past event or time period. Use the simple past to describe the later event or time period.

LATER TIME   EARLIER TIME
She **learned** *that she* **had been** *part of a secret study.*
LATER TIME   EARLIER TIME
The twins **discovered** *that they* **had** *both* **studied** *psychology.*

b. The prepositions *before, by,* or *until* can introduce the later time period.

EARLIER TIME   LATER TIME
Their mother **had known** *about the study before her death.*
EARLIER TIME   LATER TIME
Sue **hadn't met** *her sister until last year.*
EARLIER TIME   LATER TIME
Studies on twins **had become** *common by the 1960s.*

c. The past perfect is often used to give reasons or background information for later past events.

REASON
She was late. She **had forgotten** *to set her alarm clock.*
BACKGROUND INFORMATION   LATER PAST EVENT
He **had** *never* **taken** *a subway before he moved to New York.*

Data from the Real World 🌐

In writing, these verbs are commonly used in the past perfect: *come, have, leave, make,* and *take.*
Had been is the most common past perfect form in speaking and writing.

The twins **had not gone** *to the same school as children.*
The family thought that they **had made** *the right decision.*
Psychologists praised the study because the researchers **had been** *very careful in their work.*
The researchers **had not been** *aware of each other's work on twins until they met.*

▶ **Grammar Application**

Exercise 2.1 Past Perfect

Complete the sentences about twins who met as adults. Use the past perfect form of the verbs in parentheses.

1. Two separate Illinois families ___*had adopted*___ (adopt) Anne Green and Annie Smith before the twins were three days old.
2. When the girls met, they were fascinated by their similarities. For example, they _____ (live) near each other before the Greens moved away.
3. As children, both Anne and Annie _____ (go) to the same summer camp.
4. Anne _____ (not / go) to college, and Annie _____ (not / attend) college, either.
5. Both _____ (marry) for the first time by the age of 22.
6. Anne _____ (get) divorced and _____ (remarry). Annie _____ (not / get) divorced and was still married.
7. Both Anne and Annie were allergic to cats and dogs and _____ never _____ (own) pets.
8. Both _____ (give) the same name – Heather – to their daughters.
9. Both _____ previously _____ (work) in the hospitality industry.
10. Anne _____ (work) as a hotel manager. However, Annie _____ (not / work) in hotels; she _____ (be) a restaurant manager.

Theme-related exercises allow students to **apply the grammar** in a variety of natural contexts.

A **wide variety** of exercises introduce new and stimulating content to keep students engaged with the material.

Students learn to *Avoid Common Mistakes* based on research in student writing.

Exercise 4.2 Past Perfect Progressive, Past Perfect, or Simple Past?

A Complete the interview with a woman who found her three siblings after many years. Use the past perfect progressive, the past perfect, or the simple past form of the verbs in parentheses. Use contractions when possible. Sometimes more than one answer is possible.

Vijay Tell us how you found your family.

Paula I *'d been looking* (look) for my sister all my life. I _____
(1)
_____ (not / have) much luck, though. Then one day, I turned on the TV. A talk show was
(2)
on. The host of the show was interviewing three siblings – two brothers and a half
sister.[1] Different families _____ (adopt) the siblings many
(3)
years before.

Vijay And?

Paula They _____ (talk) about me before I turned on the program.
(4)
The siblings had recently reunited, and they _____ (search)
(5)
for a fourth sibling for the past several months. I called the TV station, and we all
finally _____ (meet).
(6)

Vijay So, you _____ (look) for a sister all your life, and you found
(7)
three siblings!

Paula Yes, it was wonderful! We all met at one of the network offices the following week.
After we _____ (speak) for a while, it was obvious to me that
(8)
they _____ (look) for me all their lives, too.
(9)

[1]**half sister:** a sister who is biologically related by one parent only

B *Pair Work* Discuss these questions with a partner.

- Choose a sentence in A in which you can use either the past perfect or the past perfect progressive. Why are both possible here?
- In which sentence in A is only the past perfect correct?

C *Over to You* Do an online search for twins, siblings, or other family members who reunited after many years. Write five sentences about their experiences. Use the past perfect and the past perfect progressive.

5 Avoid Common Mistakes ⚠

1. **Use the past perfect or past perfect progressive to give background information for a past tense event.**
   had
   I have never seen my sister in real life, so I was nervous the first time we met.
   had been dreaming
   I have dreamed about meeting her, and I finally did.

2. **Use the past perfect or past perfect progressive to give a reason for a past event.**
   had been crying
   Her eyes were red and puffy because she cried.

3. **Use the past perfect (not the past perfect progressive) for a completed earlier event.**
   arranged
   They had been arranging a time to meet, but both of them forgot about it.

4. **Use the past perfect (not present perfect) to describe a completed event that happened before a past event.**
   had
   I have visited her in Maine twice before she came to visit me.

Editing Task

Find and correct seven more mistakes in the paragraphs about sibling differences.

I have never really thought about sibling differences until my own children were
had
born. When we had our first child, my husband and I have lived in Chicago for just a few
months. We have not made many friends yet, so we spent all our time with our child. Baby
Gilbert was happy to be the center of attention. He depended on us for everything.

5   By the time our second son, Chase, was born, we have developed a community of
friends and a busier social life. We frequently visited friends and left the children at home
with a babysitter. As a result of our busy schedules, Chase was more independent. One
day I had just been hanging up the phone when Chase came into the room. Chase picked
up the phone and started talking into it. I thought he was pretending, but I was wrong. He
10 had been figuring out how to use the phone!

When my husband came home, he was tired because he worked all day. When I
told him about Chase's phone conversation, though, he became very excited. Gilbert has
never used the phone as a child. At first, we were surprised that Chase was so different
from Gilbert. Then we realized that because of our busy lifestyles, Chase had learned to be
15 independent.

After studying what **common mistakes** to avoid, students apply the information in **editing tasks**.

Grammar for Writing connects the unit's grammar to specific **applications** in writing.

The final writing exercise **brings everything together** as students apply their knowledge of the unit's grammar in a level-appropriate **writing task.**

Grammar for Writing 🖊

Using Past Perfect to Provide Background Information and Reasons

Writers use the past perfect to provide background information and reasons for past situations and actions. Read these examples:

I had always thought that I was an only child, but I recently discovered that I have a sister. My parents had given me up for adoption. When I was 15, I decided to find my biological parents.

Pre-writing Task

1 Read the paragraph. What does the writer believe about the influence of the environment on relationships? What example does the writer use to explain this?

The Effects of Friends on Sibling Relationships

I believe that the experiences that a person has outside the home can be as influential as experiences inside the home. Examples of this are siblings who start out very similar but become very different from one another as they grow older. For example, Andy and Frank are two brothers who are only two years apart. They did everything together
5 and were best friends until they started junior high. After Andy had been in seventh grade for a little while, he started to change. He had made new friends at school, so he and Frank did not see each other much during the day. Frank had made new friends, too. In fact, Andy's new friends did not like Frank very much, so Andy did not feel comfortable asking Frank to spend time with them. By the time Andy and Frank were in high school, they had
10 grown very far apart. They had made different friends and they had developed different interests. They had been similar when they were young, but Andy and Frank had very little in common as young adults.

2 Read the paragraph again. Underline the sentences that contain both simple past and past perfect verbs. Double underline the sentences with verbs only in the past perfect. Circle the time clauses. Notice how the time clauses help clarify the earlier time period.

Writing Task

1 *Write* Use the paragraph in the Pre-writing Task to help you write about different conditions that influence people's behavior. Give examples from events and situations you have observed to support your opinion.

2 *Self-Edit* Use the editing tips to improve your paragraph. Make any necessary changes.

1. Did you use the past perfect to give background information and provide reasons?
2. Did you use time words and time clauses to clarify the time periods in your sentences or emphasize that some events happened earlier than others?
3. Did you avoid the mistakes in the Avoid Common Mistakes chart on page 59?

A **Pre-writing Task** uses a model to guide students' **analysis** of grammar in **writing.**

14 Negative Questions and Tag Questions

Geographic Mobility

---

1 | Grammar in the Real World

A Have you moved very often in your life? If so, why did you move? Read the interview about geographic mobility. What are some of the reasons why people move?

Geographic Mobility Across Cultures

Interviewer Today we're speaking with two specialists in geographic mobility. They will discuss some reasons why people move from one place to another. Professor O'Neill is from Carlow University in the United States, and Professor Tabenkin is from Zala University in Russia. Let's start with Professor O'Neill. Professor, you have been interested in geographic mobility for a long time, **haven't you**?

O'Neill Well, yes. When I was a boy, my best friend moved away, and that affected me deeply. As I grew older, I saw more people move away. I noticed that the population decrease affected local businesses. As a result, I got interested in the choices people make about moving.

Interviewer People are very mobile and are moving a lot. But most people aren't moving long distances, **are they**? **Isn't** that curious?

O'Neill Yes. That's interesting. In fact, I've been studying the connection between moving and distance recently. Every year, about 11.6 percent of people in the United States move, and of these, about 14.8 percent move to a different state.

Interviewer **Doesn't** that surprise you?

O'Neill No, not really. Often, people who change jobs have to move long distances. On the other hand, people looking for better housing usually stay near their original home. And people who relocate¹ for family reasons may move far away or stay nearby.

¹**relocate:** move to a new place

Interviewer So, I guess it depends on the situation, **doesn't it**?

O'Neill That's right. It's more complicated than you may think. For example, my wife was living in California when we met. When we got married, she moved a long distance to live with me in Chicago. Now her sister, who lives near Chicago, is expecting a baby. She and her husband plan to move a short distance to be closer to us.

Interviewer Professor Tabenkin, people in Russia have the same issues, **don't they**?

Tabenkin To a certain extent, yes. It's harder to find housing in Russia, so people tend to move less frequently. In fact, the mobility rate in Russia is less than 2 percent. In my research, I found that young people often decide not to move because available, affordable housing would take them further from family.

Interviewer OK. But **don't** people sometimes have to move long distances for economic reasons?

Tabenkin Yes, that's true. Personally, I had to move a very long distance ten years ago because there were no jobs nearby. However, my experience doesn't seem to be the norm.[2]

Interviewer Mobility isn't easy to explain, **is it**? Thank you both for your thoughts on this issue.

[2]**norm**: an expected situation or a situation considered to be typical

B *Comprehension Check* Answer the questions.

1. What are some reasons why people move long distances?
2. What are some reasons why people stay nearby when they move?
3. Why is the mobility rate in Russia lower than in the United States?

C *Notice* Find the sentences in the article and complete them.

1. Professor, you **have been** interested in geographic mobility for a long time, _____ you?

2. Mobility **isn't** easy to explain, _____ it?

Look at the verbs you wrote and the verbs in bold. What do you notice about the use of *not*?

2 | Negative Questions

▶ Grammar Presentation

Negative questions are similar to *Yes/No* questions in that they begin with an auxiliary verb, a modal, or a form of *be*.	*Haven't you moved recently?* *Aren't there many reasons why people move?*

2.1 Forming Negative Questions

a. Negative questions usually begin with a contraction.	***Don't*** *you live around here?* ***Can't*** *you help me move?* ***Wasn't*** *he living in Chicago?*
b. The full form of *not* in negative questions is very formal. The word *not* comes between the subject and the main verb.	*Were they* **not** *living in Chicago?* *Have you* **not** *moved recently?*
c. With a contraction, use *are* instead of *am* with *I*. Use *am* when you use the full form.	***Aren't I*** *correct?* ***Am I not*** *correct?*

2.2 Using Negative Questions

a. Use negative questions when you think the information is true and you expect people to agree.	*Don't people often move when they change jobs?* (My experience tells me people often move when they change jobs.) *Isn't it unusual for people to move in Russia?* (I've read that it's unusual to move in Russia.)
b. Use negative questions to show surprise or disbelief.	*"Tom has changed his major to English."* *"Really?* **Isn't he still planning to work at a bank?***"*
c. Use negative questions to show annoyance or anger.	*Didn't you say you would call me?* (I'm angry that you didn't call me.) *Shouldn't Bob have finished that report by now?* (I'm annoyed because Bob hasn't finished the report.)

2.3 Answering Negative Questions

Respond to a negative question just as you would a regular *Yes/No* question. Typically, we answer negative questions with *yes* or *no* and an explanation.	*"Don't you want to move?"* (Do you want to move?) *"***Yes**, I do. I'd like to live somewhere else."* *"***No**, I don't. I really want to stay here."*

▶ Grammar Application

Exercise 2.1 Negative Questions

A family is packing for a big move. Complete the negative questions with the correct form of the words in parentheses.

1. _____*Didn't I tell*_____ (I told) you to be careful with that lamp?
2. _____ (you have been listening) to what I've been saying?
3. _____ (you can stop) texting and help me?
4. _____ (you should have bought) bigger boxes?
5. _____ (I am) correct that you promised to help?
6. _____ (you were going to take) the baby to the neighbor's?

Exercise 2.2 More Negative Questions

Read the sentences about moving and migration. Then write negative questions with the information in parentheses. Use contractions when possible.

1. A lot of people left Ireland in the 1800s.
   Didn't a lot of people leave because of a famine?
   (You heard that a lot of people left because of a famine.)

2. Hope of employment brings a lot of immigrants to rich countries.
   _____
   (You heard that good schools have made rich countries more attractive, too.)

3. Some people move great distances.
   _____
   (You heard that some people move great distances to reunite with family members.)

4. Some corporations require their employees to move to another country.
   _____
   (You think that this is happening more because of globalization.)

5. People are able to move around more freely because of globalization.
   _____
   (You heard that the laws are changing to allow even more movement.)

Exercise 2.3 Responding to Negative Questions

Pair Work Read the chart on migration in the United States. Study it for 30 seconds. Then cover it. What details can you remember? Ask your partner negative questions. Then switch roles, and answer your partner's negative questions.

A *Haven't 60 percent of men moved?*
B *Yes, that's right.*
A *And haven't 50 percent of college graduates moved?*
B *Actually, no. Seventy-seven percent of college graduates have moved.*

People Who Move: Percentages of people who have moved at least once in their lifetimes	% of People Who Have Moved	% of People Who Have Never Moved
Total	63	37
By Gender		
Men	60	40
Women	65	35
By Education		
College graduates	77	23
High school graduates	56	44

www.pewsocialtrends.org/2008/12/17/who-moves-who-stays-put-wheres-home

3 | Tag Questions

▶ Grammar Presentation

Use tag questions to confirm information or ask for agreement.	*You're a professor, **aren't you**?* *He hasn't been studying, **has he**?*

3.1 Forming Tag Questions

a. The verb in a tag question is an auxiliary verb, a modal, or a form of *be*.	*Your parents have never moved, **have** they?* *She got the job, **did**n't she?* *You can't stay, **can** you?*

3.1 Forming Tag Questions *(continued)*

b. The pronoun in a tag question agrees with the subject.	*The students will be on time, won't **they**?* *Your sister lives close by, doesn't **she**?*
Use *it* when the subject is *that* or *something*.	*That's amazing information, isn't **it**?*
Use *they* when the subject is *someone* or *everyone*.	*Someone recorded the interview, didn't **they**?* *Everyone respects the professor, don't **they**?*

c. Use an affirmative tag with a negative statement.

NEGATIVE STATEMENT	AFFIRMATIVE TAG
They don't live in Chicago,	***do they**?*
You're not from Russia,	***are you**?*

Use a negative tag with an affirmative statement.

AFFIRMATIVE STATEMENT	NEGATIVE TAG
Geography is interesting,	***isn't it**?*
Her sister moved to Chicago,	***didn't she**?*

3.2 Answering Tag Questions

a. In negative tags, we expect the listener to answer *yes*, but it is possible to answer *no*.

"They moved from Miami to Chicago, didn't they?"
> *"**Yes**, they got jobs in Illinois."* (That's right, they moved.)
> *"Actually, **no**."* (That's not right. They didn't move.)

b. In affirmative tags, we expect the listener to answer *no*, but it is possible to answer *yes*.

"They didn't move from Miami to Chicago, did they?"
> *"**No**, they decided to stay."* (You're right, they didn't move.)
> *"**Yes**, they had to move for work."* (Actually, they did move.)

c. You cannot answer *Yes . . . not.*

"They didn't move from Miami to Chicago, did they?"
> *"**Yes, they did.**"*
> OR *"**No, they didn't.**"*
> NOT *"~~Yes, they didn't.~~"*

▶ Grammar Application

Exercise 3.1 Tag Questions

Match the statements and tags about a friend who is moving.

1. Erica and her family are moving overseas, _d_   a. do they?
2. You knew about their move, _____   b. didn't you?
3. Erica's company is relocating to London, _____   c. aren't you?
4. Erica's husband won't get a new job, _____   d. aren't they?
5. They don't have a place to live yet, _____   e. don't I?
6. Erica will get an international driving permit, _____ f. isn't it?
7. I have a lot of information about their move, _____   g. will he?
8. You're giving them a going-away party, _____   h. won't she?

Exercise 3.2 Tags

Complete the questions about the stresses of moving. First underline the subject and circle the auxiliary verb in each sentence. Then write the correct tag.

1. Moving (can) be stressful as well as expensive, _can't it_ ?
2. People can sometimes deduct moving costs from their income taxes, _____ ?
3. Things have sometimes disappeared from a moving truck, _____ ?
4. Your friends will give you boxes, _____ ?
5. Everyone should read reviews of a moving company before hiring one, _____ ?
6. Marta has been disorganized since the move, _____ ?
7. Vinh and Ahn weren't moving today, _____ ?
8. It's been a stressful time for you, _____ ?

Exercise 3.3 Statements in Tag Questions

Complete the questions about people who are moving. Use the words in parentheses with the correct verb forms.

1. _____ Mary is retiring to Florida _____ , isn't she?
                        (Mary / retire / Florida)
2. _____ , hasn't he?
                        (Raul / relocate / London)
3. _____ , didn't she?
                        (Annette / attend school / France)
4. _____ , won't they?
           (Miriam and Amir / turn down the promotion / New York)

5. _____ , did you?
   (You / like / the air quality / Hong Kong)

6. _____ , will he?
   (Bernard / take the children / with him / Texas)

Exercise 3.4 Answering Tag Questions

Complete the conversations with the expected answers.

Conversation 1

Paolo I'm interviewing for a job in New York. You grew up there, didn't you?

Luis _Yes, I did_ . What do you want to know?
(1)

Paolo Well, I'm worried about housing. Apartments aren't cheap there, are they?

Luis _____ . They're also hard to find.
(2)

Conversation 2

Phoebe You've read the article on migration patterns for class today, haven't you?

Alex _____ . It was interesting.
(3)

Phoebe Oh, good. You don't have time to tell me about it before class, do you?

Alex _____ . But you can borrow my copy of the article.
(4)

Conversation 3

Claudia I heard the company is moving to Dallas, Texas. Some of us will have to move, won't we?

Jun _____ . I'll know exactly who next week.
(5)

Claudia You have family there, so you won't mind moving, will you?

Jun _____ . My family's excited.
(6)

Conversation 4

Fen There are a lot of new families moving into the neighborhood, aren't there?

Bin _____ . I'm glad to see new faces.
(7)

Fen It's nice to see a lot of young children around again, isn't it?

Bin _____ . It's wonderful!
(8)

Exercise 3.5 ◄))) Pronunciation Focus: Intonation and Meaning in Tag Questions

Use rising intonation in the tag when you are not certain your statement is true.	*"Moving wasn't difficult, **was it**?"* *"Yes, it was!"* *"There won't be a quiz tomorrow, **will there**?"* *"No, there won't."*
Use falling intonation when you expect the listener to agree with you.	*"His research is really boring, **isn't it**?"* *"Yes, it is."* *"You didn't go to class, **did you**?"* *"No, I didn't."*

A ◄))) Listen and repeat the questions in the chart above.

B ◄))) Listen to the conversations about a student moving far away to attend college. Draw the intonation pattern above the tag. Then write *U* if the speaker is uncertain of the information or *E* if the speaker is expecting agreement.

Conversation 1

1. You're not still thinking about going to college in Pennsylvania, are you? ___U___

2. But that college doesn't offer the major you want, does it? _____

Conversation 2

3. Your son is thinking of going to college far from home, isn't he? _____

4. Duquesne University is in Pittsburgh, isn't it? _____

Conversation 3

5. You're excited about moving to Pennsylvania for college, aren't you? _____

6. You're not worried about moving so far from home, are you? _____

Conversation 4

7. Your son is worried about moving so far from home, isn't he? _____

8. But you and your wife feel OK about him moving so far away, don't you? _____

C *Pair Work* Find out information about your partner by asking tag questions. Use both intonation patterns. Use rising intonation when you are uncertain and falling intonation when you expect agreement.

A You're from Egypt, aren't you?
B Yes, I am. You're studying culinary arts, aren't you?
A Actually, no. My major is geography.

4 Avoid Common Mistakes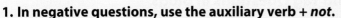

1. In negative questions, use the auxiliary verb + *not*.

Didn't she
~~She no~~ call you?

2. Answer negative questions the same way as regular *Yes/No* questions.

"Aren't you coming with us?"

No, I'm not.   *Yes, I am.*
"~~Yes.~~" (I'm not coming.)   "~~No.~~" (I'm coming.)

3. In tag questions, remember to use an auxiliary verb + a pronoun in the tag.

wasn't it
The research was old, ~~no~~?

4. In the tag, use an auxiliary verb that agrees with the main verb + the correct pronoun for the subject.

aren't they
They are still living in their hometown, ~~isn't it~~?

Editing Task

Find and correct six more mistakes in the conversation about economic mobility.

wasn't it
A That article on economic mobility in America was really interesting, ~~no~~?

B It sure was. Some of the facts were surprising, isn't it? I was especially surprised that there is more economic mobility in countries like France and Germany.

A I was, too. I thought there was more mobility here. By the way, don't you have a class right now?

5 B Yes. I'm finished for today. I'm free for the evening.

A But you're working tonight, no?

B No, I quit my job.

A Really? Why? You no like it?

B The job was fine. The truth is I'm moving to Florida with my family at the end of the semester,

10 so I'm really busy.

A You're kidding! Why? Your family no like it here?

B They like it here, but there aren't many good jobs. We're moving where the jobs are.

A But you only have one semester left, isn't it?

B That's right, but I have to go with them.

5 Grammar for Writing

Using Negative Questions and Tag Questions in Blogs

Students are often asked to post comments on online message boards about topics they discussed in class. Negative questions and tag questions are useful to confirm understanding or check information. Read this example blog:

Miguel More journalists should be writing about the impact of the new immigration laws.

Stephanie Miguel, aren't a lot of reporters already writing about immigration? I've seen a lot of articles about that.

Theresa Didn't our teacher say that there has been a lot of news on this issue?

Miguel Yes, Theresa, I think you're right. However, there haven't been many articles on the impact of these new laws on people's lives, have there?

Note that negative questions and tag questions are not used in academic writing.

Pre-writing Task

1 A group of students is working on a class project. Read the entries from their online message board. What are "boomerang kids"? What are some reasons students move back home?

Thread: Moving Back Home Project

Damien: So, we've all agreed to focus the project on students moving back in with their parents after college, haven't we? The textbook said that there are more of these "boomerang kids" than before. Jo said she thought it was because of the bad job market. I agree that is one reason, but shouldn't
5   there be other reasons, too? I think young people might be closer to their parents than they used to be. Wouldn't you guys agree?

Moving Back Home Project, Feb. 3, 3:30

Jo: I agree that many young people seem closer to their parents, but I don't know if that is a reason to move back home with them. Gabriel, you said that you
10   think family is generally more important to people these days, didn't you?

Moving Back Home Project, Feb. 3, 7:45

Gabriel: Yes, I did. I'll try to find some articles. Don't you think that the economy has something to do with it? Young people feel insecure about their future. We could write about positive and negative reasons why young people live
15   at home after college, couldn't we? What do you think?

---

2 Read the online message board again. Circle the tags in tag questions. How are they used? Underline the negative questions. How are they used?

Writing Task

1 *Write* Use the online message board entry in the Pre-writing Task to help you write comments for an online message board. You can write about one of these topics or use your own ideas.

- geographic mobility
- issues that people have when they move away from family and friends

2 *Self-Edit* Use the editing tips to improve your online message board comments. Make any necessary changes.

1. Did you use negative questions? What is the purpose of each of your negative questions?
2. Did you use tag questions? What is the purpose of each of your tag questions?
3. Did you avoid the mistakes in the Avoid Common Mistakes chart on page 199?

That Clauses

Cultural Values

1 | Grammar in the Real World

A Is it possible to identify "typical" American values? Theories exist about the values
Americans hold today – and why. Read the article about one view of American values.
Do you agree with the writer's point of view?

U.S. Cultural Values

Values are beliefs held in common by members
of a group. They often come from shared
experiences. For example, some historians assert[1]
that the settlement of the American West in
5 **the nineteenth century shaped many American
values.** These include the importance of hard work,
optimism, and individualism.

Countless U.S. children have learned in school
that hard work is essential. In fact, many
10 Americans believe **that they must work hard in
order to be happy.** How did this belief develop?
According to some researchers, as Americans moved
deeper into the continent, they discovered **that the
West was mostly wilderness.**[2] Their lives were
15 difficult, and they had to work hard to survive. Some
historians are convinced **that their success helped form a general belief
in the value of hard work.**

Furthermore, many Americans believe **that they should have a positive
view of the future.** A few historians suggest **that this perspective helped**
20 **put men on the moon.** What is the origin of this optimism? Some research
suggests **that struggles on the frontier[3] encouraged this attitude.**
People found **that they could survive, even in difficult situations.**

Another common belief about Americans is **that they are individualistic.**
Traditionally, American children have learned **that they are responsible for**
25 **their own lives.** This way of thinking supports the idea **that every person**

[1]**assert:** to state an opinion | [2]**wilderness:** an area of land that has not been farmed or had towns and roads built on it
[3]**frontier:** the western area of the United States that did not have many white settlers from the eastern part of the United States

can succeed through hard work. In addition, Americans tend to believe **that they can start over when they make mistakes**. Why do they feel this way? It is the belief of some historians **that this idea developed as a result of frontier life**. Because there were few towns and traditions, settlers created
30 their own rules. Each new settlement developed its own ways of getting things done. When settlements faced problems, they had no choice but to try new and different approaches.

Not all historians agree **that frontier life influenced modern American values**. Furthermore, the United States is becoming more and more culturally
35 diverse all the time. Undoubtedly, this is already affecting the values held by its citizens. In what way might American values change?

B *Comprehension Check* Match the two parts of the sentences.

1. According to some historians, the difficulty of living on the frontier led to _____

2. Survival under difficult circumstances may have led to _____

3. The lack of towns and traditions may have led to _____

a. optimism.

b. the value of hard work.

c. individualism.

C *Notice* Find the sentences in the article and complete them.

1. Many Americans _____ they must work hard in order to be happy.

2. Traditionally, American children _____ they are responsible for their own lives.

3. Not all historians _____ frontier life influenced modern American values.

How many subjects are in each of these sentences? What word connects the two clauses?

2 *That* Clauses

▶ Grammar Presentation

Noun clauses function like nouns in sentences. They often begin with the word *that*.	*Many people believe **that they must work hard in order to be happy**.*

2.1 Forming *That* Clauses

a. *That* clauses have their own subject and verb.

MAIN CLAUSE		THAT CLAUSE	
SUBJECT	VERB	SUBJECT	VERB

*Many Americans think **that anyone can succeed**.*

b. In conversation and informal writing, *that* is often omitted. In academic writing, *that* is usually not omitted.

*Most people recognize **cooperation is important**.* (informal)

*Most people recognize **that cooperation is important**.* (formal)

2.2 Using *That* Clauses

Use *that* clauses after the following verbs that express mental activity: *assume, believe, decide, discover, expect, feel, find (out), guess, hear, hope, imagine, know, learn, notice, read, realize, recognize, say, see, show, suppose, think, understand*	*Can we assume **that the core values have remained basically the same**?* *Some people believe **that hard work brings happiness**.* *I've discovered **that some cultures don't have a positive view of the future**.* *I read **that American values developed during the colonial period**.*

▶ Grammar Application

Exercise 2.1 Forming *That* Clauses

Combine the sentences about employees in the United States. Use *that* clauses.

1. Many Americans notice something. They are working harder but have less money.

   Many Americans notice that they are working harder but have less money.

2. In fact, recent research has found something. Hard work doesn't always lead to wealth.

   _____

   _____

3. Many older Americans are realizing something. They are unable to retire after working hard all their lives.

   _____

   _____

4. Many employees assumed something. Their companies would reward them for their hard work.

   _____

   _____

5. Researchers recently reported something. Job satisfaction has declined in recent years.

   _____

   _____

6. Employers are beginning to understand something. It is important to give people some freedom at work.

   _____

   _____

Exercise 2.2 Using *That* Clauses Without *That*

Over to You Do you believe that money makes people happy? Why or why not? Write five sentences. Use *that* clauses but do not use *that* in your sentences. Then share your sentences with a partner.

A *I don't think money makes people happy because having money causes many problems.*

B *I disagree. I believe you need a certain amount of money to feel secure, and this makes people happy.*

Exercise 2.3 Using *That* Clauses

A Write statements with *that* clauses using the words in parentheses.

1. Europeans work fewer hours than Americans. (I / understand)

    I understand that Europeans work fewer hours than Americans.

2. The average European gets about two months' vacation every year. (Michael / read)

    _____

3. The average American works 46 weeks per year. (international labor statistics / show)

    _____

4. Culture may be one reason for the difference in attitudes toward work.
   (some experts / believe)

    _____

5. Europeans tend to value leisure more highly than Americans.
   (a group of scholars / found)

    _____

6. Americans tend to value earning money more highly than Europeans.
   (some scholars / believe)

    _____

7. Many Americans seem to use possessions as a measure of success.
   (a professor at Gradina University / wrote)

    _____

B *Group Work* As a group, talk about differences between Americans and Europeans.
You may also include another culture that you know about. Discuss the following
questions, or use your own ideas.

- How much vacation time do Americans usually get?
- How much vacation time do Europeans usually get?
- How much vacation time do people from other cultures usually get?
- Who tends to relax on vacation?
- Who tends to bring work to do on vacation?

Use the following verbs in your discussion:

believe	hear	imagine	read	see	suppose	think

A *I've heard that Americans get less vacation time than Canadians.*
B *I think that's true. My brother lives in Canada, and he told me the same thing.*

3 | Agreement Between *That* Clauses and Main Clauses

▶ Grammar Presentation

Use a past form in a *that* clause when the verb refers to a past event. When it refers to a present event or state, use a present form.

Some historians believe that American values **developed** a long time ago. (present belief about a past action)

Some historians believe that early American history **explains** certain American values. (present belief about a present state)

3.1 *That* Clauses in Sentences with Present Verbs in the Main Clause

a. When the main clause is in the present, use a present form in the *that* clause to express a fact or general truth.

*Many Americans feel **that nothing is impossible**.*

*Some cultures think **that cooperation is very important**.*

b. When the main clause is in the present, use a past form in the *that* clause to describe a past event.

*Some historians don't think **that early American history influenced American culture**.*

c. When the main clause is in the present, use a future form in the *that* clause to describe a future event.

*I assume **that you are going to do more research**.*

3.2 *That* Clauses in Sentences with Past Verbs in the Main Clause

a. When the main clause is in the past, use a past form in the *that* clause to describe an event or idea that happened at the same time as the event in the main clause.

*Nineteenth-century Americans knew **that hard work was necessary**.*

*My professor noticed **that many students were writing about the nineteenth century**.*

b. When the main clause is in the past, use a present form in the *that* clause to express a universal truth or a fact that applies to the present.

*Who discovered **that the Earth is round and not flat**?*

*Scientists discovered **that DNA holds the code for life**.*

*When I started living on my own, I found out **that life is sometimes very hard**.*

3.2 *That* **Clauses in Sentences with Past Verbs in the Main Clause** *(continued)*

c. Use the past perfect or past perfect progressive when the event in the *that* clause happened before the event in the main clause.	I _discovered_ **that she <u>had been copying</u> my history research for years**! I _heard_ **that she <u>had failed</u> the test**.
d. Use *would* or *was / were going to* when the event of the *that* clause happened after the event of the main clause.	I _heard_ **that a famous historian <u>would be speaking</u> at the conference**. We _discovered_ **that we <u>were going to study</u> twentieth-century history**.

▶ Grammar Application

Exercise 3.1 *That* Clauses in Sentences with Present Verbs in the Main Clause

Complete the sentences about the influence of Latin American cultures on mainstream U.S. culture. Use a *that* clause with the correct verb form. Sometimes more than one answer is possible.

1. Anthropologists agree / there be / links between Latin American cultures and U.S. culture (present for general truth)

   Anthropologists agree that there are links between Latin American cultures and U.S. culture.

2. Research / shows / contemporary Latin American cultures / have / roots in African, European, and indigenous cultures (present for general truth)

   _____

3. Sociologists / believe / Latin American cultures / influence / world culture as well as U.S. culture (past event)

   _____

4. Many musicologists / agree / modern U.S. music / be / derived in part from Latin American cultures (present for general truth)

   _____

5. Many language experts / assert / Spanish speakers / contribute / a great many words to the English language (past event)

   _____

6. Most sociologists / agree / Latin American cultures / continue / to influence U.S. culture (future for future action)

   _____

That Clauses

Exercise 3.2 ◄)) *That* Clauses in Sentences with Past Verbs in the Main Clause

Listen to part of a lecture on westward movement in nineteenth-century North America. Complete the sentences with the words you hear.

In the nineteenth century, many people _believed that_ Americans _had_ the right
(1)   (2)
to expand across the continent. John Quincy Adams, the sixth president of the United

States, _____ one large country
(3)
_____ good for all Americans.
(4)
However, some people _____
(5)
the westward expansion _____
(6)
some negative consequences. For example, some people _____
(7)
westward expansion _____ a negative impact on Native American
(8)
culture. In fact, some Americans at the time _____ the U.S. government
(9)
_____ Native American land unfairly. They also
(10)
_____ westward expansion _____
(11)   (12)
many wars, such as the Mexican-American War of 1836. Most people

_____ Americans _____ native plants and
(13)   (14)
wildlife as well.

Exercise 3.3 Agreement Between *That* Clauses and Main Clauses

Group Work Do Internet research on how a culture, such as Irish-American or Latin American culture, has influenced culture in the United States or Canada. Write statements with *that* clauses. Use simple present for general truths, simple past for past events, and future for future action. Share your sentences with your group members. Use the following phrases in your sentences:

- I learned / discovered / found that . . .
- Another area that . . .
- For example, . . .
- A recent study showed / found that . . .

I learned that Indian culture has influenced American culture. One area that Indian culture has influenced is entertainment. Many film specialists agree that Bollywood movies are influencing American movies.

4 | *That* Clauses After Adjectives and Nouns

▶ Grammar Presentation

That clauses can follow some adjectives and nouns.	I'm sure **that a cultural group shares at least some values**. I have the feeling **that our values are quite different**.

4.1 *That* Clauses After Adjectives

a. You can use a *that* clause after adjectives that express certainty or emotion.	I'm <u>certain</u> **that I haven't read enough about American culture**. The conference organizers were <u>pleased</u> **that he accepted the invitation**.
b. You can use *that* clauses after *It + be +* certain adjectives. These adjectives often express emotions or degrees of certainty. They include: *certain, clear, evident, (un)fortunate, interesting, (un)likely, surprising, understandable*	It is <u>evident</u> **that many other cultures have influenced U.S. culture**. It is <u>unfortunate</u> **that many students don't know more about their country's history**. It is <u>unlikely</u> **that we'll finish the unit by the next class**. It is <u>understandable</u> **that historians disagree about the development of cultural values**.

4.2 *That* Clauses After Nouns

a. You can use *that* clauses after nouns that express thoughts and ideas, such as *belief, feeling, impression,* and *possibility*.	It was our <u>impression</u> **that the historian was wrong**. There was no <u>possibility</u> **that he was going to convince us**.
b. You can use noun *+ be + that* clauses with these commonly used nouns: *concern, difference, hope, idea, impression, point, problem, saying,* and *views*.	The <u>concern was</u> **that we would never find out the truth**. The <u>point is</u> **that the United States is a very large country**. The <u>problem is</u> **that very individualistic people can find it hard to work in a group**.

Data from the Real World 🌐

Research shows that the following nouns frequently occur with *that* clauses:

assumption, belief, claim, conclusion, doubt, fact, hope, idea, impression, possibility, report, suggestion, view	Is it your **assumption** that we cannot find jobs in other companies? We came to the **conclusion** that he would never understand our point of view.

▶ Grammar Application

Exercise 4.1 *That* Clauses After Adjectives

Complete the magazine interview with a cultural studies expert. For each item, use the words in parentheses with the correct form of *be* and a *that* clause.

U.S. Culture and the World

Interviewer Some experts are studying culture, and they have expressed some concerns. What are they concerned about?

Dr. Green *They are concerned that U.S. culture may have a negative impact on global culture.*

(1. they / concerned / U.S. culture may have a negative impact on global culture)

Interviewer Why are they worried?

Dr. Green _____

_____

(2. some people / worried / Americanization is making everything the same)

Interviewer Why do they think this?

Dr. Green _____

_____

(3. they / aware / Hollywood and fast-food chains are influencing culture)

Interviewer What's your opinion?

Dr. Green _____

(4. I / convinced / culture is a two-way street)

Interviewer Why do you think that?

Dr. Green _____

_____

_____

(5. I / positive / other cultures influence U.S. culture as much as U.S. culture influences them)

Interviewer	Can you give some examples?
Dr. Green	_____
	(6. a lot of people / surprised / the French invented movies)
Interviewer	What else?
Dr. Green	_____
	_____
	(7. they / surprised / the British invented one of the original fast foods, fish and chips)
Interviewer	So what can we conclude?
Dr. Green	_____
	(8. I / sure / we all benefit from global cultural exchange)

~⊷~

Exercise 4.2 *That* Clauses After Nouns and Adjectives

A *Group Work* Complete the answers to these questions about the spread of U.S. culture worldwide. Explain your answers.

1. Is the exportation of U.S. culture to the rest of the world a good thing?

    It is my belief that *the exportation of U.S. culture is in some ways a good thing and in some ways a bad thing* .

2. Survey your group members: Do you think that most people outside of the United States have a favorable opinion of U.S. popular culture?

    It is our feeling that _____ .

3. Does your group think that most people outside of the United States have good feelings about American fast-food restaurants opening up in cities around the world?

    It is our group's impression that _____ .

B *Over to You* Read the results of a survey about the exportation of U.S. culture. Write three sentences about the survey results. Use the following adjectives: *amazed, disappointed, glad, pleased, relieved, surprised*. Discuss your reactions with a partner.

What is your opinion of U.S. popular culture, such as music, TV shows, and movies?

Very favorable	21%	Somewhat unfavorable	25%	No Answer	1%
Somewhat favorable	39%	Very unfavorable	14%		

I'm not surprised that most people have mixed feelings about U.S. culture.

5 Avoid Common Mistakes ⚠

1. Do not use a comma before a *that* clause.

Their parents are pleased, that they are getting married.

2. Remember that *that* clauses need a complete verb.

I noticed that she _∧leaving.
was

3. *That* clauses must have a subject.

Records show that _∧hoped to return east later.
many settlers

4. In academic writing, do not omit *that*.

Some cultures believe _∧individuals should put other people first.
that

Editing Task

Find and correct six more mistakes in the paragraphs about a famous American of the mid-nineteenth century.

Settlers from the east who traveled across the American West in the mid-nineteenth century understood they faced a difficult journey across deserts and mountains. They knew, that the trip would take years and that some people lose their lives. However, they were optimistic.

5   Michael T. Simmons was one of those determined travelers. Someone told him to go to the Pacific Northwest for new opportunities. He sold his business to pay for the supplies that he and his family needed. He knew that the area was largely unknown. He also knew that was dangerous. This did not stop him.

When Simmons and his group reached Oregon, he announced that was going

10 to continue north. The Hudson's Bay Trading Company heard the news, and they discouraged him. However, Simmons was certain, that the trip going to be successful, and he did not listen. Instead, he continued north as planned. After he arrived, he helped to establish the first settlement in the territory that is now known as Washington State. Documents show that Simmons built the first mill using water from the

15 Tumwater waterfall for power. For this, he is sometimes called the father of Washington industry.

6 | Grammar for Writing ✎

Using *That* Clauses to State Reasons, Conclusions, Research Results, Opinions, and Feelings

That clauses are very common in academic writing. They are particularly useful for stating:

- reasons and conclusions
- research results or information from other sources
- opinions and feelings

Sociologists agree that it can be very difficult to adapt to a different culture.

One reason for this may be that people arrive in new cultures with unrealistic expectations.

The teachers were frustrated that they couldn't communicate well with the international students.

For expressing opinions and feelings, the following expressions are common before *that* clauses in academic writing: *It is (not) clear, It is (not) possible, It is likely / unlikely,* and *It is obvious.* Read these examples:

It is unlikely that people from different cultures will change many of their beliefs and values to match the values of a new culture.

It is possible that some cultures have become stronger because of globalization.

Pre-writing Task

1 Read the paragraph below. What problems did the students have? Where did the writer's information come from?

Cultural Differences in the Classroom

The first semester at college can be very difficult for international students. A recent study investigated the main difficulties international students had in their first semester in colleges in the United States and Canada. Ten students participated. The first difficulty that students had was speaking in class. There were a few reasons for
5 this. One reason was that the students were embarrassed about their English. They felt that it was not good enough. However, it was unlikely that their English was not good. After all, each student had to receive a high score on an entrance exam in English. It is possible that the students did not have enough confidence at first. Many of the students were not used to speaking in class because they did not speak in class in their
10 home countries. Another problem many students had was that they did not know what to call their teachers. The reason for this is that the students call their teachers

"Teacher" as a sign of respect when they are in their home countries. However, they discovered that *Teacher* sounded rude to some U.S. teachers. The teachers asked the students to call them by their first names, although they realized that some students

15 would be uncomfortable with this at first. It was interesting that many of the students reported having these problems in the beginning. However, most found that they were able to adjust fairly quickly.

2 Read the paragraph again. Underline the *that* clauses. Find and label one noun clause for each of these purposes: (1) reasons and conclusions, (2) research results and information, and (3) opinions and feelings. Circle the expressions *It is (not) possible that* and *It was likely / unlikely that*. Do these expressions introduce the writer's opinions and feelings or the international students' opinions and feelings?

Writing Task

1 *Write* Use the paragraph from the Pre-writing Task to write about cultural differences. You can write about one of these topics or use your own ideas.

- classroom practices
- dating
- dealing with teachers
- eating
- family life
- making friends
- studying
- taking tests

2 *Self-Edit* Use the editing tips to improve your paragraph. Make any necessary changes.

1. Did you use the correct verb forms in your noun clauses with *that*?
2. Did you use any of the common expressions that come before noun clauses with *that*?
3. Did you avoid the mistakes in the Avoid Common Mistakes chart on page 213?

16 Noun Clauses with *Wh-* Words and *If / Whether*

Inventions They Said Would Never Work

1 Grammar in the Real World

A Have you ever thought of inventing something? If so, what was it? Read the article about inventors. What obstacles did Edison and the Wright brothers face?

Inventions People Said Would Never Work

Throughout history, new ideas have often faced skepticism[1] from society. Skepticism, however, has never stopped the creation of new inventions. Three important American inventors,
5 Thomas Edison and Orville and Wilbur Wright, faced strong public doubt, but they persevered,[2] and the results were the invention of the electric light bulb and the airplane.

While Edison may now be considered a brilliant inventor, in his lifetime
10 he faced much criticism. Most inventors in his day would not announce an invention until they had a model. Edison, however, stated that he had invented the light bulb, but he had no actual evidence for it. Thus, scientists doubted **what he said**. Also, most inventors had a schedule for their projects, but Edison did not. No one knew exactly **when he would complete it**. Moreover,
15 his experiments failed repeatedly, and this added to the skepticism. However, in 1882, Edison succeeded in lighting up an entire New York neighborhood, and the world finally understood **what he had accomplished**.

Many inventors in the early 1900s wondered **whether it was possible to fly**. The Wright brothers proved **what others doubted** by inventing the
20 first airplane. However, they faced many obstacles along the way. First, most inventors were highly educated, but the Wright brothers had little formal education. Second, the success of inventors often depended on **whether they had financial support**. The Wright brothers had none. Finally, most inventors

---

[1]**skepticism:** doubting the truth or value of an idea or belief | [2]**persevere:** continue doing something in a determined way despite difficulties

publicized their research, but the Wright brothers did not. No one knew
25 exactly **what they were doing**. Consequently, the public did not believe
that the Wright brothers would succeed. Wilbur himself was not sure **what
would happen**. He could not predict **if their airplane would fly or not**.
Then, in 1903, the Wright brothers flew their airplane for 12 seconds in
Kitty Hawk, North Carolina. No one could believe **what they were seeing**.
30 Five years later in France, they flew another plane higher and longer.

Inventors almost always face public disbelief. Some people have trouble
believing that new ideas are possible, but they certainly are. No one can be
sure about **what the future holds**.

B *Comprehension Check* Answer the questions.

1. Why did people doubt Thomas Edison?
2. How did Edison convince the world of his accomplishment?
3. What were the obstacles the Wright brothers faced?

C *Notice* Find the sentences in the article and complete them.

1. No one knew exactly _____ .

2. Second, the success of inventors often depended on

   _____ .

3. He could not predict _____ .

Look at the sentences again. Answer the questions.

1. In sentence 1, what type of question is the missing clause similar to?
   a. an information question   b. a *Yes / No* question

2. In sentences 2 and 3, what type of question is the missing clause similar to?
   a. an information question   b. a *Yes / No* question

2 Noun Clauses with *Wh-* Words

▶ Grammar Presentation

Noun clauses with *wh-* words can act as subjects, direct objects, or objects of prepositions.	***What they wanted*** *was financial support.* *The inventor understood* ***how we should build the machine***. *I learned about* ***how many inventions are made every year***.

2.1 Forming Noun Clauses with *Wh-* Words

a. Noun clauses with *wh-* words use statement word order (subject + verb).	*I've just realized **what he did**!* *I don't know **when Edison invented the light bulb**.*
b. When noun clauses with *wh-* words *who*, *what*, and *which* act as subjects, they take a singular verb.	***What happened next** is going to surprise you.*

2.2 Using Noun Clauses with *Wh-* Words

a. Noun clauses with *wh-* words often appear after the following verbs: Thoughts and opinions: *consider, know, remember* Learning and perception: *figure out, find out, see, understand, wonder* Emotions: *care, doubt, hate, like, love*	*I don't <u>remember</u> **who invented the airplane**.* *We need to <u>figure out</u> **why our invention failed**.* *Our professor <u>cares</u> **how we do our work**.*
b. Noun clauses with *wh-* words often follow verbs + prepositions, including *care about, decide on, find out about, forget about, know about, learn about, read about,* and *see about*.	*We shouldn't <u>forget about</u> **which inventions succeeded and which didn't**.* *I <u>read about</u> **where Edison grew up**.*

2.3 Reduced Noun Clauses with Infinitives

Noun clauses with *wh-* words can often be reduced to *wh-* word + infinitive. Common infinitives used this way include *to ask, to consider, to decide, to figure (out), to find (out), to forget, to know, to learn, to remember, to say, to see, to show, to understand,* and *to wonder*.	*We're not sure **who / whom[1] to ask for information**.* *= We're not sure **who / whom[1] we should ask for information**.* *I don't know **what to say about your invention**.* *= I don't know **what I can say about your invention**.*

[1]The use of *whom* is infrequent, except in very formal writing.

▶ Grammar Application

Exercise 2.1 Noun Clauses with *Wh-* Words

A 🔊 Listen to the conversation among a group of students doing Internet research on recent inventions and inventors. Complete the sentences with the noun clauses you hear.

Peter   OK, let's start with Randi Altschul.

Larry   I don't know <u>*who Randi Altschul is*</u> .

(1)

Paula   Neither do I. I don't know _____ .
(2)

Peter   I know _____ . She invented the disposable
(3)

   cell phone.

Paula   I'm impressed! I wonder _____ .
(4)

Larry   I don't know.

Peter   Got it! It says here her cell phone wasn't working well, and she felt like throwing it away.

Larry   Let's find out _____ .
(5)

Peter   It says here she got a patent for it in 1999.

Larry   I just found out _____ at the time.
(6)

   It was Florida.

Paula   I wonder _____ .
(7)

Peter   It says here that it was only 2 inches by 3 inches – kind of like a

   credit card.

Larry   I wonder _____ .
(8)

Peter   It was made of recycled paper.

B *Pair Work*   With a partner, talk about what you know or don't know about other inventions. Use the verbs in A with *wh-* noun clauses.

I know when the smartphone was invented. It was in 2007. I remember what company first made it, but I don't know who invented it.

Exercise 2.2 Reduced Noun Clauses with *Wh-* Words + Infinitives

Some college students are talking to a business adviser about their new product. Rewrite the sentences with *wh-* words + infinitives.

1. We don't know where we should start.

   We don't know where to start.

2. Amy wonders where she could find a good patent lawyer.

   _____

3. I don't know how I can find a manufacturer for our product.

   _____

4. Binh is wondering who he can ask for money for our invention.

   _____

5. I'll figure out who we can contact for financial advice.

_____

6. I wonder what we should charge for our product.

_____

3 | Noun Clauses with *If* / *Whether*

▶ Grammar Presentation

Noun clauses can begin with *if* or *whether*. These noun clauses are similar in some ways to *Yes* / *No* questions, but they follow statement (subject + verb) word order.	*I'm not sure **if the Wright brothers invented the airplane**.* *He doesn't know **whether we will get money for our experiment**.*

3.1 Forming Noun Clauses with *If* / *Whether*

a. Use statement word order (subject + verb) for noun clauses with *if* / *whether*.	*I don't know **if the public will accept our idea**.* *I don't know **whether Edison really invented the light bulb**.*
b. You can use the words *or not* at the end of both *if* and *whether* clauses.	*The scientist didn't know **if** / **whether you would understand her invention or not**.*
Or not can immediately follow *whether*, but not *if*.	*The scientist didn't know **whether or not you would understand her invention**.* NOT *The scientist didn't know if ~~or not~~ you would understand her invention.*
c. You can use *if* / *whether* to introduce two options.	*We don't know **whether the new phone or the new tablet will come out first**.*

3.2 Using Noun Clauses with *If* / *Whether*

a. You can use noun clauses with *if* / *whether* after the following verbs: Thoughts and opinions: *decide, know, remember* Learning and perception: *figure out, find out* Emotions: *care, doubt, matter, mind*	*I haven't decided **if I'm going to write a report about the Wright brothers**.* *He can't find out **if Edison first tried the light bulb in New York**.* *They doubted **whether anyone would steal their idea**.*

3.2 Using Noun Clauses with *If / Whether* (continued)

b. You can also use noun clauses with *whether* after verbs + prepositions, including *care about, decide on, find out about, forget about, know about,* and *read about.*
You cannot use *if* after prepositions.

You should <u>forget about</u> ***whether you'll make a lot of money with that invention.***
NOT *You should forget about* ~~if you'll make a lot of money with that invention.~~

c. You can use an infinitive with *whether.*
You cannot use an infinitive with *if.*

He didn't know ***whether to share his discovery.***
(= *He didn't know whether he should share his discovery.*)
NOT *He didn't know* ~~if to share his discovery.~~

Data from the Real World

Noun clauses with *if* are much more frequent than noun clauses with *whether. Whether* is more frequent in writing than in speaking.

► Grammar Application

Exercise 3.1 Forming Noun Clauses with *If / Whether*

Combine the sentences. Use a noun clause with *if* or *whether.* Sometimes more than one answer is possible.

1. Scientists have not decided something. Is time travel possible?

   Scientists have not decided whether time travel is possible.

2. Many people don't know something. Do some robots think like humans?

   _____

3. Many people don't know this. Can we invent a nonpolluting fuel?

   _____

4. We can't remember this. Has anyone invented a self-cleaning house?

   _____

5. Many people don't know about this. Are hybrid cars good for the environment?

   _____

6. Scientists haven't figured this out. Are there other planets humans can live on?

   _____

Exercise 3.2 Using Clauses with *If / Whether*

A Read the inventor's list of questions about her invention. Rewrite the questions as sentences. Use noun clauses with *if* or *whether*.

Notes on My Invention – Key Questions

---

1. Can I really invent a solar-powered car?

    I don't know if I can really invent a solar-powered car.

2. Will it take a long time to invent it?

    _____

3. Am I smart enough to do it by myself?

    _____

4. Do people really want solar-powered cars?

    _____

5. Will a solar-powered car work on cloudy days?

    _____

6. Is my car going to be too expensive?

    _____

B Read more questions from the inventor in A. Rewrite the questions as sentences. Use *whether or not* with an infinitive.

1. Should I get some help?

    I can't decide whether or not to get some help.

2. Should I take out a loan from the bank?

    _____

3. Should I patent my idea first?

    _____

4. Should I see a lawyer?

    _____

4 Noun Clauses in Direct and Indirect Questions

▶ Grammar Presentation

Wh- noun clauses and noun clauses with *if* and *whether* can be used in direct and indirect questions.

Do you know **when New York got electricity?** (direct question)
I was wondering **when New York got electricity**. (indirect question)

4.1 Forming Direct and Indirect Questions

a. Direct questions with noun clauses have question word order and end with a question mark.
Common phrases include:
Do you know . . . ? Can you tell me . . . ? Would you know . . . ?

<u>Do you know</u> **who invented the first calculator?**
<u>Are you trying to find out</u> **if Edison was born in this country?**
<u>Can anyone tell me</u> **if Edison was born in Scotland?**

b. Indirect questions with noun clauses have statement word order and end with a period.
Common phrases include:
I want to find out . . . I'd like to know . . . I don't know why . . .

<u>I have been wondering</u> **what a patent is.**
<u>My group really needs to find out</u> **if the Wright brothers had financial support for their invention.**
<u>I'd like to know</u> **if people need to get patents for their inventions.**

▶▮ Verbs and Fixed Expressions that Introduce Indirect Questions: See page A10.

▶ Grammar Application

Exercise 4.1 Direct and Indirect Questions

Complete the interview with artist and inventor Crispiano Columna. Rewrite the questions in parentheses as noun clauses in direct and indirect questions. Sometimes more than one answer is possible.

ArtOnline I'm wondering _if you are both an artist and an inventor_ .
(1. Are you both an artist and an inventor?)

Crispiano Columna Yes, I'm both.

ArtOnline I'd like to know _____ .
(2. What is your most famous invention?)

Crispiano Columna I make sculptures that you can wear as gloves.

ArtOnline I was wondering _____ .
(3. Can you show us an example?)

Crispiano Columna Yes, I'm wearing a pair right now.

ArtOnline I'm interested in knowing _____ .
(4. Do you market your gloves?)

Crispiano Columna Not yet. I'm still trying to get funding to manufacture my gloves.

ArtOnline Can you tell us _____ ?
(5. Where were you born?)

Crispiano Columna I was born in San Pedro Sula, Honduras.

ArtOnline I was wondering _____ .
(6. Did you study art in college?)

Crispiano Columna No. In fact, I studied literature.

ArtOnline I'd like to know _____ .
(7. How did you become an artist?)

Crispiano Columna I taught myself. I learned about color and drawing from books.

ArtOnline Please tell us _____ .
(8. What is your self-regenerating car?)

Crispiano Columna It's an electric car that you never have to stop and recharge.

ArtOnline Please let us know _____ .
(9. How does it work?)

Crispiano Columna It uses solar power. The solar power charges the batteries.

ArtOnline I'd like to know _____ .
(10. What was your first invention?)

Crispiano Columna I invented a toy airplane for my nephew when I was a teenager.

Exercise 4.2 More Indirect Questions

A Look at the pictures of inventions. Write one indirect question about each picture.
Use the following phrases:

I wonder / I'm wondering...   I'd like to know...   I'm interested in knowing...

| The hair protector | The food cooler | The baby mop | The butter stick |

I wonder who invented the hair protector.

1. _____
2. _____
3. _____
4. _____

B *Pair Work* Take turns reading your questions.

5 Avoid Common Mistakes ⚠

1. Remember that a noun clause with a *wh-* word follows statement word order.

                                              will

  No one knows what ~~will~~ the next great invention ^ be.

2. Be careful to spell *whether* correctly.

                                             whether

  The success of the invention depended on ~~wether~~ people would buy it.

3. Do not confuse *whether* and *either*.

                                             whether

  The newest electronic devices will always tempt us, ~~either~~ we like them or not.

Editing Task

Find and correct the mistakes in the paragraphs about the importance of the Internet in daily life.

Many inventions make life more convenient, but the Internet is the most essential one today. The Internet is a part of daily life. Although some people worry about _whether_ ~~wheather~~ this fact is harmful or not, many agree that they do not know what would they do if they could not go online.

5   First of all, the Internet helps people communicate instantly with family and friends who are far away. In the past, people had to write a letter or pay for a long-distance call to find out how were they doing. While they waited, they worried about whether their loved ones were all right. Now there are many ways to contact people and find out if they are well.

10   In addition, the Internet helps people find information. If we want to know what is the temperature in Seoul today, we only have to type the question. Also, it is very easy to look for employment, research solutions to a problem, and even find out wether a movie is playing nearby.

It is too early to tell either the Internet causes serious problems for society or not.

15 To me, it seems extremely valuable because it connects me to people I care about and to information I need.

6 Grammar for Writing

Using Noun Clauses with *Wh-* Words and *If / Whether*

Noun clauses that begin with *wh-* words, *if*, or *whether* are useful when describing how events happened. They are particularly useful for explaining what people think, feel, or know. Read these examples:

Some inventors don't care if their inventions change the world.
Many doctors wonder when scientists will discover cures for all kinds of cancer.
The Facebook creators had no idea how fast the site would grow.

Pre-writing Task

1 Read the paragraph below. What discovery is the story about? What things did the discoverer not realize during the discovery process?

An Accidental Discovery

Penicillin is effective against many serious bacterial infections. Alexander Fleming, a Scottish scientist, discovered penicillin in 1928. However, he did not immediately understand what he had discovered. At the time, he was observing substances that could destroy bacteria. However, Fleming was not a very neat scientist. He often left
5 trays of bacteria around his lab. In August 1928, he went away for a vacation. When he returned, he found that something strange had happened to one of the trays. A fungus had grown on the bacteria and killed them. At first, Fleming did not understand why this had happened, but he later realized what he had discovered. He realized that the fungus was powerful and could be useful in curing bacterial infections, but he still
10 had not understood how important it was. He doubted whether the fungus could be effective long enough to kill bacteria inside a human body. The penicillin he grew in the first few years was too slow in taking effect, so he stopped working on it. After a few years, he returned to it. Fleming and other scientists discovered ways to make the substance work more rapidly, and it soon became the most effective antibiotic in
15 existence. This discovery has saved millions of lives.

2 Read the paragraph again. Underline the noun clauses with *whether* and *wh-* words. Notice how they help to tell the story of the discovery.

Writing Task

1 *Write* Use the paragraph in the Pre-writing Task to help you write the story of a discovery or an invention. You may need to do some research. Include discoveries that the inventor or discoverer made along the way. You can write about inventions or discoveries that were:

- accidental
- controversial
- extremely popular
- never popular
- unnecessary
- life-saving

2 *Self-Edit* Use the editing tips to improve your story. Make any necessary changes.

1. Did you use noun clauses to help to tell the story?
2. Did you begin indirect questions with a *wh-* word, *whether*, or *if*?
3. Did you avoid the mistakes in the Avoid Common Mistakes chart on page 225?

Direct Speech and Indirect Speech
Human Motivation

1 | Grammar in the Real World

A What makes people work hard at their jobs? Read the article about employee motivation. What type of reward is particularly effective in motivating workers?

Workplace Motivation

Motivation is the desire to do something. Billionare Donald Trump **said**, "Money was never a big motivation for me. . . . The real excitement is playing
5 the game." Trump meant that he enjoys doing the work more than making millions of dollars. Can that be true? What other factors are important in motivating employees?

10   Many psychologists believe that there are two types of rewards that affect motivation: external rewards and internal rewards. External rewards are rewards that someone gives you. A pay raise is a common external reward. A good grade at school is also an example of an external reward. Internal rewards are connected to the feelings people have about the work they do. The satisfaction
15 you get when you do something well is an internal reward. Researcher Frederick Herzberg (1923–2000) studied motivation in the workplace for many years. Herzberg **said that** employers must think about factors that affect employees' feelings of satisfaction. Herzberg **explained that** working conditions and relationships among co-workers affect workers' motivation. Therefore,
20 employers need to create an environment that makes employees feel safe, valued, and accepted.

Some studies on workplace motivation have focused on autonomy, which is the freedom to work independently. This is an important internal reward. Daniel Pink, the author of a book on motivation, **told** an audience once **that** Google
25 was a good example of a company that supported autonomy. One day each week, Google engineers focus on their own ideas. Pink **informed** the audience **that** Google News and Gmail had been created during this free time.

Research also shows that appreciation is a powerful reward. In his book *The 1001 Rewards and Recognition*[1] *Fieldbook*, Bob Nelson described a study on the
30 effects of appreciation on motivation. The study **asked**, "What motivates you?" Workers ranked the importance of 65 motivating factors. Nelson **indicated that** appreciation for their work ranked first for the workers.

The subject of worker motivation is complex. People expect fair pay for their work. However, research **shows that** people find internal rewards more
35 meaningful than a high salary.

[1]**recognition:** special positive attention

B *Comprehension Check* Complete the chart. Check (✓) whether each reward is external or internal.

	External Reward	Internal Reward
1. Pay raise		
2. Feeling successful		
3. Freedom to work independently		
4. Good salary		
5. Good grades		

C *Notice* Find similar sentences in the article and complete the sentences below.

1. Donald Trump _____ , "Money was never a big motivation for me.... The real excitement is playing the game."

2. Daniel Pink, the author of a book on motivation, _____ an audience once that Google was a great example of a company that supported autonomy.

3. Pink _____ the audience that Google News and Gmail had been created during this free time.

Each sentence tells what someone says. Which sentence gives the actual words of the speaker? How do you know?

2 | Direct Speech

▶ ## Grammar Presentation

Direct speech repeats people's exact words.	Donald Trump said, "Money was never a big motivation for me. . . . The real excitement is playing the game."

2.1 Forming Sentences with Direct Speech

a. Direct speech consists of a reporting clause and a person's exact words.	REPORTING CLAUSE *Donald Trump said, "Money was never a big motivation for me."*
The most common reporting verb is *said*. Use a comma after the verb.	*Our manager **said,** "Treat the customers like family, and they will come back."*
To quote speech, use quotation marks and a capital letter to begin the direct speech. End the direct speech with punctuation inside the quotation marks.	*My colleague said, **"We** are going to lead the company in sales next year**!"***
b. The reporting clause can also come at the end or in the middle of direct speech. Notice that the verb can also come before the subject in the reporting clause when the reporting clause comes at the end or in the middle.	*"The company pays its workers fairly," **the president said**.* *"We didn't do well this year," **said Liz,** "so we won't get a sales bonus."*
c. Use the verb *asked* to quote a question.	*Mr. Smith **asked,** "What do you hope to accomplish in this job**?"***

▶ ## Grammar Application

Exercise 2.1 Statements in Direct Speech

A Rewrite the quotations about motivation as direct speech. Sometimes more than one answer is possible.

1. in my experience, there is only one motivation, and that is desire –Jane Smiley

   Jane Smiley said, "In my experience, there is only one motivation, and that is desire."

2. the ones who want to achieve and win championships motivate themselves
   –Mike Ditka

   _____

   _____

3. the ultimate inspiration is the deadline –Nolan Bushnell

   _____

   _____

4. motivation is the art of getting people to do what you want them to do because
   they want to do it –Dwight D. Eisenhower

   _____

   _____

5. I'm a great believer in luck, and I find the harder I work, the more I have of it
   –Thomas Jefferson

   _____

   _____

6. great work is done by people who are not afraid to be great –Fernando Flores

   _____

   _____

7. nothing great was ever achieved without enthusiasm –Ralph Waldo Emerson

   _____

   _____

8. you miss 100 percent of the shots you don't take –Wayne Gretzky

   _____

   _____

9. the journey of a thousand miles begins with a single step –Lao Tzu

   _____

   _____

B *Over to You* Choose two of the quotations, and write a sentence that explains what
each one means.

*When Jane Smiley said, "In my experience there is only one motivation, and that is
desire," she meant that the only real motivation is wanting to do something.*

C *Pair Work* Share your sentences with a partner. Discuss whether you agree or
disagree with your partner's interpretation.

Exercise 2.2 Questions in Direct Speech

A Read the transcript of an online discussion about motivating employees. Then rewrite each question as a direct speech question. The information in parentheses tells you where to put the reporting clauses – at the beginning or end of the sentences.

Working Today

Today, motivational expert Camila Valdez is here to answer your questions.

Claire **Is money the best way to get employees to work harder?**
(1)

Camila No. Studies show that appreciation and recognition are the best ways.

Pedro **Do you have guidelines for rewarding employees?**
(2)

Camila Try to match the size of the reward to the size of the accomplishment.

Roxana **When should you give the rewards?**
(3)

Camila It's really best to give them as soon as possible after employees have accomplished something.

Hong **What are some ways to motivate employees?**
(4)

Camila Give rewards that fit your employees' working style.

Chelsea **Can you give an example of what you mean?**
(5)

Camila Certainly. For example, give a more flexible schedule to working parents. They will feel more focused at work because they will be able to take care of their home-related responsibilities.

1. (beginning) *Claire asked, "Is money the best way to get employees to work harder?"*

2. (end) _____

3. (beginning) _____

4. (end) _____

5. (beginning) _____

B *Over to You* Ask two classmates these questions: Would money motivate you to work harder? Why or why not? Then write a short report on your interviews with direct speech statements and questions.

I talked to Anne and Mike. I asked, "Would money motivate you to work harder?" Anne said, "No, it wouldn't." I asked, "Why not?" Anne said, "I work to please myself. That's my reward." Then I asked Mike, "Would money motivate you to work harder?" Mike said, "Yes, it would."

3 Indirect Speech

▶ Grammar Presentation

Indirect speech tells what someone says in another person's words. Indirect speech is also called reported speech.	*Donald Trump said, "Money was never a big motivation for me."* (direct speech) *Donald Trump said that money had never been a big motivation for him.* (indirect speech)

3.1 Forming Indirect Speech

An indirect speech statement consists of a reporting verb such as *say* in the main clause, followed by a *that* clause. The word *that* is optional and is often omitted when speaking.	*She said, "The boss is angry."* (direct speech) *She **said (that)** the boss was angry.* (indirect speech)

3.2 Tense Shifting in Indirect Speech

a. After a past verb in the reporting clause, the verb form in indirect speech usually changes. The verb shifts to express a past time.

DIRECT SPEECH	INDIRECT SPEECH
*She said, "The boss **is** angry."*	*She said that the boss **was** angry.*
*He said, "She **is enjoying** the work."*	*He said that she **was enjoying** the work.*
*They said, "The store **closed** last year."*	*They said that the store **had closed** last year.*
*The manager said, "The group **has done** good work."*	*The manager said that the group **had done** good work.*

b. The following forms usually change in indirect speech.

DIRECT SPEECH	INDIRECT SPEECH
*He said, "The department **will add** three new managers."*	*He said that the department **would add** three new managers.*
*She said, "They **are going to hire** more people soon."*	*She said that they **were going to hire** more people soon.*
*The teacher said, "The students **can work** harder."*	*The teacher said that the students **could work** harder.*
*Their manager said, "Money **may not be** very important to them."*	*Their manager said that money **might not be** very important to them.*

c. The forms of *should*, *might*, *ought to*, and *could* are the same in direct and indirect speech.

DIRECT SPEECH	INDIRECT SPEECH
*The boss said, "He **should go** home."*	*The boss said that he **should go** home.*

3.2 Tense Shifting in Indirect Speech (continued)

d. Do not change the form of verbs in general truths or facts.	She said, "Martin Luther King, Jr. **was** a great man."
	She said (that) Martin Luther King, Jr. **was** a great man.
	NOT She said that Martin Luther King Jr. ~~had been~~ a great man.

▶▶ Tense Shifting in Indirect Speech: See page A11.

▶ Grammar Application

Exercise 3.1 Tense Shifts in Indirect Speech

Read the quotes about a psychology course. Then rewrite each quote as indirect speech. Sometimes more than one answer is possible.

1. The professor said, "Psychology 101 includes a unit on motivation."

   The professor said that Psychology 101 included a unit on motivation.

2. A student said, "The class is discussing motivation and personality this week."

   _____

   _____

3. The professor said, "The class is reading about Abraham H. Maslow's theories on motivation."

   _____

   _____

4. One student said, "I'm learning a lot in the class."

   _____

   _____

5. Another student said, "I don't understand the lectures."

   _____

   _____

6. The teaching assistant said, "The readings have great practical value."

   _____

   _____

Exercise 3.2 Modals and Future Forms in Indirect Speech

Read the excerpt from a lecture on how to motivate adult learners. Then complete the e-mail. Rewrite each sentence from the lecture as indirect speech. Sometimes more than one answer is possible.

Welcome to Motivating Adult Learners. This class is for people who teach adults. Participants in the course are going to learn all about motivating adult learners. The course will rely heavily on participants' own experiences. Students should come to class prepared to discuss their own experiences. We may occasionally have guest speakers. The course will include presentations, homework, and weekly quizzes. There will be three papers and two oral presentations. Participants can substitute an oral presentation for one of the papers.

Send   Attach   Save Draft   Spelling ▾   Cancel

To: jake15@cambridge.org
From: marta34@cambridge.org
Subject: First Class Meeting

Hi Jake,
    Here's what happened in class today. The instructor welcomed us, and then she said Motivating Adult Learners was for people who teach adult learners.

1. *She said that participants in the course were going to learn all about motivating adult learners.*

2. _____

_____

3. _____

_____

4. _____

_____

5. _____

_____

6. _____

_____

4 Indirect Speech Without Tense Shift

▶ Grammar Presentation

Indirect speech usually includes a shift in verb tense. However, in some cases the form of the verb does not change.	*The president announced that she **was going** to start an employee program next year.* *The president announced that she **is going** to start an employee program next year.*

4.1 Keeping the Original Tense in Indirect Speech

You may use the tense in the original direct speech clause when you report statements that are still true now, such as:	
Facts or general truths	*He said, "A pay raise **is** a common reward."* *He said that a pay raise **is** a common reward.*
Habits and routines	*Leo said, "Our meetings always **begin** on time."* *Leo said that their meetings always **begin** on time.*
Actions in progress	*Eve said, "I**'m studying** hard for the exam.* *Eve said that she **is studying** hard for the exam.*

▶▶ Tense Shifting in Indirect Speech: See page A11.

4.2 Using Present Tense Reporting Verbs

Use a present tense verb in the reporting clause when what was said relates to the present and is still important at the moment of speaking. Keep the same tense as in the quote.	*Everybody always **says**, "Employees **need** to be motivated."* *Everybody always **says** that employees **need** to be motivated.*

▶ Grammar Application

Exercise 4.1 Keeping the Original Tense in Indirect Speech

Read the quotes from a business meeting. Then rewrite the quotes as indirect speech. Use the same tense as the direct speech. Sometimes more than one answer is possible.

1. "We are trying to improve our new marketing plan." –the marketing manager

   The marketing manager said that we are trying
   to improve our new marketing plan.

2. "The client loves it." –the manager

_____

3. "We have always solved these problems in the past." –Janet

_____

4. "Staff satisfaction has been very important." –Janet

_____

5. "Tomorrow, we are going to have a half-day training session on giving constructive feedback." –Rodrigo

_____

_____

6. "We will all work together, as a team." –Rodrigo

_____

Exercise 4.2 Using Present Tense Reporting Verbs

A Complete the sentences. Use the correct form of the verbs in parentheses.

1. My father always says that money _makes_ (make) the world go round.

2. My friend Amanda insists that a good night's sleep _____ (be) more important than studying.

3. Donald Trump says that he _____ (enjoy) doing the work more than making money.

4. My friend says that he _____ (enjoy) having autonomy at work.

5. My colleague says that it _____ (not / be) always easy to stay motivated.

6. My manager says that you _____ always _____ (should / ask) questions if something is not clear.

B _Pair Work_ Discuss the sentences in A. Do you agree with the statements?

5 | Other Reporting Verbs

▶ Grammar Presentation

Although *say* is the most common reporting verb, many other verbs can introduce indirect speech.	The president **explained** that our company's workers deserved higher pay. The president **told us** that our company's workers deserved higher pay.

5.1 Other Reporting Verbs

a. *Tell* is a common reporting verb. Always use a noun or object pronoun after *tell*.	The president **said** that he was doing a great job. The president **told him** that he was doing a great job.
b. You can use these verbs in place of *say*: *admit, announce, complain, confess, exclaim, explain, mention, remark, reply, report, state,* and *swear*.	"The workers need recognition," **said** the manager. The manager **admitted** that the workers needed recognition.
When used with an object, the object comes after *to*.	He **swore** <u>to us</u> that he'd be on time in the future.
c. You can use these verbs in place of *tell*: *assure, convince, inform, notify,* and *remind*. Always use a noun or object pronoun with these verbs.	The president **told the managers**, "All workers need to be creative." The president **reminded them** that all workers need to be creative.

▶▌ Reporting Verbs: See page A11.

Data from the Real World

Commonly used reporting verbs in formal writing include *claim, explain, find, show, state,* and *suggest*.	The author **claimed that** internal motivation was more effective than external motivation. The results of the study **showed that** money was not always an effective way to motivate employees.

Grammar Application

Exercise 5.1 Other Reporting Verbs

Complete the excerpt from an e-mail about a presentation on cultural differences in motivation. Circle the correct verbs.

> **Send** **Attach** **Save Draft** **Spelling ▼** **Cancel**
>
> Wei **said /(told)** me that he had attended a presentation on the cultural differences that
> (1)
> affect motivation. He **said / told** that an expert on motivation gave the presentation. He
> (2)
> **said / told** me that the expert was Dr. Ghosh. He **reminded / mentioned** me that we had
> (3)   (4)
> read one of her articles in class.
>
> Anyway, Dr. Ghosh **said / informed** the group that the typical workplace included
> (5)
> people with various cultural backgrounds. She **explained / reminded** that these workers
> (6)
> had different expectations. She **informed / explained** the group that these workers often
> (7)
> had different motivations.
>
> At the same time, Dr. Ghosh **reminded / remarked** that there was no one way to
> (8)
> motivate all workers. She **admitted / reminded** that in multicultural settings, it was even
> (9)
> more complicated.
>
> She **stated / reminded** the group that managers shouldn't make generalizations about
> (10)
> cultures. She **assured / remarked** that the "human touch," getting to know employees as
> (11)
> individuals, was the best way to motivate them.

Exercise 5.2 More Reporting Verbs

A 🔊 Listen to the conversation about a presentation on cultural differences in classrooms. Complete the sentences with the words you hear.

David What happened in class today?

Mira We had a guest speaker. He _told us_ about the importance of motivation in
(1)
the language classroom. He _____ there are two kinds
(2)
of motivation: intrinsic and extrinsic.

David Right. Last week, the professor _____ there were two
(3)
different types, and she gave examples.

Mira Yes. So anyway, the speaker _____ he had done
(4)
a study of students in Japan and students in the United States. He

_____ both groups had native-speaking English
(5)
teachers. He _____ the purpose of the study was to see
(6)
whether the teachers' remarks had a negative effect on the motivation of the

Japanese students.

David What did he find out?

Mira He _____ the study found four ways in which the teachers'
(7)
behavior had a negative effect on Japanese students' motivation.

David Did he give any examples?

Mira He _____ classroom discussion is one area where there
(8)
are key differences. He _____ in the Japanese classroom,
(9)
students generally listen more and talk less.

David And as we know from our reading, Porter and Samovar

_____ in the U.S. classroom, some students speak up
(10)
spontaneously, and that a lot of teachers encourage discussion.

Mira Right. So, he _____ when a teacher criticizes a Japanese
(11)
group for not participating, it has a bad effect on motivation.

B ◄») Listen again and check your answers.

C *Over to You* Compare the behavior of American and Japanese students to students
from another culture that you are familiar with. Use sentences with indirect speech.

The speaker said that in the Japanese classroom, students listen more and talk less.
That is true in my culture, too. Students show respect that way.

6 Avoid Common Mistakes

1. **For verbs such as *admit, announce, complain, explain,* and *mention,* the object pronoun comes after the preposition *to*.**

   $\overset{to\ us}{}$
   He explained ~~us~~ the objective.

2. **Change the form of the verb in indirect speech in most cases.**

   $\overset{had}{}$
   He claimed that they followed the directions.

3. **Use beginning and ending quotation marks with direct speech.**

   The director said, "All designers may work from home on Fridays."

Editing Task

Find and correct the mistakes in the paragraphs about a memorable event.

One of the highlights of my life happened through an experience at work. It started when my manager announced ~~us~~ some interesting news. He said, I am starting a company band. Then he asked, "Who wants to join?" I mentioned him that I had played guitar for many years. He said, You should definitely try out.

5   On the day of tryouts, I was a little nervous because everyone played extremely well. After I auditioned, the manager thanked me and explained me that he will let me know soon.

I forgot about it, so I was very surprised when I got a phone call from my manager a few days later. He said, You can play lead guitar. I said, Wow! That's great! After that, the

10 band practiced a few times a week. A few months later, we played at the company party. We were nervous, but we played well. The president of the company spoke to me later and said I have a lot of talent. I was embarrassed by his compliment, but I said I am proud to play for the company. I will never forget that experience.

7 | Grammar for Writing ✎

Using Descriptive Reporting Verbs

There are a number of verbs that writers can use in indirect speech. Some of these verbs add additional meaning; others are more neutral. Read these examples:

The teacher <u>argued</u> that he could motivate students from any culture with special rewards.
Many of his students <u>claimed</u> that the rewards did not motivate them, however.
A few students <u>pointed out</u> that many of their teachers offer rewards for good work.

Notice that *argued* and *claimed* show that the speaker is sharing an opinion or feels strongly about the statement, whereas *pointed out* is more neutral.

The following reporting verbs are especially useful in academic writing.

These are more neutral:	*announce, ask, explain, inform, mention, note, notify, observe, point out, remark, remind, reply, report, say, state, tell*
These add more precise meaning:	*admit, advise, argue, assure, claim, complain, confess, convince, exclaim, suggest, swear*

Pre-writing Task

1 Read the paragraphs below. Where did the survey take place? What was the purpose of the survey? What did the writer decide to do?

A Motivation Survey

I find it hard to motivate myself to exercise, so I went to a gym to get some advice. I asked people what motivated them. A few of the people said that they made exercise a routine or habit. They explained that they didn't think about whether or not to go to the gym on any particular day. They just went on the same days every week. One of the trainers
5 there swore that money was one of the most important motivators. She argued that people who paid for something tended to use it more.

Two other people told me that they promised themselves a reward each week that they went to the gym three times. They claimed that they wouldn't reward themselves if they missed a day. I asked them what their rewards usually were, and they explained that
10 they often went out to dinner with friends as a reward. I pointed out that having dinner in a restaurant might ruin the benefits of going to the gym, but they assured me that they always ate healthy meals at restaurants. I decided I could use all of these ideas for motivation, so I joined the gym.

2 Read the paragraphs again. Circle the reporting verbs. Underline the reporting verbs that add meaning to the writer's statements.

Writing Task

1 *Write* Use the paragraphs in the Pre-writing Task to help you write about what motivates people to do something. Survey four people. Then write a paragraph reporting your results. You can write about how they motivate themselves to:

- do laundry
- lose weight
- get enough sleep
- eat well
- not procrastinate
- study hard

2 *Self-Edit* Use the editing tips to improve your paragraph. Make any necessary changes.

1. Did you choose neutral reporting verbs where appropriate?
2. Did you use reporting verbs that add meaning to your statements?
3. Did you use the correct verb form after each reporting verb?
4. Did you avoid the mistakes in the Avoid Common Mistakes chart on page 241?

Indirect Questions; Indirect Imperatives Requests, and Advice

Creative Problem Solving

1 Grammar in the Real World

A When you have to solve a problem, what strategies do you use? Read the article about brainstorming. Would you prefer traditional brainstorming or "brainwriting"?

Brainstorming as a Problem-Solving Tool

There is more than one way to solve a problem. One method many people use is brainstorming. Brainstorming is an activity designed to produce a number of ideas in a
5 short time. Alex Osborn invented the word in 1939. In his book *Unlocking Your Creative Power*, Osborn said that the word *brainstorm* means using the brain to solve a problem creatively. Although he **said that groups should**
10 **brainstorm** in a particular way, variations on his technique have also become popular.

Osborn's original brainstorming method had four rules. First, he **told participants not to judge** other people's ideas. Second, he welcomed all ideas, even wild ideas. Osborn said that crazy ideas could get people thinking along new lines and could
15 lead to effective solutions. Therefore, he **asked participants to shout out** even unusual ideas. Third, Osborn **asked group members to produce** a large number of ideas. He thought that the group would find a few really good ideas if many different ones were available. Finally, Osborn **asked the brainstorming group if they could improve** the ideas that had been suggested.

20 One alternative to brainstorming is brainwriting. Brainwriting is a silent version of brainstorming. With brainwriting, participants write down their ideas instead of shouting them out. In his book *Thinkertoys*, creativity expert Michael Michalko suggests that brainwriting may be more productive than traditional brainstorming. This is because people often think of additional ideas as they write. He also asserts
25 that this method is better for quieter individuals because they do not have to express their ideas out loud.

> Brainstorming and brainwriting are flexible methods. Anyone can use them because they do not require a lot of training or expensive materials. These processes are all effective tools for creative problem solving in professional, academic, and
> 30 personal situations.

B *Comprehension Check* Answer the questions.

1. What are the four rules of brainstorming?
2. Why does Michalko believe that brainwriting may be more productive than brainstorming?
3. According to the writer, who can use brainstorming?

C *Notice* Find the sentences in the article and complete them.

1. First, he told participants _____ other people's ideas.

2. Therefore, he asked participants _____ even unusual ideas.

What are the forms of the missing verbs?

2 Indirect Questions

Grammar Presentation

Indirect questions tell what other people have asked. There are two kinds of indirect questions: *Yes/No* questions and information questions.	*He asked, "Are your jobs satisfying?"* *He asked if our jobs were satisfying.* *The director asked, "Which technique do you prefer?"* *The director asked us which technique we preferred.*

2.1 Forming Indirect Questions

a. Use *asked* in the reporting clause and *if* to introduce an indirect *Yes/No* question.	*"Will we start attending brainstorming sessions?" Mia **asked**.* *Mia **asked if** we will/would start attending brainstorming sessions.*
Use *asked* in the reporting clause and the same *wh-* word to introduce an indirect information question.	*"**When** will the training begin?" our manager **asked**.* *Our manager **asked when** the training will/would begin.*

2.1 Forming Indirect Questions (continued)

b. Use statement word order in the indirect question.	*He asked if Rita was one of our most productive employees.*
c. After *ask*, you can use a direct object. The direct object can be a noun or pronoun.	*She **asked the students** if they understood.* *She **asked me** when I wanted to leave the company.*

▶ Grammar Application

Exercise 2.1 Forming Indirect Questions

Read the interview between Joanna and Dr. Martin, a critical thinking expert. Then rewrite each of Joanna's questions as an indirect question.

    Joanna Dr. Martin, why is creative thinking in the business world so important?

Dr. Martin Companies need very creative people to help design and market new products.

5 **Joanna** Why will creative thinking be even more important in the future?

Dr. Martin Competition is getting stronger. You have to be creative to stay competitive.

    Joanna What techniques have worked to get
10   people to think creatively?

Dr. Martin One technique that really works is to move the body. I tell people who are sitting at a desk to move into the conference room or take a walk outside.

    Joanna How does moving promote creativity?

15 **Dr. Martin** Moving stimulates the brain.

    Joanna Are there any other ideas like this?

Dr. Martin Of course. Try putting colorful pictures on the wall. Never try to be creative in an empty room.

    Joanna Do objects and colors stimulate creative thinking?

20 **Dr. Martin** They definitely do.

1. What did Joanna ask Dr. Martin about creative thinking in the business world?

   Joanna asked Dr. Martin why creative thinking in the business
   world was important.

2. What did Joanna ask Dr. Martin about the future?

   _____

3. What did Joanna ask about creative techniques?

   _____

4. What did Joanna ask about moving?

_____

5. What did Joanna ask about other ideas?

_____

6. What did Joanna ask about stimulating creative thinking?

_____

Exercise 2.2 More Forming Indirect Questions

Read the conversation about a company's creativity exercises. Then rewrite each of Ahmet's questions as an indirect question.

Ahmet How was your creativity session yesterday?
Irina It was fun, and we had some really good ideas, too.
Ahmet Was the session here?
Irina Yes, it was here.
5 _Ahmet_ Who was your leader?
Irina It was Dr. Martin, a creativity expert. She gave us a problem to solve. Then she gave us large pieces of white paper and markers in a lot of different colors.
10 _Ahmet_ What did you do with the paper and the markers?
Irina We drew pictures of things that we wanted to say, that is, the solutions we had for the problem.
Ahmet Interesting. How long were you drawing pictures?
Irina We did that for about an hour. Then we had a thing called "incubation." We stopped
15 working, had lunch, and then watched a TV show!
Ahmet Why did you watch TV in the office?
Irina The idea was to forget about everything and then come back to the problem. When we went back to work, we then found the best solution.
Ahmet Are you going to continue tomorrow?
20 _Irina_ Yes.

1. What did Ahmet ask Irina about yesterday?

   He asked her how her creativity session was.

2. What did Ahmet ask Irina about the location?

   _____

   _____

3. What did Ahmet ask Irina about the leader?

   _____

   _____

4. What did Ahmet ask Irina about the paper and the markers?

   _____

5. What else did Ahmet ask Irina about the activity with the paper and markers?

_____

_____

6. What did Ahmet ask Irina about watching TV in the office?

_____

7. What did Ahmet ask Irina about tomorrow?

_____

Exercise 2.3 Using Indirect Questions

Group Work Ask and answer the questions about creativity with two students. Then share your answers with the whole class.

- What are some situations in which people have to be creative?
- Why is creativity difficult for some people?
- When you have to be creative, do you have any techniques to stimulate your thinking? What are they?

3 | Indirect Imperatives, Requests, and Advice

▶ Grammar Presentation

Imperatives, requests, and advice are usually made indirect with an infinitive.	*"**Please sit down**."* *He asked us **to sit down**.* *"**Would** you **please turn off** your phones?"* *He asked us **to turn off** our phones.*

3.1 Indirect Imperatives, Requests, and Advice

a. Use an infinitive in indirect imperatives. Use *not* + infinitive in negative indirect imperatives. You can use *tell* or *say*.	*"**Don't make** a lot of noise," said Mr. Jung.* *Mr. Jung <u>said</u> **not to make** a lot of noise.*
Use an infinitive in indirect requests. You can use *ask*, *tell*, or *say*.	*"**Please turn off** your cell phones," said Mr. Cho.* *Mr. Cho <u>told</u> us **to turn off** our cell phones.*
Use an infinitive to report advice given with modals such as *should*. Use *not* + infinitive to report advice with *should not*. You can use *tell* or *say*.	*"You **shouldn't reject** any ideas," Carl said.* *Carl <u>told</u> us **not to reject** any ideas.*

3.1 Indirect Imperatives, Requests, and Advice *(continued)*

b. Always use an object after *tell*.

Ms. Ali **told** us to work quietly.
NOT ~~Ms. Ali told to work quietly.~~

Use a pronoun or noun after *ask* to show the person who is the object of the request.

Sam **asked** her to share her ideas with the group.

Grammar Application

Exercise 3.1 Indirect Imperatives and Requests

Read the directions that a trainer gave to a group of employees. Then rewrite the steps with infinitives and the words in parentheses.

1. "Get into groups of three or four."
2. "Don't get into a group with someone you usually work with."
3. "Cut out pictures from magazines that show your ideal working environment."
4. "Don't criticize your group members' choices."
5. "Present your picture to the other groups."
6. "Comment on the other groups' pictures, but don't criticize people's choices."
7. "Discuss the emotions that the pictures suggest."

I attended a problem-solving session with Dr. Martin yesterday. The goal was to help us get along better with each other. She helped us a great deal. Here's what she did:

1. (First / she / tell) _First, she told us to get into groups of three or four._
2. (Then / she / say) _____
   _____
3. (She / tell) _____
   _____
4. (Dr. Martin / say) _____
   _____
5. (Then / she / tell) _____
   _____
6. (After that / she / say) _____
   _____
7. (Finally / Dr. Martin / say) _____
   _____

Exercise 3.2 🔊 Indirect Requests and Advice

Listen to the marriage counseling session. Then answer the questions. Use the words in parentheses and *ask*, *say*, or *tell*.

1. What did the therapist tell the husband and wife to do?

   The therapist told them to take a pad

   of paper and a pencil.

   (take a pad of paper and a pencil)

2. What did the husband ask?

   _____

   _____

   (take a different pencil)

3. What did the wife ask?

   _____

   (use her own pen)

4. What did the therapist say?

   _____

   (write for 15 minutes without stopping)

5. What did the therapist tell the clients?

   _____

   (not look at each other's writing during the activity)

6. What did the therapist say?

   _____

   (not talk to each other)

7. What did the therapist tell the clients?

   _____

   (be prepared to read their descriptions to each other)

8. What did the husband ask?

   _____

   (have a little more time to write)

Exercise 3.3 Indirect Advice

A *Over to You* Think of some good and bad advice you or people you know have received. What was the advice? Write six sentences.

Good Advice

My father's doctor told him not to eat meat and to exercise more.

1. _____

2. _____

3. _____

Bad Advice

Economists told Americans in 2005 to buy real estate because prices would increase.

4. _____

5. _____

6. _____

B *Group Work* Compare your answers with your group members. Discuss why the advice was good or bad. Take notes on your group members' answers.

A *My father's doctor told him not to eat meat and to exercise more. This was good advice because it helped him to get into better shape.*

B *Many economists told their clients to buy real estate because prices would increase. This was bad advice because real estate prices went down.*

Avoid Common Mistakes ⚠️

1. Use infinitives in indirect imperatives.

The leader asked us ~~that we~~ write for 5 minutes about the topic.

(inserted: *to*)

2. In indirect *Yes/No* questions, remember to use an *if* clause.

He asked me ~~did I want~~ to be the group leader.

(inserted: *if wanted*)

3. Remember to use an object pronoun or noun after *tell*.

I told ∧ my ideas, and we ended up using two of them in the project.

(inserted: *them*)

Editing Task

Find and correct the mistakes in the paragraph about a brainstorming session.

When my psychology professor asked our class ~~did~~ we ~~want~~ to try brainstorming as
(inserted: if wanted)
part of our next group project, I had no idea that the experience would be so challenging
or successful. First, when we started, one of our members asked many unimportant
questions. When the team leader asked her that she asks the questions later, that person

5 began complaining. Then the team leader asked the person did she want to be the group
leader. The rest of us told this was a bad idea, and there was an argument. A different
problem arose when we met the second time. The leader asked one student that he takes
electronic notes, but he forgot. As a result, when we met the third time, the leader had to
tell the information again. She asked me that I write the notes this time, and I did. Aside

10 from these minor problems, the group generated a lot of ideas and finally came up with
a successful proposal for a project. So, if someone asked me do I want to work as a group
again, I would say yes because even though it is hard to work as a group, the outcome can
be better.

5 | Grammar for Writing

Using Indirect Questions, Imperatives, Requests, and Advice

Students often communicate with other students through online message boards and chat rooms, especially when they are working together on an assignment. In these situations, it is often necessary to report what other people have asked, commanded, requested, or advised. Read these examples:

Marielle asked when the first draft is due. Does anyone know? (question)
Professor Harper told us to make a list of creative problem-solving strategies. (command)
Jorge asked us not to have our meetings on Friday because he works on Fridays. (request)
He also said to use a different strategy for each problem we have to solve. (advice)

Pre-writing Task

1 A group of students is working on a project. They are using an online message board to talk to each other. Read their entries. What is the focus of their project, and how many students are in the group?

Thread: Study skills project

Clara: Professor Moss asked us to write outlines for our reports on good problem-solving strategies. He said to identify our own creative problem-solving processes before we try to find new ones. I'll start. When I have a problem I can't solve, I think about my older sister,
5 Susannah. She's really good at solving difficult problems. I ask myself how Susannah would solve the problem. That helps me to think about things in a different way.

Study skills project, May 9, 7:30

Carmen: That's interesting, Clara. I never thought of doing that. I have a different technique. A few years ago, I had a teacher who always told
10 us to try to solve problems by thinking of the end result we wanted and working backward. I try to do that sometimes. Why don't we try everyone else's creative thinking processes and see how they work? Also, could everyone say when they can meet next?

Study skills project, May 9, 8:41

Jun: I don't think I use any special creative problem-solving strategies.

15   Hao: Jun, Carmen asked if we could try each other's strategies. If you don't have one, why don't you just try everyone else's and let us know how they work for you?

Study skills project, May 12, 10:07

Carmen: I just realized it's already Thursday and no one has written here for a while. We have to get working. Does anyone remember when we have

20   to turn in our outline?

Study skills project, May 12, 10:14

Jun: Yes, I asked Prof. Moss when our outline was due. Prof. Moss asked if we could turn it in by Friday. He said he could get us some feedback by Monday. He told us not to spend too much time on the outline, though, because he wants to approve our ideas before we

25   write our report.

2 Read the online message board again. Underline the examples of indirect speech. Label each example as *I* (for an imperative), *Q* (for a question), or *A* (for advice). Which verbs show you that the sentence reports advice?

Writing Task

1 *Write* Use the online message board in the Pre-writing Task to help you write a paragraph. Get into pairs and interview each other about one of the following problem-solving strategies. Get instructions and advice from your partner. Then write a paragraph reporting what you asked your partner and what your partner said. You can write about one of these topics or use your own idea.

- backward problem solving
- journaling
- talking about problems with others
- thinking about possible outcomes

2 *Self-Edit* Use the editing tips to improve your paragraph. Make any necessary changes.

1. Did you use the correct tenses after the reporting verbs?
2. Did you use the correct form for indirect questions?
3. Did you avoid the mistakes in the Avoid Common Mistakes chart on page 251?

The Passive (1)

English as a Global Language

1 Grammar in the Real World

A Should everyone speak English? Why or why not? Read the web article on the use of English around the world. Why is English important to learn?

English Is Spoken Here

An Italian businesswoman in Russia speaks English in meetings. Teenagers from Argentina, Turkey, and Japan chat online – in English. Learning English is clearly important in today's
5 world. David Crystal, a linguist[1] who studies the English language, believes that English has become a global language, although it is not an official language in many countries. According to Crystal, no other language **has been spoken** in
10 so many countries and by so many speakers. Currently, over 275 million people speak English as a first language around the world, and approximately one billion speak it as a second language. This means that there are more nonnative speakers of English than native speakers. How **is** English **used** by nonnative speakers? Employees of international companies **are** often **asked** to learn
15 English for their jobs. In addition, the Internet **is dominated**[2] by English. Some experts say that more than half of the information on the Internet is in English. Also, English **has** long **been viewed** as a common language among travelers from different countries. The use of English worldwide appears to have clear benefits for everyone.

20 Does this increase in the use of English worldwide have any disadvantages? Some say that cultures may lose some of their identity if people use English instead of their native languages. For example, much of a culture's identity

[1]**linguist:** someone who studies languages and their structures | [2]**dominate:** control a place or person, want to be in charge, or be the most important person or thing

is reflected in its music and literature. Would these songs and stories be as effective in English? Others say that the English language itself could change.

25 In fact, this is happening now. When English **is spoken** by a group of people whose native language is not English, words from the native language **are** sometimes **mixed in**, and the pronunciation of words is different from British or American English. This means that dialects[3] and different forms of English **are being spoken** in various areas around the world. Sociologists

30 **are** currently **studying** this phenomenon. The loss of cultural identity and the creation of varieties of English are two areas of interest for sociologists and linguists.

English **is being used** worldwide more and more, and for many people, learning it is necessary for their personal and professional lives. There are

35 obvious advantages to learning English. The disadvantages remain unclear. It is clear that varieties of English will continue to evolve. How will this affect how English **is taught**? In the future, will greater numbers of people have to decide which variety of English they learn?

[3]**dialect:** a local variety of language that differs in its pronunciation and word usage

B Comprehension Check Answer the questions.

1. Where is English being spoken?
2. When do people around the world speak English?
3. What might be some disadvantages of English being a global language?

C Notice Match the sentences in A with the sentences in B that mean the same thing.

A	B
_____ 1. International companies **ask** their employees to learn English for their jobs.	a. How **is** English **used** by nonnative speakers?
_____ 2. In addition, English **dominates** the Internet.	b. Employees of international companies **are** often **asked** to learn English for their jobs.
_____ 3. How do nonnative speakers **use** English?	c. In addition, the Internet **is dominated** by English.

Look at the forms of the verbs in bold in each of the matched sentences. How are the verbs in column B different from the verbs in column A?

2 | Active vs. Passive Sentences

▶ Grammar Presentation

A passive sentence and an active sentence have similar meanings, but the focus of the sentences is different. In the passive sentence, the focus is on the action or on the person or thing receiving the action.	The president **asked** <u>the employees</u> to speak English. (active) *<u>The employees</u> **were asked** to speak English.* (passive)

2.1 Passive Sentences with *By* + Agent

a. In active sentences, the agent (or doer of the action) is in subject position. In passive sentences, the object of the active sentence becomes the subject. The word *by* comes before the agent.

AGENT   OBJECT
*<u>People</u> **spoke** <u>English</u> at the meeting.* (active)

*<u>English</u> **was spoken** <u>by people</u> at the meeting.* (passive)

b. The agent is not always necessary.

*English **was spoken** at the meeting.* (We assume *people* were doing the speaking.)

c. Use the *by* + agent phrase if the agent is important or if the meaning of the sentence would be unclear without it.

*The Internet **is dominated** by English.*
NOT *The Internet is dominated.* (By who or what?)

2.2 Present and Past Forms of the Passive

a. For the simple present form of the passive, use the present form of *be* + the past participle of the main verb.

*Some international companies **ask** their employees to learn English.* (active)
*Employees **are asked** to learn English by some international companies.* (passive)

b. For the present perfect form of the passive, use *has / have* + *been* + the past participle of the main verb.

*The company **has told** the employees to speak English.* (active)
*The employees **have been told** to speak English.* (passive)

c. For the present progressive form of the passive, use the present form of *be* + *being* + the past participle of the main verb.

*These days, people around the world **are speaking** many dialects of English.* (active)
*These days, many dialects of English **are being spoken** by people around the world.* (passive)

2.2 Present and Past Forms of the Passive *(continued)*

d. For the simple past form of the passive, use the past form of *be* + the past participle of the main verb.

This form is the most common.

*Years ago, people **did** not **consider** English a global language.* (active)
*Years ago, English **was** not **considered** a global language.* (passive)

e. For the past progressive form of the passive, use the past form of *be* + *being* + the past participle of the main verb.

This form is rare.

*Ten years ago, fewer people **were using** English online.* (active)
*Ten years ago, English **was being used** by fewer people online.* (passive)

f. In passive sentences, do not use a form of *do* in questions and negative statements in the simple present and simple past.

***Do** most travelers **speak** English?* (active)
***Is** English **spoken** by most travelers?* (passive)
*Turkish teenagers **didn't use** English to chat online a decade ago.* (active)
*English **wasn't used** by Turkish teenagers to chat online a decade ago.* (passive)

 Research shows that the simple present, present perfect, and simple past forms of the passive are much more frequent than the present progressive, past progressive, and past perfect forms of the passive.

▶▶Irregular Verbs: See page A1.
▶▶Passive Forms: See page A12.

Data from the Real World

Research shows that in academic writing, these are the most common verbs used in the passive:

analyze, calculate, carry out, collect, determine, expect, find, measure, observe, obtain, prepare, see, set, show, test, and *use.*

▶ Grammar Application

Exercise 2.1 Active and Passive Sentences

A Complete the online interview with a reporter from BusinessTimes Online and the CEO of an international company. Circle the correct verb forms.

Reporter I would like to ask some questions about your use of English here at BR Corporation. **Do people speak English /(Is English spoken)** by
(1)
most executives?

CEO Yes, most executives **speak / are spoken** English at this branch.
(2)

Reporter Do only executives speak English? I mean, do lower level employees **use / are used** English here, too?
(3)

CEO No, English **isn't used / doesn't use** by them much.
(4)

Reporter Why is English necessary for some employees?

CEO English **is needed / needs** by executives who travel. Also, we
(5)
are expected / expect them to read technical documents in English.
(6)

Reporter **Does BR Corporation support / Is BR Corporation supported** English
(7)
language learning?

CEO Yes, BR Corporation **is offered / offers** onsite English courses.
(8)

Reporter **Are the courses taught / Do the courses teach** by native English speakers?
(9)

CEO Yes, native speakers **are conducted / conduct** all of our English classes.
(10)

Reporter Thank you for speaking with me today.

B *Pair Work* Which sentences in A are in the passive? Rewrite them as active sentences.

Do most executives speak English?

C *Group Work* Rewrite the active sentences in A as passive sentences. In which sentences is the *by* + agent phrase necessary? Share your answers with the group.

Exercise 2.2 Present Forms of the Passive

Complete the article about foreign-language teaching. Use the simple present or present perfect form of the passive with the verbs in parentheses. Sometimes more than one answer is possible.

English _has been taught_ (teach) in
(1)
many countries all over the world for years.

It _____ currently _____
(2)   (2)
(speak), at least to some degree, by

one–quarter of the world's population.

Schools in the United States also recognize

the importance of learning other languages.

For some time, languages other than English _____ (include) in
(3)
these schools' programs. Recently, a growing number of languages has become

available. Which languages _____ (offered) by U.S. high schools
(4)
nowadays? The results may surprise you.

French is one of the most popular foreign languages for high school students.

It _____ (teach) in most U.S. high schools for many years. Arabic
(5)
is becoming more and more popular. In fact, Arabic _____ (offer)
(6)
at many Massachusetts public schools these days. Chinese is also beginning

to gain popularity. An increase in the number of students learning Chinese

_____ (report) for several years in various states across the
(7)
country. It _____ (estimate) that more than 50,000 U.S. high
(8)
school students are now enrolled in Chinese classes.

Exercise 2.3 Past Forms of the Passive

A Read the active sentences about language. First underline the object in each sentence. Then rewrite the sentences as passive sentences. Sometimes more than one answer is possible.

1. At one time, many people used <u>Latin</u> as a global language.

   At one time, Latin was used as a global language by many people.

2. The ancient Romans spoke Latin.

   _____

3. Ancient Roman authors wrote many important manuscripts.

   _____

4. For many centuries, the Romans conquered neighboring nations.

   _____

5. These conquered groups spoke versions of Latin.

   _____

6. Conquered people from Britain to Africa used Latin.

   _____

7. People were still speaking Latin after the Roman Empire fell.

   _____

8. Scholars and scientists were using Latin until the eighteenth century.

   _____

B Read the sentences in A again. In which sentences are the agents not important? Discuss the reasons for your answers with a partner. Then rewrite these sentences in the passive without the agent.

   A *In the first sentence,* many people *isn't important because we know that only people use language.*

   B *You're right. The sentence could be* At one time, Latin was used as a global language.

3 | Verbs and Objects with the Passive

▶ Grammar Presentation

Transitive verbs (verbs that take an object) can occur in the passive.	Someone **saw** her at the conference. (transitive)
	She **was seen** at the conference.
Intransitive verbs (verbs that do not take an object) cannot occur in the passive.	I **fell** asleep. (intransitive)

3.1 Transitive and Intransitive Verbs

a. Some common transitive verbs that occur in the passive are *call, concern, do, expect, find, give, know, left, lose, make, put, see, take,* and *use.*

*Improvement of your language skills **is expected**.*
*I **was given** a new English textbook.*
*The reasons for his success **were not known**.*

b. *Born* is the past participle of *bear. Born* is used almost exclusively in the passive.

*I **was born** in a small town.*
*Where **were** you **born**?*

c. Some common intransitive verbs, which have no passive form, include *appear, arrive, come, die, fall, go, happen, live, look, occur, sit, smile, stay, wait,* and *walk.*

*When **did** your symptoms first **appear**?*
NOT *When were your symptoms first appeared?*
*Globalization of some languages **happens** over time.*
NOT *Globalization of some languages is happened over time.*

3.2 Passive Forms with Direct and Indirect Objects

Some verbs, such as *give, offer, show,* and *tell,* can have two objects: a direct and an indirect object. In passive sentences, either the direct object or the indirect object can become the subject. Use *to* before an indirect object that is not in subject position.

INDIRECT OBJ   DIRECT OBJ
The team gave the manager the report.
*The manager **was given** the report by the team.*
*The report **was given** to the manager by the team.*

Grammar Application

Exercise 3.1 Transitive or Intransitive?

Read the sentences about "dead" languages. Underline the verb in each sentence. If the sentence can occur in the passive, write the passive sentence on the line. Do not use an agent. Write ✗ if a passive form is not possible.

1. People in Ancient Rome spoke Latin.
   Latin was spoken in Ancient Rome.

2. People don't use Latin for everyday communication today.
   _____

3. Some languages die.
   _____

4. This occurred with Dalmatian.
   _____

5. People spoke Dalmatian in Croatia. _____

6. Dalmatian speakers lived in coastal towns of Croatia. _____

7. Groups in different regions developed dialects of Dalmatian.

_____

8. Native speakers didn't record the grammar of Dalmatian.

_____

Exercise 3.2 Using Transitive and Intransitive Verbs

A *Over to You* Answer the questions about a language you know. Use the underlined verbs in your answers. Use passive sentences when possible. Use the indirect object as the subject of the passive sentence when possible. Write sentences that are true for you.

1. What is a computer <u>called</u> in this language?

   A computer is called "bilgisayar" in Turkish.

2. What English words are <u>used</u> in this language?

   _____

3. Do any other foreign words <u>occur</u> in this language? If so, what are they?

   _____

4. Is this language <u>spoken</u> by more people or fewer people than it was 50 years ago?

   _____

5. What advice is frequently <u>given</u> by teachers to people learning this language?

   _____

6. Do speakers of this language <u>tell</u> their children traditional stories?

   _____

B *Group Work* Share your sentences with your group members.

Exercise 3.3 Direct Objects in Passive Sentences

A Read the sentences about Esperanto, a language that was created as a global language. Underline the agents.

1. The first book about Esperanto was published by <u>a company</u> in 1887.
2. Esperanto was invented by L. L. Zamenhof.
3. Esperanto was created by its inventors to be a very easy language to learn.
4. The grammar was designed by Zamenhof to be simple and clear.
5. It is spoken by about 10,000 people.
6. It is being used by people in about 115 countries.
7. It has not been recognized as an official language by any country.
8. The language is used by some international travelers.

B *Pair Work* Read the sentences in A again. Circle the direct objects. Compare your answers with a partner.

4 | Reasons for Using the Passive

▶ Grammar Presentation

The passive is used to describe processes and to report news events. The agent is not important. The focus is on the action or on the person or thing receiving the action.	First, the students **were shown** a video in English. A "dead" language **has been brought** back to life in one community.

4.1 Reasons for Using the Passive

a. Use the passive to describe a process or a result. Common verbs to describe a process or a result are *compare, develop, examine, make, measure, study,* and *test.*

*First, the information **was studied**. Then recommendations **were made**.* (process)
*Therefore, English **was made** the official language of the company in 2010.* (result)

b. Use the passive when you don't know who performed the action. You can also use the passive to avoid directly blaming or criticizing someone.

*The report **was poorly written**.* (We don't know, or we don't want to say, who wrote the report.)

c. Use the passive to report news events.

*Recommendations for the teaching of languages **were published** today.*

▶ Grammar Application

Exercise 4.1 Describing Processes and Results

A ◀)) Listen to a report on a language study of English as a Second Language (ESL) students. Then complete the answers to the questions. Use the passive and the words in parentheses.

1. How many groups of students were there? (put into)

   The students _were put into two groups_____ .

2. What was the assignment at the beginning of the semester? (give)

   Students in each group _____ .

3. What did group 1 study? (teach)

   Group 1 _____ .

4. What did group 2 study? (teach)

   Students in group 2 _____ .

5. Who read the essays? (read)

The first and final essays _____ .

6. What did the judges do with all of the final essays? (put)

All of the final essays from group 1 and group 2 _____

_____ .

7. How did the judges rate all the final essays? (rate)

The essays _____ .

8. What rating did the essays produced by group 1 receive? (give)

Most of the final essays produced by group 1 _____ .

9. What did the results seem to indicate? (include)

ESL students' writing improves when grammar and writing instruction

_____ .

B ◀))) Listen again and check your answers.

Exercise 4.2 Reporting News Events

Read the sentences about preserving two Native American languages. Then rewrite each
sentence in the passive. Do not use an agent. Sometimes more than one answer is possible.

1. In 2009 in Minnesota, the legislature established a volunteer group
   to preserve Native American languages.

   In 2009 in Minnesota, a volunteer group was
   established to preserve Native American languages.

2. The legislature recognized the importance of preserving the Native
   American languages.

   _____

   _____

3. The volunteer group collected data on the use of the Ojibwe and
   Dakota languages.

   _____

4. In Minnesota, many Native American people no longer spoke the Ojibwe and
   Dakota languages.

   _____

5. The volunteer group developed a strategy to teach the Ojibwe and Dakota languages
   in schools.

   _____

6. The group is developing teacher-training programs.

   _____

7. In 2011, a nonprofit business released software for teaching the Ojibwe language.

_____

8. The preservation of the languages will strengthen the Native Americans' cultural identities.

_____

Exercise 4.3 Avoiding Blame and Criticism

Read each classroom scenario and pretend you are the teacher. Then write passive statements to avoid directly blaming or criticizing someone. Use the underlined sentences in your answers. Sometimes more than one answer is possible.

1. Someone stole some valuable equipment from the classroom. You think that someone in the class is responsible, but you aren't sure. You tell the class:

   Some valuable equipment was stolen from the classroom.

2. One student's essay contained plagiarized material. The student copied some material in his essay from the Internet. You tell the student:

   _____

3. A hacker broke into the school's e-mail system last night. No one knows who is responsible, but you must inform the students. You tell the class:

   _____

4. A student hands in the second draft of an essay. You see a lot of grammar mistakes. The student did not edit the paper carefully. You tell the student:

   _____

5 Avoid Common Mistakes ⚠

1. Remember to use a form of *be* in passive sentences.

    is
English ∧ spoken at most airports.

2. Always use the past participle form of the verb in passive sentences.

    translated
The words have been ~~translating~~ into Spanish, Arabic, Chinese, and Urdu.

3. Do not use the passive form when the subject is the doer of the action.

    studying
I have been ~~studied~~ English for 5 years.
Most students have ~~been~~ used an English dictionary.

4. With questions, remember to put *be* before the subject.

    was
Why ∧ he ~~was~~ given an award?

Editing Task

Find and correct the mistakes in the paragraphs about English spelling.

Even good writers will tell you that English spelling has ~~been~~ confused them at one time or another. The same sound spelled many different ways. For example, the words *lazy* and *busy* are pronouncing with a /z/ sound, but they are not consistent in their spelling because of strange rules that are being related to the vowels. Why English is written this

5　way? English is an ancient language that contains old spelling rules. Also, other languages have been contributed many words to English.

Some experts who have been studied the English language for years would like to see English spelling simplified. They ask important questions: Why so much time is wasted on spelling lessons? Why is literacy lower in English-speaking countries than in countries

10　with simplified spelling? They point to the fact that many other languages simplified successfully. They suggest that in places such as Sweden, France, and Indonesia, changes to the written form have helped make learning to read easier.

6 | Grammar for Writing ✎

Using the Passive to Write About the Object of an Action

Writers often use passive sentences when the main topic of their writing is a noun that does not usually perform an action. For example, the nouns *English*, *idea*, and *information* usually receive an action rather than perform an action. Read these examples:

English <u>is spoken</u> very differently in different parts of the world.
Maxwell's ideas <u>are</u> always <u>expressed</u> in a way that makes people angry.
The information <u>was provided</u> in both English and Spanish.

Pre-writing Task

1 Read the paragraph below. What forms of English are being compared?

Jamaican English

English is spoken in many countries around the world, but in most places, it is more similar to British English than it is to American English. However, Jamaican English is different. The English that is spoken in Jamaica has similarities to both British and American English. Because Jamaica was once a British colony, Jamaican English used

5 to be similar to British English. However, because Jamaican people get more exposure to American media than to British media these days, and because Jamaica is so close to North America, many changes have occurred. For example, in Jamaica, people say *do you have* instead of the British *have you got.* In addition, *you don't need to do that* is used instead of the British expression *you needn't do that.* Also, many American English words are used

10 in Jamaica in place of their British equivalents. For example, baby beds are *cribs* rather than the British *cots,* and people live in *apartments* rather than the British *flats.* Despite the changes in expressions and vocabulary, the words are pronounced in a more British way than in an American way. As English becomes more of a global language, it will be interesting to see what other changes occur.

2 Read the paragraph again. Underline the passive verbs. Draw arrows to the nouns that receive the action. What is the agent in each clause with a passive verb? In each case, is it unknown, unimportant, or obvious?

Writing Task

1 *Write* Use the paragraph in the Pre-writing Task to help you write about language use or language change. You can write about one of these topics or use your own ideas.

- the languages that are spoken in your home
- the use of English or another language in a country you know well
- the use of foreign words in a language you know

2 *Self-Edit* Use the editing tips to improve your paragraph. Make any necessary changes.

1. Did you use the passive to place the focus on the action or on the person or thing receiving the action?
2. Did you use active sentences to place the focus on the doer of the action?
3. Did you avoid the mistakes in the Avoid Common Mistakes chart on page 265?

The Passive (2)
Food Safety

1 | Grammar in the Real World

A What do you know about genetically modified food? Read the article about genetically modified food. What are some genetically modified foods?

 ## Genetically Modified Food

Genetically modified[1] (GM) foods come from plants that **have been changed** in a laboratory. This technology alters the genes[2] of the plants. It was developed so that food could have specific, desirable traits. For example, the first GM crop in the United States consisted
5 of tomatoes that were genetically changed to stay firmer longer.

Many people have strong opinions about the potential[3] benefits and risks of GM agriculture. For example, those in favor of GM foods believe that crops **should be designed** to resist insects. They point to the example of sweet corn. They say that sweet corn **used to be destroyed** by pests. This created serious problems. Farmers lost
10 money. Crops **got damaged** and **could not be eaten**. Therefore, they say that a great benefit **can be found** in GM sweet corn, which has been modified to resist insects that cause damage. People who oppose GM foods see the issue differently. They cite[4] a study that links GM corn to organ[5] damage in rats. They claim that the safety of these crops has not been tested adequately.[6]

15 GM supporters see GM soybeans as another beneficial crop. These crops are not harmed by a powerful weed-killing chemical. This chemical kills weeds the first time it is applied, so farmers use less of it. Supporters say that this improves air and water quality since fewer pollutants enter the environment. Critics argue that the weeds are no longer affected by the weed killer, and new "superweeds" are growing. Therefore, farmers have
20 to use more chemicals to save their crops.

[1]**modify:** change something in order to improve it | [2]**gene:** a code that controls the development of particular characteristics in a plant or animal | [3]**potential:** possible but not yet achieved | [4]**cite:** mention something as an example or proof of something else | [5]**organ:** a vital part of the body, like the heart, lungs, and kidneys | [6]**adequately:** good enough but not very good

Finally, those in favor of GM foods say that better control of pests and weeds has made it possible for GM crops to produce more food in a shorter time. They believe this increased production will help feed a world population which is expected to grow to 9 billion by 2050. Opponents insist that the problem of world hunger **will**
25 **not be solved** by producing more food. They argue that farmers grow enough food now and that global hunger is a result of unequal food distribution, not the result of a food shortage.[7]

Clearly, there are pros and cons to this debate. GM foods seem to have the potential to benefit the world. However, **should** extra care **be taken** until the
30 long-term risks are known?

[7]**shortage:** a lack of something needed

B *Comprehension Check* Answer the questions.

1. What are genetically modified foods?
2. What are some advantages of genetically modified foods?
3. What are some concerns about genetically modified foods?

C *Notice* Find the sentences in the article and complete them.

1. For example, those in favor of GM foods believe that crops _____ to resist insects.

2. Opponents insist that the problem of world hunger _____ by producing more food.

3. However, _____ extra care _____ until the long-term risks are known?

What verb comes after modals in passive verb forms?

The Passive with *Be Going To* and Modals

Grammar Presentation

You can use the passive with *be going to* and modals.	GM foods **will replace** natural foods. (active) Natural foods **will be replaced** by GM foods. (passive)

2.1 Forming the Passive with *Be Going To* and Modals

a. For the passive with *be going to*, use *be going to* + *be* + the past participle of the main verb. *Not* comes before *be going to* in the negative form.	*Only natural foods **are going to be served** in our house. The food **is not going to be eaten** immediately. **Is** more GM food **going to be grown** in the future?*
b. For the passive with modals, use a modal + *be* + the past participle of the main verb. *Not* follows the modal in the negative form.	*People **could be harmed** by GM food. People **must be informed**. Food **should not be eaten** if it isn't fresh. **Will** questions about GM food **be answered** by scientists?*

▸▸ Passive Forms: See page A12.

▶ Grammar Application

Exercise 2.1 The Passive with *Will* and *Be Going To*

Complete the interview about plans for a food conference. Circle the passive form of the verbs.

Reporter A conference called *The Future of Food* **will hold / (will be held)** at
(1)
Bay City Tech next week. Issues concerning the food industry
will be discussed / will discuss by experts from a variety of fields. We
(2)
interviewed two participants, Dr. Fred Bell, a biologist, and Deniz Martin,
the president of the *Traditional Food Society*. First, what major issues
are going to address / are going to be addressed at next week's
(3)
conference?

Dr. Bell Policies on food aid **are going to debate / are going to be debated** in
(4)
one session.

Reporter What are the issues there?

Dr. Bell Well, GM plants **are going to be promoted / are going to promote**
(5)
as the main solution to hunger in poor nations.

Reporter World hunger is a serious problem. What's your opinion as a biologist?
Will the situation **improve / be improved** by GM plants?
(6)

Dr. Bell No, the problem of world hunger **will not solve / will not be solved** by
(7)
GM crops, in my opinion.

> *Reporter* Don't some experts believe that GM food will help increase crop production?
>
> *Dr. Bell* In my opinion, crop production **will not be increased / will not increase** by GM plants. In fact, there is no proof of this so far.
> ₍₈₎
>
> *Reporter* Ms. Martin, what *Traditional Food Society* issues **will be presented / will present** at the conference?
> ₍₉₎
>
> *Ms. Martin* The issue of sustainable food production – growing food without harming people or the environment – **will address / will be addressed**. For example, ways to improve organic farming methods **will be demonstrated / will demonstrate**.
> ₍₁₀₎ ₍₁₁₎
>
> *Reporter* Thank you both for your time.

Exercise 2.2 The Passive with Modals

A Read the facts that a student collected for a report on pesticides.[1] Rewrite the facts as passive sentences. Sometimes more than one answer is possible.

1. Pesticides can harm humans, animals, and the environment.

   Humans, animals, and the environment can be harmed by pesticides.

2. Pesticides can cause air pollution.

   _____

3. In the United States, scientists can find pesticides in many streams.

   _____

4. Pesticides may have harmed some farm animals.

   _____

5. Pesticides may have affected meat from farm animals.

   _____

6. Pesticides in water could affect fish.

   _____

7. In some cases, pesticides can affect humans.

   _____

[1]**pesticide:** a weed-killing chemical

B *Pair Work* Compare your sentences with a partner.

Exercise 2.3 More Passive with Modals

Complete the web article about a government recall. Rewrite the steps as passive sentences with modals. Use the indirect object as the subject of the passive sentence when possible. Sometimes more than one answer is possible.

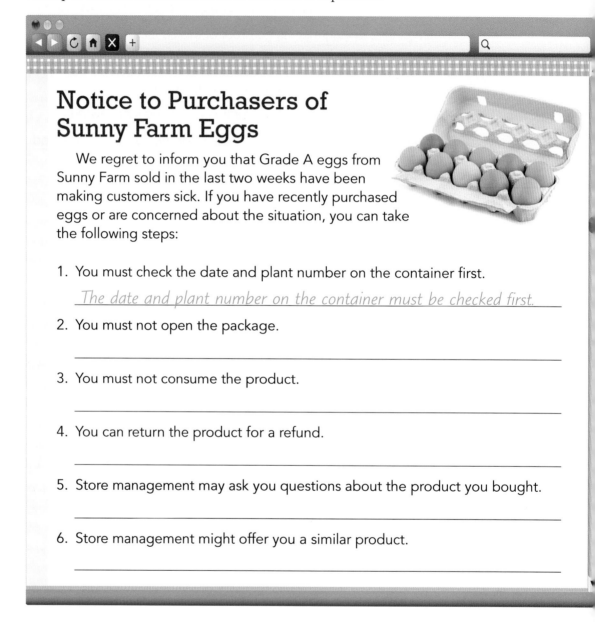

Notice to Purchasers of Sunny Farm Eggs

We regret to inform you that Grade A eggs from Sunny Farm sold in the last two weeks have been making customers sick. If you have recently purchased eggs or are concerned about the situation, you can take the following steps:

1. You must check the date and plant number on the container first.

   The date and plant number on the container must be checked first.

2. You must not open the package.

   _____

3. You must not consume the product.

   _____

4. You can return the product for a refund.

   _____

5. Store management may ask you questions about the product you bought.

   _____

6. Store management might offer you a similar product.

   _____

Exercise 2.4 Using Passive Forms of Modals

Group Work Discuss the questions about GM food. Use passive sentences with modals.

- Should food be genetically modified? Why or why not?
- In your opinion, can people be harmed by eating genetically modified food? If yes, in what ways?
- Should genetically modified food be labeled in the United States? Why or why not?

A *In my opinion, food should not be genetically modified because we don't know the dangers.*

B *I disagree. I think food should be genetically modified because it's the best way to end world hunger.*

3 Get Passives

Grammar Presentation

Passive sentences with *get* instead of *be* are more informal and are often used to express stronger emotions.	*The storm **destroyed** the crops.* (active) *The crops **got destroyed** by the storm.* (passive)

3.1 Forming *Get* Passives

a. For the *get* passive, use a form of *get* + the past participle of the main verb.	*He **is getting transferred** to the research department.* *Our orange trees **got damaged** last night.*
b. For negative statements and questions in the simple present and simple past, use a form of *do* + *get* + the past participle of the main verb.	*In my opinion, food **doesn't get inspected** carefully enough.* ***Did** your crops **get damaged** in the hurricane?*

3.2 Using *Get* Passives

We often use *get* passives to talk about negative situations or situations we think are beyond our control.	*Some food companies **are getting fined** for using unsafe equipment.*

speaking	
general writing	
formal academic writing	

Say: "She **got arrested and charged** with murder."
Write: She **was arrested and charged** with murder.

▶ Grammar Application

Exercise 3.1 *Get* Passives

Complete the interview about food contamination. Write *get* passives with the words in parentheses. If there is a line through the agent, do not use it in the passive.

Alternative Review

Interviewer There's been another case of contaminated[1] lettuce. How does this happen? An anonymous lettuce grower agreed to be interviewed if we did not mention his name. So, I hear

you're getting investigated by the FDA
(1. the FDA[2] is investigating you)

for problems with food safety. What happened?

Grower _____ .
(2. ~~Something~~ contaminated our lettuce)

Interviewer _____ ?
(3. Did the FDA recall the lettuce)

Grower Yes, _____ .
(4. ~~The FDA~~ recalled it)

Interviewer What happened, exactly?

Grower I'm not sure. As you know, _____
(5. ~~workers~~ pick our produce)

right here on the farm. _____ here.
(6. ~~Workers~~ also pack it)

_____ . This can cause contamination.
(7. ~~Workers~~ sometimes mishandle it)

[1]**contaminated:** less pure and potentially harmful | [2]**FDA:** Food and Drug Administration, a U.S. government agency

Interviewer Don't you have strict procedures?

Grower Yes, but it's been very hot lately. Working conditions have been difficult. Perhaps

_____ .
(8. ~~something~~ distracted the workers)

Interviewer _____ before it goes to the stores?
(9. Doesn't ~~someone~~ check your produce)

Grower No, _____ . That's our responsibility, and
(10. ~~people~~ don't inspect it)

my company is very sorry that we didn't catch it.

Interviewer I see. Well, thank you very much for agreeing to be interviewed.

Exercise 3.2 More *Get* Passives

A *Over to You* Look at the following statements about food safety. Check (✔) the statements you agree with.

- ☐ 1. When a restaurant gets inspected, the results should be posted on the restaurant's front door.
- ☐ 2. Food recalls get publicized too much. This hurts farmers, and a lot of perfectly good food gets thrown away.
- ☐ 3. If a supermarket sells spoiled food, the manager should get fired.
- ☐ 4. If a restaurant gets temporarily shut down for food safety problems, no one should ever eat there again.
- ☐ 5. All foreign fruit and vegetables should get inspected before entering the country.

B *Group Work* Compare your answers with your group members. Discuss your reasons. Use *get* passives.

A I think that when a restaurant gets inspected, the results should be posted on the restaurant's front door.

B I disagree. If a restaurant gets inspected and receives a low rating, it's bad for business.

4 | Passive Gerunds and Infinitives

▶ Grammar Presentation

Gerunds and infinitives can occur in the passive.	*Some people worry about genetically modified food **harming** them.* (active)
	*Some people worry about **being harmed** by genetically modified food.* (passive)
	*Consumers should expect food companies **to give** them accurate information about their food.* (active)
	*Consumers should expect **to be given** accurate information about their food.* (passive)

4.1 Forming Passive Gerunds

a. To form passive gerunds, use *being* + the past participle of the main verb.

*Consumers are afraid of food companies **harming** them.* (active)
*Consumers are afraid of **being harmed** by food companies.* (passive)

b. Common verbs that are followed by passive gerunds include *avoid, consider, dislike, enjoy, like, miss, quit,* and *remember*.

*I remember **being given** information about GM foods in the supermarket.*

c. Common verbs + prepositions that are followed by passive gerunds include *complain about, keep on, succeed in,* and *worry about*.

*The restaurant worried about **being closed** by the food inspectors.*

d. Common adjectives + prepositions that are followed by passive gerunds include *afraid of, aware of, concerned about, content with, interested in, tired of,* and *worried about*.

*The company was interested in **being seen** as a socially responsible company.*

▸▸ Verbs Followed by Gerunds Only: See page A7.
▸▸ Verbs Followed by Gerunds or Infinitives: See page A7.
▸▸ Verbs + Prepositions: See page A9.
▸▸ Adjectives + Prepositions: See page A10.

4.2 Forming Passive Infinitives

a. To form passive infinitives, use *to be* + the past participle of the main verb.

*Food companies are not likely **to solve** the problem of world hunger.* (active)
*The problem of world hunger is not likely **to be solved** by food companies.* (passive)

4.2 Forming Passive Infinitives *(continued)*

b. Common verbs followed by passive infinitives include *ask, expect, hope, manage, refuse, seem,* and *want.*

*The manager of the restaurant expected **to be told** that the restaurant passed the inspection.*

▸▸| Verbs Followed by Infinitives Only: See page A7.
▸▸| Verbs Followed by Gerunds or Infinitives: See page A7.

Grammar Application

Exercise 4.1 Passive Gerunds and Infinitives

Complete the sentences about restaurant food safety. Circle the correct passive forms of the verbs.

1. Customers at Corner Café recently complained about **being** / **to be** served undercooked food.

2. The manager of the café was concerned about **to be** / **being** inspected.

3. The owners were afraid of **to be** / **being** told they must close the cafe if the problems were not corrected.

4. The owners expected **being** / **to be** cited by the county food safety bureau.

5. The staff hoped **to be** / **being** paid for the time that the restaurant was closed.

6. The manager was not happy about **being** / **to be** told to close the restaurant.

Exercise 4.2 More Passive Gerunds and Infinitives

A ◀)) Listen to an interview with consumers about food labeling. Write the passive gerund or infinitive forms you hear.

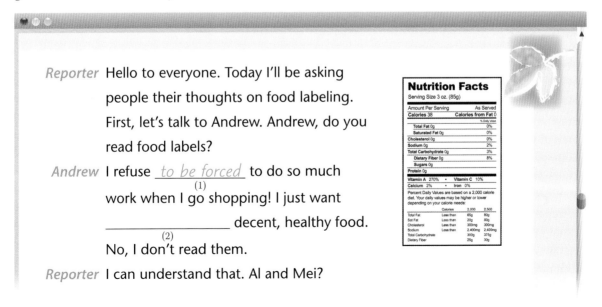

Reporter Hello to everyone. Today I'll be asking people their thoughts on food labeling. First, let's talk to Andrew. Andrew, do you read food labels?

Andrew I refuse *to be forced* to do so much
          (1)
          work when I go shopping! I just want
          _____ decent, healthy food.
          (2)
          No, I don't read them.

Reporter I can understand that. Al and Mei?

Nutrition Facts
Serving Size 3 oz. (85g)

Amount Per Serving	As Served
Calories 38	Calories from Fat 0

Al We expect _____ the truth by food companies,
(3)
but we know labels aren't always accurate.

Mei You have to inform yourself. All consumers have to start
_____ better _____ , so we always read them.
(4)   (4)

Reporter OK. And you, Roxana, do you read food labels?

Roxana Yes, because I'm a pretty informed consumer. I'm not too
concerned about _____ by food companies, but
(5)
I'm not interested in _____ , either!
(6)

Reporter Thank you, Roxana. And finally, Jessica. What do you think?

Jessica It's sometimes easy _____ by product labeling, so
(7)
I don't read them much because they don't matter. Take the
word *natural*, for example. You expect it _____ for
(8)
food that has few or no artificial ingredients. However, the word
natural can be used for genetically modified food products.

Reporter Thanks to you all. It appears that consumers are tired of
_____ by food companies.
(9)

B *Over to You* Complete the sentences about food labeling with passive gerunds or infinitives and the verbs in the box. Write sentences that are true for you.

~~confuse~~	give	lie to	tell
do	inform	sell	use

1. I'm tired of *being confused by food labels* _____

2. I expect _____

3. I'm (not) concerned about _____

4. I hope _____

5. It's (not) easy _____

C *Pair Work* Compare your answers with a partner.

A *I'm tired of being confused by food labels. I don't want to be told something is "organic" when it really isn't.*

B *Well, I know what you mean, but actually, I'm tired of being told to eat organic and healthy food all the time. Why can't I enjoy a candy bar once in a while?*

5 Avoid Common Mistakes ⚠

1. In passive sentences, use a past participle after *be*, not the base form of the verb.

produced
Unintended side effects can be ~~produce~~ by new technologies.

2. Don't forget to use *be* + the past participle to express a passive meaning.

be caused
An allergic reaction can ~~cause~~ by many different kinds of foods.

Editing Task

Find and correct seven more mistakes in the paragraph about some GM food concerns.

made
It is certain that many advances in technology will be ~~make~~ in the twenty-first century. Although many of these advances will improve our future, others may do as much harm as good. GM foods are one example. Currently, many new foods are creating by scientists. For instance, many people suffer from food allergies. Certain GM
5 foods may help avoid this problem; the food's DNA has been change so that the food no longer causes allergic reactions. Also, one day, the world's growing population may be feed with GM foods that grow quickly. This will make it possible for more food to be produce. These new foods can be use to feed more people. However, GM foods have another side. Because these foods have not existed very long, scientists do not know all
10 their effects. For example, some people fear that cancer can cause by GM foods. This is especially troubling because GM foods might not mark as such, so consumers may not know what they are buying. When they develop new foods, scientists should be aware of the concerns that consumers have. In my view, we should be careful with any new technology.

6 Grammar for Writing

Using the Passive with Modals, Gerunds, and Infinitives

> Writers use the passive to focus on actions, results, or processes rather than on the agents of action. Read these examples:
>
> *The origin of grocery products <u>has to be included</u> on labels.*
> *Local farmers are happy about their food <u>being purchased</u> by the restaurants in town.*
> *Organic food is likely <u>to be priced</u> higher than nonorganic food.*

Pre-writing Task

1 Read the paragraph below. What two reasons does the writer give for not buying certain organic products all the time?

Are Organic Foods Always the Best Choice?

Buying organic foods has been popular for a long time, but it can be expensive. Some organic foods may not be worth the extra expense. For example, consumers do not necessarily have to buy organic bananas. The reason for this is that the banana itself seems to be protected from the pesticides by the thick banana peel. Other
5 nonorganic foods that have thick peels or skins and that can be eaten safely are avocados and watermelons. There are also some nonorganic foods that are safe for other reasons. For example, some foods are simply not attractive to bugs, so it is a waste of farmers' time and money to spray pesticides on these foods. No one is sure why, but the reason for this might be that insects don't like the taste of these foods.
10 Broccoli, cabbage, and onions fall into this category. However, these nonorganic foods can still be priced higher because no chemical residue can be found in them. Should the public be informed of this? Consumers should be worried about not being made aware of this information since they could be spending more than they need to.

2 Read the paragraph again. Underline the passive forms of modals. Circle the passive gerund. <u>Double underline</u> the passive infinitive.

Writing Task

1 *Write* Use the paragraph in the Pre-writing Task to help you write about some aspect of food. You can write about one of these topics or use your own ideas.

- children and food choices
- the lack of healthy fast-food options
- eating vegetarian or vegan
- pros and cons of GM foods

2 *Self-Edit* Use the editing tips to improve your paragraph. Make any necessary changes.

1. Did you use the passive to place the focus on the action or process?
2. Did you use different forms of the passive?
3. Did you use passive gerunds and infinitives correctly?
4. Did you avoid the mistakes in the Avoid Common Mistakes chart on page 279?

Subject Relative Clauses (Adjective Clauses with Subject Relative Pronouns)

Alternative Energy Sources

1 | Grammar in the Real World

A What are some alternative sources of energy (other than oil or coal)? Read the article about one type of alternative energy. Is "people power" an efficient energy source? Why or why not?

Exercising for Electricity

Much of the world's energy comes from sources like oil and coal, **which cannot be replaced when used up**. Renewable sources – water, wind, and
5 the sun – are better for the environment. However, these alternative sources of energy have not always been sufficiently explored for political and economic reasons. People **who care**
10 **about the environment** are looking for more alternative sources that might appeal to people **who make decisions about these things**. One source **that is becoming popular** uses energy
15 **that is generated by humans**, sometimes called "people power."

With people power, people create electricity through exercise. People exercise in green gyms, **which**
20 **contain special treadmills**. These machines convert human energy into electricity **that helps run the lights and air-conditioning**. People power also helps prevent air pollution.
25 Someone **who exercises for one**

hour can feel good about the fact that he or she is helping prevent carbon dioxide from going into the air. Professional athletes, **whose exercise**
30 **routines can last for several hours**, could help power a house!

Exercise is not the only way people can make energy. One company has created surfaces **which are powered**
35 **by humans**. People dance or walk on special dance floors and sidewalks. This movement generates electricity, **which can light up the dance floor or power street lamps**. Body heat
40 is used for power, too. One system in Sweden gathers the body heat from

commuters in a train station. This heat, **which is sent to a nearby building**, cuts the energy bill by 25 percent.

45 People power is not perfect, though. Large gyms need a lot of energy to run. People power, **which only generates a part of the total electricity needed**, does not lower the gym's electric bill

50 much. Also, the use of this technology is moving slowly. Business leaders, **who must focus on making a profit**, do not always want to be the first to create new products. They are afraid to spend

money on technology **which might not** 55 **be successful**. However, people **who support green energy** are confident that this technology will catch on in the near future.

People power is not a major 60 energy source yet, but it could be soon. Meanwhile, this "green energy" encourages people to exercise, and it makes people more aware of the environment. It is one kind of 65 technology **that helps people and the planet** at the same time.

B *Comprehension Check* Answer the questions.

1. What are some ways that people can make energy?
2. How can "people power" help the environment?
3. What are some problems with people power?

C *Notice* Find the sentences in the article and complete them. Then draw an arrow from each missing word to the word that it refers to.

1. Professional athletes, _____ **exercise routines** can last for several hours, could help power a house!

2. This heat, _____ **is sent** to a nearby building, cuts the energy bill by 25 percent.

3. However, people _____ **support** green energy are confident that this technology will catch on in the near future.

Look at the words in bold that follow the words you wrote. What parts of speech are the words in bold?

2 Identifying Subject Relative Clauses

Grammar Presentation

Relative clauses modify – define, describe, identify, or give more information about – nouns. In a subject relative clause, the relative pronoun is the subject of the clause. An identifying relative clause gives essential information about the noun it modifies.	SUBJECT *I go to a gym. The gym creates its own electricity.* RELATIVE PRONOUN *I go to a gym **that creates its own electricity**.*

2.1 Forming Identifying Subject Relative Clauses

a. The subject of an identifying subject relative clause is the relative pronoun. The relative pronoun refers to the noun before it. Use *who* or *that* for people, and *which* or *that* for things.	NOUN RELATIVE PRONOUN *Nowadays, people often drive cars **that don't use a lot of gas.***
Do not add a second subject to the clauses.	*People **that exercise** can use special machines to create electricity.* NOT *People that ~~they~~ exercise can use special machines to create electricity.*
b. The information in an identifying subject relative clause is essential. Do not add a comma before this type of clause.	*People **who care about the environment** often recycle their garbage.* (The relative clause tells which people.) *The school uses the electricity **that comes from the exercise machines in the gym**.* (The relative clause tells which electricity.)
c. The verb in the relative clause agrees with the noun that the relative pronoun modifies.	SINGULAR NOUN SINGULAR VERB *Someone **that supports** the environment recycles.* PLURAL NOUN PLURAL VERB *Many people **that support** the environment recycle.*

: Relative Clauses: See page A13.

2.2 Using Identifying Subject Relative Clauses

a. Use an identifying relative clause to give essential information about a noun. These clauses are also called restrictive subject clauses.	*People power is a kind of energy.* (What kind of energy? What is important about it?) *People power is a kind of energy **that creates electricity**.* (The relative clause gives essential information.)
b. Use an identifying relative clause in definitions, especially with words such as *anyone, people, someone,* or *something*.	*Green energy is something **which doesn't hurt the environment**.* *Environmentalists are people **who care about the environment**.*

Grammar Application

Exercise 2.1 Subject Relative Pronouns

A Complete the article about people power. Use *who* or *which* and the simple present form of the verbs in parentheses.

> Silvia is a student at Bay City University (BCU) _who works out_ (work out) at
> (1)
> the campus gym every day. Today, she is exercising on a bike _____
> (2)
> (connect) to a power grid. Silvia is possibly producing the energy _____
> (3)
> (keep) the gym lights on or _____ (power) a professor's laptop in
> (4)
> another part of the campus. BCU and Bay City Tech are just two educational
> institutions _____ (use) human energy as power.
> (5)
> We interviewed Mark Sandoval, a BCU employee _____ (run)
> (6)
> campus operations. He said, "This is not a program _____ (save)
> (7)
> the university money. It's more of an experiment _____
> (8)
> (illustrate) to the students how they affect their environment." GreenGo is a Bay
> City human energy company _____ (provide) BCU with the exercise
> (9)
> equipment. Rita Crane, a GreenGo spokesperson, said, "We enjoy working with
> students and faculty_____ (take) their impact on the environment
> (10)
> very seriously."

B 🔊 Listen to the article and check your answers.

Exercise 2.2 Definitions with Identifying Relative Clauses

A Complete the energy definitions with *who* or *that* and the correct form of the verbs in parentheses. Sometimes more than one answer is possible.

1. Geothermal energy is heat _that comes_ (come) from inside the earth.

2. Renewable energy is something _____ (not / disappear).

3. Ecologists are people _____ (study) the relationship between organisms and the environment.

4. A green politician is someone _____ (put) environmental issues ahead of other issues.

5. A sustainable engineer is anyone _____ (design) objects to protect the environment.

B Complete the energy definitions with subject relative pronouns and the words in the box.

chemicals / trap / heat in the atmosphere	a type of energy / come / from human exercise
~~fuel / come / from vegetable oil or animal fat~~	
people / be / part of a political group focused on good environmental policy	a type of energy / use / the sun as its source
someone / work / to protect the environment	a vehicle / use / two sources of power to run
structures / not have / a large negative impact on the environment	

1. Biodiesel is a kind of _fuel that/which comes from vegetable oil or animal fat_ .

2. A conservationist is _____ .

3. "Greens" are _____ .

4. Greenhouse gases are _____ .

5. A hybrid car is _____ .

6. Solar energy is _____ .

7. People power is _____ .

8. Green buildings are _____ .

Exercise 2.3 Sentence Combining

A Combine the sentences from an alternative energy company's advertisement. Use *who*, *that*, or *which* in subject relative clauses. Sometimes more than one answer is possible.

1. GreenGo is a company. It develops renewable energy systems.

   GreenGo is a company that/which develops
   renewable energy systems.

2. GreenGo developed a technology. The technology turns exercise machines into power generators.

   _____

   _____

3. GreenGo builds machines like exercise bikes. These exercise bikes let exercisers generate electricity from their workouts.

   _____

   _____

4. The electricity connects to a power grid. The power grid covers a large geographic area.

   _____

   _____

5. Sachiko Hanley is the woman. The woman invented this technology.

_____

6. Many GreenGo clients are colleges and other institutions. The institutions have on-site gyms.

_____

_____

7. GreenGo provides an energy source. The energy source is good for the environment.

_____

8. "We are proud to work with institutions. They have the same environmental goals that we do."

_____

_____

B In each of the sentences you wrote in A, underline the subject relative clause and draw an arrow from the relative pronoun to the noun in the main clause it refers to.

GreenGo is a company that develops renewable energy systems.

3 | Nonidentifying Subject Relative Clauses

Grammar Presentation

Nonidentifying subject relative clauses have the same form as identifying clauses. Unlike identifying clauses, nonidentifying clauses provide additional, not essential, information about the nouns they modify.

Biodiesel fuel, **which often comes from plants**, *is an economical source of energy.* (Where the fuel comes from is extra information. It is not essential information about *Biodiesel fuel.*)

3.1 Forming Nonidentifying Subject Relative Clauses

a. Like identifying subject relative clauses, the subject of a nonidentifying subject relative clause is the relative pronoun. The relative pronoun refers to the noun before it.

Use *who* for people and *which* for things. Do not use *that* in a nonidentifying clause.

People power, **which** *is a way to create energy, is popular.*

NOT *People power,* ~~that~~ *is a way to create energy, is popular.*

3.1 Forming Nonidentifying Subject Relative Clauses *(continued)*

b. Use commas before and after the nonidentifying subject relative clause. The commas indicate that the information is not essential to the meaning of the noun. It is extra information.

Hybrid cars, **which are better for the environment,** *use less gas.*

3.2 Using Nonidentifying Subject Relative Clauses

a. Use a nonidentifying subject relative clause to give nonessential information about a noun. These clauses are also called nonrestrictive clauses.

People power, **which is a way to create energy,** *is popular with environmentalists.*

b. Nonidentifying relative clauses are more common in writing and formal speaking than in informal speaking.

3.3 Identifying vs. Nonidentifying Subject Relative Clauses

a. Identifying relative clauses provide essential information about the noun. The information in the clause identifies or distinguishes the noun.

Renewable energy **that comes directly from the sun** *is called solar energy.* (The information identifies a particular type of renewable energy – not all types of renewable energy.)

My sister **who lives in Maine** *loves being outside.* (The information distinguishes this sister from the other or others; it implies there is more than one sister.)

b. Nonidentifying clauses give extra information about a noun. The information is not essential. In speaking, use a short pause before and after the clause. In writing, separate the clause between commas.

Renewable energy, **which releases fewer greenhouse gases,** *is becoming more popular.* (The information does not identify the type of renewable energy; it gives more information about it.)

My sister, **who lives in Maine,** *loves being outside.* (The information is extra, not essential; it also implies the speaker has only one sister.)

▶ Grammar Application

Exercise 3.1 Identifying or Nonidentifying?

A Read the news report on building affordable green homes in New Orleans. Underline the relative clauses. Label each of the relative clauses *I* (for identifying) or *NI* (for nonidentifying).

As the environment changes, hurricanes and other severe storms have become a

serious problem in the United States and Latin America. Hurricanes, which primarily attack
NI

southern and southeastern parts of the United States, have been increasing in severity.
The hurricane that did the most damage in recent history was Hurricane Katrina. Since then,
5 a great number of Americans, including many celebrities, have helped the people of New
Orleans rebuild their homes.

The celebrity who is best known for building homes in New Orleans is Brad Pitt.
Pitt, who created a foundation called Make It Right, helps build new "green" homes in
New Orleans. The goals of this foundation are admirable. Make It Right volunteers, who
10 work for free, want to build 150 new green homes in the Lower 9th Ward.

The foundation is not simply providing new homes. Make It Right homes have
many features which are environmentally sound. For example, Make It Right homes
have metal roofs which absorb heat and keep them cool. It is possible that Make It
Right homes will inspire new home builders not only in New Orleans but around the
15 world as well.

B *Pair Work* Compare your answers with a partner. Discuss the reason for each of
your answers.

The relative clause which primarily attack southern and southeastern parts of
the United States *is nonidentifying, because it is not essential to understanding the
sentence. You can say* Hurricanes have been increasing in severity, *and the idea is
complete.*

Exercise 3.2 Nonidentifying Subject Relative Clauses

Combine the facts and the additional information about green architecture. Use
nonidentifying relative clauses.

1. **Fact:** Green architecture is becoming more common.
   Additional Information: Green architecture considers
   both design and the environment.

   *Green architecture, which considers both design
   and the environment, is becoming more common.*

2. **Fact:** The Turning Torso building uses only renewable energy.
   Additional Information: The Turning Torso building is
   located in Malmö, Sweden.

   _____

   _____

   _____

   _____

3. **Fact:** The Turning Torso building was inspired by a sculpture of a twisting human being.
   Additional Information: The Turning Torso building is the tallest building in Sweden.

   _____

   _____

4. **Fact:** The Burj al-Taqa will be a wind- and solar-powered green skyscraper.
   Additional Information: The Burj al-Taqa will be in Dubai.

   _____

   _____

5. **Fact:** Eckhard Gerber has also designed a green building in Riyadh.
   Additional Information: Eckhard Gerber designed the Burj al-Taqa.

   _____

   _____

6. **Fact:** Architect Eric Corey Freed believes that people will pay more for green buildings.
   Additional Information: Eric Corey Freed has written several books on building green structures.

   _____

   _____

4 Subject Relative Clauses with *Whose*

▶ Grammar Presentation

Subject relative clauses that begin with the pronoun *whose* show possession.	In Sweden, there are train commuters. *The commuters' body heat supplies energy for a building.* In Sweden, there are train commuters **whose body heat supplies energy for a building**.

4.1 Forming Relative Clauses with *Whose*

a. The pronoun *whose* shows a possessive relationship between the noun before and after it.	They are the scientists **whose research** has won awards. (The research belongs to the scientists.) That is the product **whose inventor** attended this college. (The product is related to the inventor.)
b. The verb in the relative clause agrees with the noun following *whose*.	WHOSE + SINGULAR NOUN + SINGULAR VERB He's the scientist **whose newest idea is often quoted.** WHOSE + PLURAL NOUN + PLURAL VERB He's the scientist **whose ideas are often quoted.**

4.2 Using Relative Clauses with *Whose*

Relative clauses with *whose* can be identifying or nonidentifying subject relative clauses.

IDENTIFYING RELATIVE CLAUSE

*They are the journalists **whose articles have explained green energy**.* (The information in the clause identifies which journalists.)

NONIDENTIFYING RELATIVE CLAUSE

*Brad Pitt, **whose movies are well known**, gives a lot of money to environmental causes.* (The information about his movies is not essential to identifying Brad Pitt.)

Grammar Application

Exercise 4.1 Subject Relative Clauses with *Whose*: Identifying or Nonidentifying?

A Read the article about a human-powered vehicle. Underline the subject relative clauses. Add commas when necessary.

Meet Charles Greenwood, the inventor of a new type of car. Greenwood, <u>whose human-powered car can go up to 60 miles per hour</u>, is an engineer. This inventor whose dream is to sell the cars to the public has also started a business to manufacture it. A car whose power source is human energy is obviously good for the environment. How does

5 it work? The car whose main power source is human-operated hand cranks[1] also runs with a battery. It's not expensive, either. The car – the HumanCar Imagine PS – will sell for about $15,000. A hybrid car whose selling price will only be about $15,000 should be very popular with energy-conscious consumers.

There are other benefits to a human-powered car. A car whose

10 power source is human energy might also help drivers stay fit. In addition, owners expect to save money operating the HumanCar. The HumanCar whose main source of power is human-operated hand cranks gets the equivalent of 100 miles to the gallon of gas in a regular car.

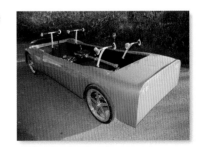

[1]**crank:** a handle or bar on a machine that you can turn to make another part turn

B *Pair Work* Compare your answers with a partner. Discuss whether each subject relative clause is identifying or nonidentifying.

The relative clause whose human-power car can go up to 60 miles per hour *is nonidentifying because it is not necessary for identifying* Greenwood.

Exercise 4.2 *That, Who,* or *Whose?*

Complete the article about green awards. Use *that, who,* or *whose.* Sometimes more than one answer is possible.

Awards for Being Green

There are many organizations _that_ offer awards to companies _____
(1)   (2)
practices help the environment and society. Some organizations recognize the work of

companies _____ focus on environmentally responsible practices. The Evergreen
(3)
Award program honors companies _____ create environmentally friendly products.
(4)
An award in 2010 went to Play Mart Inc., a maker of plastic playground equipment

_____ products were made from jugs and bottles from landfills.
(5)

The One Show is another awards organization, _____ Green Pencil award
(6)
celebrates environmentally conscious advertising. In 2009, Häagen-Dazs received the

award for their advertisements _____ raised awareness about the disappearance
(7)
of honeybees. Häagen-Dazs, _____ ice-cream is well known, also donates
(8)
money to research _____ studies honeybees. People _____ buy certain
(9)   (10)
flavors of Häagen-Dazs ice-cream help support this research.

Exercise 4.3 Subject Relative Clauses with *Whose*

Pair Work Answer the questions. Use subject relative clauses with *whose* in your sentences. Then compare your answers with a partner.

- What are the benefits of human-powered vehicles and flying machines?
- What are the disadvantages to these inventions?

A I said, "A vehicle whose power source is human energy is good for the environment."

B I said, "A vehicle whose power source is human energy probably won't go very far or very fast."

5 Avoid Common Mistakes ⚠

1. Use *which* or *that* for things, not *who*.

which / that

Scientists are looking for new energy sources ~~who~~ don't harm the environment.

2. Use *who* or *that* for people, not *which*.

who / that

Governments support researchers ~~which~~ are trying to develop alternative approaches to energy.

3. Don't use *who's* when you mean *whose*.

whose

An inventor ~~who's~~ innovative technology solves the energy crisis will help all of us.

4. Don't include a second subject in the relative clause.

A fuel that ~~it~~ is renewable will help solve the world's pollution problems.

Editing Task

Find and correct eight more mistakes in the paragraph about an alternative renewable energy source.

People think renewable energy only comes from water, wind, or the sun, but there is

which / that

another renewable energy source: biofuels. Biofuels are fuels ~~who~~ are derived from oils in plants. Farmers who's fields were once planted with food crops can now grow energy on their land. The most commonly used example of this is ethanol, a biofuel who is usually

5 made from corn and added to gasoline. However, ethanol has been criticized. Some critics say that the world, who's population continues to grow, needs all of its corn for food production. Others have argued that it takes too much energy to produce corn ethanol. Recently, scientists which do biofuels research have been working to overcome these problems. For example, some scientists have produced a genetically modified tobacco

10 that it contains more oil than usual. Other scientists have produced genetically modified tobacco plants that they produce a lot of oil. This oil can be made into ethanol. In fact, some scientists have produced ethanol from inedible grass that it grows in the wild. The scientists which made these inventions hope that biofuels will become an important part of our renewable energy future.

6 | Grammar for Writing

Using Subject Relative Clauses to Avoid Repetition

Writers use subject relative clauses to avoid repeating information and to condense – or package – the information into fewer sentences. This can improve the clarity and flow of a reading passage. Read these examples:

Hybrids have been getting more efficient every year. However, they are not getting any less expensive.

Hybrids, <u>which have been getting more efficient every year</u>, are not getting any less expensive.

The environmentalist's work was featured on a recent television program. That environmentalist is speaking today at the university.

The environmentalist <u>whose work was featured on a recent television program</u> is speaking today at the university.

Pre-writing Task

1 Read the paragraph below. What change does the writer promote and why?

Small but Effective Changes

People everywhere are concerned with the future of our planet, whose environment is rapidly deteriorating. Environmentalists who want to help protect the planet are working hard to find environmentally sound alternatives that are also economical. However, there are many changes that are relatively easy to make. One change that
5 could make a significant impact is using reusable bags instead of plastic or paper bags when shopping. Plastic bags, which might take up to 1,000 years to degrade, are very destructive for the environment. Between 500 billion to 1 trillion plastic bags are used each year around the world. In various parts of the world, laws which would stop the use of plastic bags entirely are being discussed or implemented. Paper bags are not as harmful
10 for the environment as plastic, but they still cause a significant amount of damage. Approximately 14 million trees are cut down each year just to supply Americans with paper bags. In some stores in the United States, shoppers who use their own bags are given five cents back for each bag. However, even though using reusable shopping bags instead of plastic or paper is a very easy change to make, only a small minority of people in
15 the United States have begun to do it voluntarily. In years to come, there will likely be laws that regulate the use of shopping bags to protect the environment.

2 Read the paragraph again. Underline the subject relative clauses. Circle the relative pronoun in each relative clause and draw an arrow to the noun it refers to.

Writing Task

1 *Write* Use the paragraph in the Pre-writing Task to help you write about small or big changes people can make to help the environment or about ways people can be green. You can write about one of these topics or use your own ideas.

- alternative energy
- daily life
- entertainment
- housing
- transportation
- work

2 *Self-Edit* Use the editing tips to improve your paragraph. Make any necessary changes.

1. Did you use identifying subject relative clauses to help define or clarify the noun that is being discussed?
2. Did you use nonidentifying subject relative clauses to add additional information?
3. Did you avoid the mistakes in the Avoid Common Mistakes chart on page 293?

Object Relative Clauses (Adjective Clauses with Object Relative Pronouns)

Biometrics

1 | Grammar in the Real World

A What are some techniques that the police use to solve crimes? Read the article about how the police analyze evidence. What are some modern techniques for analyzing evidence?

Forensics: An Imperfect Science

Someone steals a painting from a private home. The victim shows the police the room **in which the theft occurred**. Police collect clothing fibers and dirt left on the carpet. Experts then use the fibers
5 and dirt to identify the thief. The thief is caught, and the art is returned. The use of scientific tests to investigate crimes like this one is called forensics. Traditional forensic techniques include collecting and analyzing evidence **that police find at the**
10 **crime scene**. This evidence includes dust, hair, or fibers **that thieves leave behind**. Police sometimes use dogs to investigate a crime. Scents **that dogs are trained to recognize** include the scents of people, drugs, and explosives. Police also look for fingerprints, **which they often find on hard surfaces**. Unfortunately, fingerprints are often incomplete. However, new techniques use computer programs to help police
15 identify suspects or missing people. Computer programs can produce a list of matches for partial fingerprints. This kind of list, **which police use to narrow a large field of suspects**, helps investigators work efficiently.

In addition, new technology is being used to analyze other evidence. New video cameras can automatically identify a face **whose image police have on film**. Police
20 can compare the faces of suspects to the image of the criminal and find the actual person more quickly. There is also a new way **in which police can identify someone who may be a "missing person."**[1] This new technology compares a digital image of the person's iris[2] with the irises of people who are listed as missing in a database.

[1]**missing person:** someone who has disappeared | [2]**iris:** the colored part of the eye

Forensic evidence **that police collect** is not always accurate. For example, fiber
25 matching is inconclusive.[3] Currently, fibers **that investigators analyze** can only be
matched to a type of cloth. The fibers may not be from clothes **that the suspect owns**.
Another concern is that there are no strict training standards for forensic dogs. Therefore,
agencies like the FBI have only a few dog teams **whose work they trust**.

Combining technology with traditional methods is changing the way **that criminal
30 investigations are done**. Forensic science is not perfect, but it is still an important
tool in investigations.

[3]**inconclusive:** not leading to a definite result or decision; uncertain

B *Comprehension Check* Answer the questions.

1. What are some types of forensic evidence?
2. What is one way that police can identify someone?
3. Why can forensic evidence sometimes be inaccurate?

C *Notice* Match the first part of the sentence from the article on the left with the
second part on the right.

A	**B**
1. The victim shows the police the room _____	a. **that** thieves leave behind.
2. Traditional forensic techniques include collecting and analyzing evidence _____	b. in **which** the theft occurred.
3. This evidence includes dust, hair, or fibers _____	c. **that** police find at the crime scene.

Do the words in B in bold act as the subjects or objects of the clauses they are in?

2 | Identifying Object Relative Clauses

▶ Grammar Presentation

In an object relative clause, the relative pronoun is the object of the clause. An identifying object relative clause gives essential information about the noun it modifies.	OBJECT *Evidence is sometimes inaccurate. Police collect this evidence.* RELATIVE PRONOUN *Evidence **that police collect** is sometimes inaccurate.*

2.1 Forming Identifying Object Relative Clauses

a. The object relative pronoun follows the noun it replaces and comes at the beginning of the relative clause. In an object relative clause, the relative pronoun is the object of the clause.	*Humans aren't aware of <u>smells</u>. A dog can recognize <u>smells</u>.* RELATIVE NOUN PRONOUN *Humans aren't aware of smells **that a dog can recognize.***
b. Use the relative pronouns *who*, *that*, or *whom* with people. Use *which* or *that* for things.	*Detectives are <u>people</u> **who/that/whom** I respect tremendously.*
These pronouns are frequently omitted in speaking, but not in formal writing.	*Forensic evidence is something **which/that police count on**. (in writing)* *Forensic evidence is something **police count on**. (in speaking)*
When referring to people, *that* is more common than *who*. The pronoun *whom* is very formal and is much less common than *that* or *who* in conversation.	least formal ↑↓ most formal *Detective Paula Cho is a person **that** I admire very much.* *Detective Paula Cho is a person **who** I admire very much.* *Detective Paula Cho is a person **whom** I admire very much.*
c. Use *whose* + a noun to show possession. *Whose* cannot be omitted.	*The person **whose car the thieves stole** was a friend of mine.*

▸▸ Relative Clauses: See page A13.

2.2 Using Identifying Object Relative Clauses

Use an identifying relative clause to give essential information that defines or identifies the noun it modifies.	*Evidence **that criminals leave at the crime scene** is called forensic evidence. (That criminals leave at the crime scene identifies the evidence.)*

▶ Grammar Application

Exercise 2.1 Forming Identifying Object Relative Clauses

Complete the sentences about forensic technology. Use *who* or *which* and the verbs in parentheses.

1. *Biometrics* refers to the techniques <u>which</u> people <u>use</u> (use) to identify individuals by their physical or behavioral characteristics.

2. Biometric information _____ experts _____ (analyze) includes DNA, fingerprints, eyes, and voice patterns.

3. People _____ the police _____ (suspect) of a crime can be excluded with the use of biometrics.

4. Biometric technology can match fingerprints with ones _____ the police _____ (have) on file.

5. One type of biometric technology _____ people _____ (utilize) for security is the fingerprint scanner.

Fingerprint scanner

6. For example, people _____ Disney World _____ (admit) to the park must have their fingerprints scanned.

7. The fingerprint scanners _____ Disney World _____ (use) help to stop people from entering the park without a proper ticket.

Exercise 2.2 Using Identifying Object Relative Clauses

Complete the web interview about forensic technology. Rewrite the sentence pairs in parentheses as single sentences with object relative clauses. Sometimes more than one answer is possible.

Reporter I understand that our police department has some new forensic technology.

Mayor *Yes, it has a new system that it uses to analyze DNA.*
(1. Yes, it has a new system. It uses the system to analyze DNA.)

Reporter What does it look like?

Mayor _____
(2. It's a hand-held device. Officers bring it to the crime scene.)

_____
(3. It helps the police to analyze data. They find the data at the scene.)

Reporter I understand that not everyone is happy about this device.

Mayor _____
(4. The device has privacy issues. Some people are concerned about these privacy issues.)

Reporter Why is this a concern?

Mayor _____
(5. Well, the DNA might get the person in trouble. The device collected this DNA.)

_____
(6. For example, many people have health issues. They want to keep these issues private.)

Reporter Oh, I see. This is certainly a lot to think about. Thank you for the interview.

Exercise 2.3 Sentence Combining

A Rewrite the reporter's notes on local crimes. Use identifying object relative clauses with the relative pronouns in parentheses.

Recent Crime Reports

1. A man was arrested for theft. Police raided his house last night. (whose)

   A man _whose house police raided last night was arrested_
   for theft .

2. The detectives made their report. The police sent the detectives to the crime scene. (whom)

   The detectives _____ .

3. Several valuable items had been stolen. The police recovered the items. (that)

   Several valuable items _____ .

4. The man has not been identified. Burglars invaded the man's home. (whose)

   The man _____ .

5. Detectives have visited the house. The thief broke into the house yesterday. (which)

   Detectives _____ .

6. The man is in good condition. A car hit him last night. (that)

   The man _____ .

B *Pair Work* In which sentences in A can you omit the pronoun? Discuss the answer with a partner. Then rewrite the sentences with the pronoun omitted.

3 | Nonidentifying Object Relative Clauses

▶ Grammar Presentation

Nonidentifying object relative clauses have the same form as identifying clauses. Unlike identifying clauses, nonidentifying clauses provide additional, not essential, information about the nouns they modify.	*Evidence from crimes, **which we call forensic evidence**, can help police solve cases.* (*Which we call forensic evidence* is extra information. It is not essential to understanding *Evidence from crimes*.)

3.1 Forming Nonidentifying Object Relative Clauses

a. Use *who* or *whom* for people. Use *which* for things. Use *whose* for possessive people and things.

The Sherlock Holmes stories were written by the Scottish author Arthur Conan Doyle, **who / whom many people think was English**.

Do not use *that* in nonidentifying relative clauses.

Forensic science, **which Sherlock Holmes used**, *has been recognized as science since the 1800s.*
NOT *Forensic science,* ~~that~~ *Sherlock Holmes used, has been recognized as science since the 1800s.*

Do not omit the relative pronoun in nonidentifying object clauses.

The character Sherlock Holmes, **who Arthur Conan Doyle created**, *was a fictional detective.*
NOT *The character Sherlock Holmes,* ~~Arthur Conan Doyle created~~, *was a fictional detective.*

b. Use commas before and after the nonidentifying object relative clause.

Arthur Conan Doyle, **whose medical clinic not many patients attended,** *had time to write his stories.*

▶ Grammar Application

Exercise 3.1 Nonidentifying Object Relative Clauses

Read part of a presentation on a forensic science program. Underline the nonidentifying clauses. Add commas.

Forensic science, <u>which many of you know about from popular TV shows</u>, has become a popular career. Forensic science courses which many colleges are offering today prepare students for careers in crime scene investigation. The University of Central Florida (UCF) which I attended has a forensic science program. Your area of specialization

5 which you choose during your time here depends on your interests and skills. The area that I chose was forensic biochemistry because I wanted to study odontology. Forensic odontology which the police use to analyze teeth is challenging and fascinating. Forensic analysis which focuses on chemistry and analysis of different kinds of evidence is also available. Introduction to Forensic Science which you take after other preliminary courses

10 will help you decide on the area of specialty. I wish you all the best of luck!

Exercise 3.2 Using Nonidentifying Object Relative Clauses

Read the sentences about a TV show that popularizes forensics. Combine the sentences with nonidentifying object relative clauses. Add commas when necessary.

1. *CSI: Crime Scene Investigation* is an American TV series. Anthony E. Zuiker created it.

   CSI: Crime Scene Investigation _, which Anthony E. Zuiker created, is an_ _American TV series_ .

2. The program was an immediate hit. CBS first aired it in 2000.

   The program _____ .

3. *CSI* has been on the air for over 10 years. The entertainment industry has awarded it six Emmys.

   CSI _____

   _____ .

4. The program is shown around the world. Over 70 million people have watched it.

   The program _____ .

5. "Who Are You?" is the *CSI* theme song. Pete Townsend wrote it in the 1970s.

   "Who Are You?" _____ .

6. *CSI: Miami* and *CSI: NY* also had high ratings. CBS created the shows on the same model as the original *CSI*.

   CSI: Miami and *CSI: NY* _____

   _____ .

4 Object Relative Clauses as Objects of Prepositions

▶ Grammar Presentation

The relative pronouns in object relative clauses can be the object of prepositions.	OBJ. OF PREP. *There's the police officer. I spoke to her.* RELATIVE PRONOUN *There's the police officer **to whom I spoke**.* *There's the police officer **who I spoke to**.*

4.1 Object Relative Clauses as Objects of Prepositions

a. The prepositions in object relative clauses can come at the end of the clause in informal speaking and writing.

*The police examined the chair **that / which I was sitting on**.*
*The witness, **who / whom I spoke to yesterday**, will appear in court.*

In identifying relative clauses, use the relative pronouns *who*, *that*, or *whom* for people and *that* or *which* for things. You can also omit the relative pronoun.

IDENTIFYING RELATIVE CLAUSE
*The police examined the chair (**that / which**) **I was sitting on**.*
*The police officer (**who / that / whom**) **I met with** was robbed.*

In nonidentifying relative clauses, use the relative pronouns *who* or *whom* for people and *which* for things. You cannot omit the relative pronoun.

NONIDENTIFYING
RELATIVE CLAUSE
*The door, **which I entered through**, was broken during the crime.*
*The witness, **who / whom I spoke to yesterday**, will appear in court.*
NOT *The witness, ~~I spoke to yesterday~~, will appear in court.*

b. In more formal spoken and especially in written English, the preposition comes before the relative pronouns *whom* or *which*. Do not use *that* or *who*.

*The police examined the chair **on which I was sitting**.*
NOT *The police examined the chair on ~~that~~ I was sitting.*
*The witness, **with whom I spoke yesterday**, will appear in court.*
NOT *The witness, with ~~who / that~~ I spoke yesterday, will appear in court.*

You cannot omit the relative pronoun.

NOT *The police examined the chair ~~on I was sitting~~.*
NOT *The witness, ~~with I spoke yesterday~~, will appear in court.*

▶ Grammar Application

Exercise 4.1 Prepositions and Object Relative Clauses

A ◀)) Listen to a detective describe a crime scene. Complete the sentences with the words you hear.

I arrived at the crime scene at 11:00 a.m. The crime had taken place in a restaurant.

The room __*that*__ the crime occurred __*in*__ was the kitchen. The back door was open.
      (1)   (1)

The back wall was covered in graffiti. I found a spray can under a table. The spray can,

_____ I found fingerprints _____ , matched the color of the graffiti. I asked the
  (2)   (2)

kitchen staff to talk to me as a group. The group, _____ the chef was the only
                                     (3)

one missing, was very nervous. I learned that the chef had a lot of enemies. I spoke to a

cleaning person _____ the chef had argued _____ last week. I also interviewed
several waitresses _____ the chef had gone out _____ . One waitress showed me
the chef's locker, _____ I found more spray cans _____ .

(4) (4) (5) (5) (6) (6)

B ◀)) Listen again and check your answers.

Exercise 4.2 Using Prepositions and Object Relative Clauses

A Combine the sentences from a crime scene investigator. Use identifying object relative
clauses with a preposition at the end of the clause. Sometimes more than one answer
is possible.

1. The room was the office. I found broken furniture in it.

   The room _which/that I found broken furniture in_ was the office.

2. I found fibers on the floor. The broken furniture was lying on the floor.

   I found fibers on the floor _____ .

3. The neighbors said they heard nothing. I spoke to them.

   The neighbors _____ said they heard nothing.

4. The house was unlocked. The crime took place in it.

   The house _____ was unlocked.

5. There were fingerprints on the door. The criminal entered through it.

   There were fingerprints on the door _____ .

6. The lab matched the fingerprints immediately. I sent the evidence to it.

   The lab _____ matched the fingerprints immediately.

B Rewrite your answers in A as formal sentences.

1. _The room in which I found broken furniture was the office._

2. _____

3. _____

4. _____

5. _____

6. _____

5 Avoid Common Mistakes ⚠️

1. Use *who / whom / that*, not *which*, for people and *which / that* for things.

The investigator is someone ~~which~~ *who / whom / that* he respects.

CSI is a crime show ~~who~~ *that / which* I watch.

2. Remember to omit the object pronoun after the verb in object relative clauses.

The evidence that the police found ~~it~~ was used to find the suspect.

3. Do not use a comma before an identifying object relative clause.

The TV crime program, that people thought was the most popular, worked closely with the police to develop its stories.

4. Do not use *what* in relative clauses.

The crime ~~what~~ I am talking about happened yesterday.

Editing Task

Find and correct six more mistakes in the paragraphs about eyewitness testimony.

A victim who police have taken ~~her~~ to the police station gives testimony. She looks at a man in a police lineup and says, "That's the person which I saw in my car." During the trial, the woman gives her testimony in front of the jury, and the jury makes a decision. Soon, the man goes to jail. However, it is possible the woman whose testimony

5 was used is wrong. Researchers now claim that the eyewitness stories what courts often rely on are not always reliable.

Psychologists have conducted experiments who revealed some surprising results. They played a crime-scene video for participants and then asked the participants to remember details. Results showed that participants often described events, which

10 they knew nothing about and had not seen in the video. Similarly, the suspect what participants chose out of a police lineup was rarely the actual criminal.

Psychologists who courts have hired them have testified that eyewitness testimony is not as accurate as was once assumed. As such, psychologists have developed new rules to guide the use of eyewitness testimony.

6 | Grammar for Writing ✎

Using Object Relative Clauses to Provide Background Information

> Writers often use object relative clauses to condense information, just as they do with subject relative clauses. Read these examples:
>
> *Joaquin's brother helped solve the crime. The detective had met him years ago.*
> *Joaquin's brother, <u>whom the detective had met years ago</u>, helped solve the crime.*
>
> Writers also use object relative clauses to provide background information. Read these examples:
>
> *The detectives talked to the woman <u>whose husband they had arrested</u>.*
> *The thief stole the money <u>which the shop owner had left in the store</u>.*

Pre-writing Task

1 Read the paragraph below. Who does the Innocence Project help, and how many people has it helped?

Innocent or Guilty?

The Innocence Project is a legal organization whose purpose is to free innocent people from prison. These people have been imprisoned for crimes that they did not commit. The Innocence Project was created in 1992 by two lawyers who knew about a famous study about how unreliable eyewitness reports could be. This study showed

5 that it was important to find another way of proving a person's guilt or innocence, especially in the case of serious crimes. At that time, DNA testing was a relatively new process. The first time that DNA testing helped prove someone's innocence was in the 1980s in England. In this case, police arrested a man who had been accused of committing two serious crimes. However, the police were not convinced that they

10 had the right man, so they hired a doctor whose specialty was working with DNA. The DNA testing that the doctor performed proved that the suspect was not guilty. The founders of the Innocence Project thought that DNA testing might help prove that some prisoners were innocent of the crimes for which they had been convicted. Since the Innocence Project was established, it has been very successful. DNA testing, with

15 which most people are now very familiar, has been responsible for freeing almost 300 prisoners since 1989.

2 Read the paragraph again. Underline the object relative clauses. Double underline the subject relative clauses. Circle the relative pronouns and draw arrows to the nouns they modify. Find the one nonidentifying clause, and notice that the information is interesting but not essential. Then look at the identifying relative clauses, and notice that the information in the clauses is essential.

Writing Task

1 *Write* Use the paragraph in the Pre-writing Task to help you write about forensics or crime in general. You can write about one of these topics or use your own ideas.

- the case of a person who was convicted, then found to be innocent
- the difficulty of apprehending criminals
- the advantages and disadvantages of using DNA evidence

2 *Self-Edit* Use the editing tips to improve your paragraph. Make any necessary changes.

1. Did you use both subject and object relative clauses to condense information?
2. Did you use relative clauses to provide background information?
3. Did you avoid the mistakes in the Avoid Common Mistakes chart on page 305?

23

Relative Clauses with *Where* and *When*; Reduced Relative Clauses

Millennials

1 Grammar in the Real World

A Do you know anyone born in the 1980s or 1990s? Some studies suggest that individuals born during these years have similar traits, such as high self-confidence. Read the article about Millennials, a term for these individuals. How might these people be different from other, older people in the workplace?

Millennials in the Workforce

Millennials, **also known as Generation Y**, are people born in the 1980s and 1990s. There are over 70 million of them in the United States alone, **where they are now the fastest**
5 **growing group in the workplace**. It is hard to generalize about such a large group, but these young workers often share certain positive and negative traits.

This group has high opinions and expectations
10 of themselves. Bruce Tulgan, a **Generation Y expert**, believes this is the result of the way they were raised. They were raised at a time **when parents and teachers believed in a lot of praising and rewarding**. For example,
15 **everyone playing** a game was often given a trophy, not just members of the winning team.

In the workplace, this self-confidence shows up in several ways. Millennials expect a lot of positive feedback. For example, if they do something well, they want to be praised for it. They also want their opinions to be heard and valued.
20 In fact, they often speak out when they disagree with a boss's decision. Some employers call them challenging and demanding.

Millennials, **raised in the era of computers, cell phones, and the Internet**, understand technology very well. They are also multitasking
25 experts. They can text, listen to music, and chat online at the same time. Their experience with technology usually makes them good at technology-based jobs.

However, their technology habits can sometimes
30 serve as distractions.[1] Working while e-mailing friends can cause moments of inattentiveness,[2] **during which serious errors can occur**. Some members of Generation Y are known for being distracted on the job. Older colleagues may find
35 this trait annoying.

This generation of employees is sometimes known for being demanding and outspoken. Tulgan says that Generation Y is "the most high maintenance[3] workforce in the history of the world." However, Millennials are also smart, driven, and tech savvy.[4] These are the traits **helping them** succeed in workplaces around the
40 country.

[1]**distraction:** something that takes your attention away from what you are doing or should be doing
[2]**inattentiveness:** not listening to what is being said; not giving complete attention to what is happening
[3]**high maintenance:** requiring a large amount of attention to remain happy and efficient [4]**tech savvy:** having good skills with technology and electronics

B *Comprehension Check* Answer the questions.

1. When were Millennials born?
2. Why do Millennials have such high self-confidence and expectations?
3. What kind of jobs are they good at? Why?

C *Notice* Read the sentences. What words could you add to the words in bold to make them relative clauses? Are the new clauses subject or object relative clauses?

1. Bruce Tulgan, **a Generation Y expert**, believes this is the result of the way they were raised.

2. For example, everyone **playing a game** was often given a trophy, not just members of the winning team.

2 Relative Clauses with *Where* and *When*

▶ Grammar Presentation

<table>
<tr>
<td>The adverbs where and when can be used in relative clauses. Where is used to modify nouns of place, and when is used to modify nouns of time. In these cases, we call these words relative adverbs.</td>
<td>The computer lab is a place where many young students feel comfortable.

Night is a time when many students study for exams.</td>
</tr>
</table>

2.1 Relative Clauses with *Where*

<table>
<tr>
<td>a. Use where in relative clauses to modify a noun referring to a place.
Common nouns include area, country, house, place, and room.</td>
<td>This is the only <u>area</u> where you can find Wi-Fi outside of the office.
The United States is a <u>country</u> where a lot of research on young people is done.
The office is a <u>place</u> where workers often compete.</td>
</tr>
<tr>
<td>b. Do not use a preposition before where. Use which instead. The use of preposition + which is common in academic writing.</td>
<td>It's a city in which you can find Wi-Fi almost everywhere.
NOT It's a city <s>in where</s> you can find Wi-Fi almost everywhere.</td>
</tr>
</table>

▶◀ Relative Clauses: See page A13.

2.2 Relative Clauses with *When*

<table>
<tr>
<td>a. Use when in relative clauses to modify a noun referring to a time.
Common nouns include day, moment, period, season, time, and year.</td>
<td>The <u>day</u> when you graduate is the <u>day</u> when you will need to find a job.
Spring is the <u>time</u> when most students graduate.
The 1980s and 1990s are the <u>years</u> when many young people in the workforce were born.</td>
</tr>
<tr>
<td>b. Do not use a preposition before when. Use which instead. The use of preposition + which is very formal.</td>
<td>Summer is the time during which many jobs become available.
NOT Summer is the time <s>during when</s> many jobs become available.
The day on which you start your new job will be very busy.
NOT The day <s>on when</s> you start your new job will be very busy.</td>
</tr>
<tr>
<td>c. You can omit the relative adverb when in identifying relative clauses.</td>
<td>Ricardo remembered the moment he met his boss.
= Ricardo remembered the moment when he met his boss.</td>
</tr>
</table>

Data from the Real World

Research shows that in writing, nonidentifying relative clauses with *where* and *when* are much less common than nonidentifying relative clauses with *which*. Clauses with *when* are the least common and are used in rather formal writing.

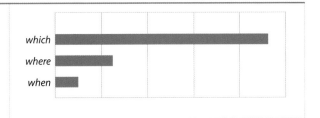

Grammar Application

Exercise 2.1 Object Relative Clauses with *Where* and *When*

Complete the sentences about Millennials. Circle the correct words. Note Ø means no relative adverb.

1. Millennials believe America is a place **where** / **when** anyone can be successful.
2. They were born at a time **in which** / **where** technology was part of everyday life.
3. They came into the workplace during a period **when** / **which** the economy was bad.
4. They came from families **when** / **in which** they were the center of attention.
5. They expect a work environment **Ø** / **where** people collaborate and work together.
6. They grew up during a period **when** / **where** national security was an issue.
7. The day **Ø** / **where** they graduate from school is a time of both joy and anxiety.

Exercise 2.2 More Object Relative Clauses with *Where* and *When*

A 🔊 Listen to an interview with a Millennial who is helping to change the world in a positive way. Circle the answers to the questions.

1. Where did Sean go?
   a. To Haiti   b. To Florida
2. When did Sean go?
   a. After a rainstorm   b. After an earthquake
3. Why did Sean go?
   a. To help people   b. To take a break from school
4. What did he do there?
   a. Work in a large city to give basic medical care   b. Work in small towns to give basic medical care

B 🔊 Listen again. Complete the interview with the words you hear.

Interviewer   Some people think that members of the Millennial generation only think about themselves, but there are a lot of young people who are making a difference. They are helping others and trying to make the world a better place. One of these young people is Sean Green. Sean is a medical student in Florida. He went to Haiti at a time *in which* they needed him the most. Sean, tell us your story.
                                                          (1)

Sean   Sure, I'd be happy to. I went to Haiti at a time _____ many people
                                                                                  (2)
were suffering – right after the 2010 earthquake.

Interviewer   Why did you go?

Sean   Haiti is a place _____ there aren't enough doctors. I'm in medical
                                        (3)
school now. So it seemed like a good opportunity for me to get experience and to help people as well.

Interviewer   What did you do there?

Sean   I worked in small towns _____ the earthquake destroyed the homes
                                                      (4)
of many people. I lived in a town _____ a lot of people were hurt, and
                                                          (5)
helped give basic medical care. It was the season _____ there is a lot
                                                                                  (6)
of rain. There was mud everywhere. It was a challenge to keep things clean.

Interviewer   Tell us a little about the people you worked with.

Sean   The people in the town _____ I worked gave us a lot of help. They
                                                  (7)
were very friendly and welcoming. It was an amazing experience.

Interviewer   Thank you for your time, Sean.

C 🔊 Listen again and check your answers.

Exercise 2.3 Relative Clauses with *When*

Look at the information in the chart. It shows three important generations in the United States and the major events or influences in their lifetimes. Then write sentences about the years in parentheses. Use relative clauses with *when*, *in which*, and *during which*. Sometimes more than one answer is possible.

	Name of Generation	Years Born	Important Lifetime Events or Influences
	Baby Boomers	1946–1964	President Kennedy dies, 1963 Vietnam War ends, 1975
	Generation X (Gen Xers)	1965–1981	The Berlin Wall falls, 1989
	Millennials	1980–2000	The Great Recession occurs, 2007–2009

1. (1946–1964)

   The years 1946–1964 are the years when the Baby Boomers were born.

2. (1963)

3. (1975)

4. (1965–1981)

5. (1989)

6. (1980–2000)

7. (2007)

3 | Reduced Relative Clauses

▶ Grammar Presentation

Relative clauses with *be* can often be reduced to phrases. There are three types of reduced relative clauses: participle phrases, prepositional phrases, and appositives.

RELATIVE CLAUSE
*The expert **who is giving tomorrow's talk on Millennials** is very well known.*

REDUCED RELATIVE CLAUSE
*The expert **giving tomorrow's talk on Millennials** is very well known.*

3.1 Forming Reduced Relative Clauses

a. Reduce a subject relative clause by omitting the relative pronoun (*that*, *which*, *who*) and *be*.	*My brother, **a Millennial**, likes a fast-paced environment.* = *My brother, **who is a Millennial**, likes a fast-paced environment.*
b. Do not shorten a subject relative clause with *be* + a single adjective. Instead, move the adjective before the modified noun.	*I know a lot of people **who are self-confident**.* *I know a lot of **self-confident people**.* NOT *I know a lot of people self-confident.*
c. Do not reduce object relative clauses.	*Our new assistant, **who I am meeting tomorrow**, is a Millennial.* NOT *Our new assistant, meeting tomorrow, is a Millennial.*

3.2 Reduced Relative Clauses with Participle Phrases

Participle phrases are a reduced form of relative clauses with a verb that includes a form of *be*.	*Students **concerned with the environment** should get involved in environmental groups on campus.* = *Students who **are concerned with the environment** should get involved in environmental groups on campus.*
This verb can be in the form of verb + *-ing* (present participle) or the past participle form. This includes progressive verbs and passive verbs.	VERB + *-ING* *He is the person **using the Internet too much at work**.* PAST PARTICIPLE *She did the things **not expected of her**.* *This is the intern **known to be the hardest working**.*

3.3 Reduced Relative Clauses with Prepositional Phrases

You can omit the relative pronoun and the verb *be* when they are followed by a prepositional phrase in identifying relative clauses.

PREP. PHRASE

The computers **in our classroom** are fast.
= The computers **that are in our classroom** are fast.

An adjective can also come before the prepositional phrase.

ADJ. + PREP. PHRASE

Young workers **low in self-esteem** are unusual.

3.4 Reduced Relative Clauses with Appositives

a. You can omit the relative pronoun and the verb *be* when they are followed by a noun phrase in nonidentifying relative clauses. This is called an appositive.

Jan Smith, **an expert on Millennials**, will be speaking at noon today.
= Jan Smith, **who is an expert on Millennials**, will be speaking at noon today.

Often the position of the modified noun and the appositive is interchangeable.

An expert on Millennials, Jan Smith, will be speaking at noon today.

b. Appositives begin and end with commas.

Résumés, **brief documents that summarize an applicant's work background,** are necessary for all job applications.

In academic writing, appositives often occur in parentheses, instead of commas.

Résumés **(brief documents that summarize an applicant's work background)** are necessary for all job applications.

► Grammar Application

Exercise 3.1 Reducing Relative Clauses

A Read the sentences about different generations. Check (✓) the sentences that can be reduced.

- ☑ 1. Young people who are entering the workforce are different from other generations.

- ☐ 2. In general, Millennials, who attentive parents raised, are confident workers.

- ☐ 3. Millennials who are in the workforce tend to have a "can-do" attitude.

- ☐ 4. Generation X, which is another large group in the workforce, does not tend to equate age with respect.

☐ 5. Baby Boomers who work with Millennials often think they do not show enough respect.

☐ 6. Baby Boomers, who are loyal employees, have started to retire from their jobs.

☐ 7. Millennials, who the recession has hurt, still tend to be optimistic.

☐ 8. Baby Boomers who were graduating from college in the 1960s lived in prosperous times.

☐ 9. Most Millennials who are not attending school say they intend to go back.

☐ 10. Many Millennials who are in school also have jobs.

☐ 11. Millennials that dress casually at work sometimes upset Baby Boomers.

B Rewrite the sentences in A with reduced relative clauses. If a sentence cannot be reduced, write ✗.

1. _Young people entering the workforce are different from other generations._
2. _✗_
3. _____
4. _____
5. _____
6. _____
7. _____
8. _____
9. _____
10. _____
11. _____

C *Pair Work* Compare your answers with a partner. Discuss what kind of reduced relative clause each sentence is. If a sentence couldn't be reduced, say why not.

A *The reduced relative clause in number 1 is a participle phrase, so it can be reduced.*

B *That's right, but the relative clause in 2 can't be reduced because it is an object relative clause.*

Exercise 3.2 Relative Clauses with *Be* + Prepositional Phrases and *Be* + Adjectives + Prepositional Phrases

Combine the sentences from a company website about the type of employees it seeks. Use relative clauses. Then rewrite the sentences using reduced relative clauses.

1. People are at JP Corporation. They represent every generation.

   People _who are at JP Corporation_ represent every generation.

   People at JP Corporation represent every generation.

2. People are good with technology. They have an advantage here.

   People _____ have an advantage here.

   _____

3. Workers are familiar with social networking. They will be able to use these skills here.

   Workers _____ will be able to use these skills here.

   _____

4. Employees are good at multitasking. They will enjoy our fast-paced environment.

   Employees _____ will enjoy our fast-paced environment.

   _____

5. Employees are high in self-esteem. They do well here.

   Employees _____ do well here.

   _____

6. People are interested in advancement. They will find it here.

   People _____ will find it here.

   _____

7. Employees are in our training programs. They appreciate learning new skills.

   Employees _____ appreciate learning new skills.

   _____

8. People are accustomed to a dynamic environment. They will be happy here.

   People _____ will be happy here.

   _____

Exercise 3.3 Relative Clauses with Adjectives

Read the advice for managers who work with Millennials. Rewrite the sentences that you can shorten. If you can't shorten the sentence, write ✗.

1. Managers should encourage Millennials who are self-assured.

   Managers should encourage self-assured Millennials.

2. Workers who are Millennials seek approval from their managers.

   _____

3. Even Millennials who are confident appreciate feedback.

   _____

4. Millennials appreciate work environments that are structured.

   _____

5. Employees who are Millennials want their managers to listen to them.

   _____

6. It's important to provide challenges for Millennials who are bored.

   _____

7. Managers must not overwork Millennials who are family oriented.

   _____

8. Managers who are Baby Boomers might expect Millennials to work longer hours.

   _____

9. Employees who are Millennials sometimes need more direction than older workers.

   _____

10. Millennials who are unemployed don't always have a lot of experience in job interviews.

    _____

Exercise 3.4 Using Adjective Phrases

Pair Work With a partner, discuss the work styles of people at your school, such as students, teachers, and administrators. Write five sentences with relative clauses. Then write shortened versions without relative clauses. Use the words in the box or your own ideas.

appreciate feedback	are family oriented	enjoy team work
appreciate work-life balance	are self-assured	have a "can-do" attitude

Students who are at this school tend to have a "can-do" attitude.
Students at this school tend to have a "can-do" attitude.

4 Avoid Common Mistakes

1. Do not use a preposition before *when*.

There was a period ~~in~~ when people did not change jobs often.

2. In clauses with *where*, remember to use a subject.

         he

The place where ∧ works is very busy.

3. When shortening relative clauses to appositives, be sure to omit both the pronoun and *be*.

My mother, ~~is~~ an office manager, often works late.

Editing Task

Find and correct eight more mistakes in the paragraphs about the separation between younger and older technology users.

Digital Natives vs. Digital Immigrants

      There was a time ~~in~~ when my mother always complained about my use of technology. She did not understand why I had to constantly text friends and go online. My mother, is a digital immigrant, grew up without a lot of tech gadgets. As a result, she is uncomfortable using technology at the office where works. On the other hand, my

5 brothers and I, are all digital natives, are happy to use technology all the time.

      Digital natives, are lifelong technology users, use electronic devices instinctively. These people do not remember a time in when they were not connected to the Internet. In fact, they find it annoying when they go to places where cannot connect to the Internet. Digital immigrants, in contrast, remember a time in when there was no Internet. As

10 a result, some of them see the Internet as useful but not essential. In addition, digital immigrants sometimes find it difficult to figure out how to use technology. For example, when my mother first began uploading information, she had to call someone for help. Lately, however, my mother has found a social networking site where often goes in her free time to stay in touch with friends and family members.

5 | Grammar for Writing ✎

Using Reduced Subject Relative Clauses to Make Ideas Clearer

Writers often reduce subject relative clauses with *be* to condense information. Reducing relative clauses makes sentences more compact and the author's ideas clearer. Read these examples:

Preteens who were raised after cell phones became common can't imagine life without them.

Preteens <u>raised after cell phones became common</u> can't imagine life without them.

Facebook and other social networking sites, which are tools that Millennials commonly use, offer new ways to communicate.

Facebook and other social networking sites, <u>tools that Millennials commonly use</u>, offer new ways to communicate.

Pre-writing Task

1 Read the paragraph below. What skills does the writer say Millennials are known for?

Technology and Millennials

Millennials, experts at multitasking, are the first generation to grow up in a digital age. Some people believe that in addition to making Millennials good at multitasking, this has also made them good at teamwork, a much valued skill in American workplaces. Because many U.S. Millennials had access to cell phones,

5 computers, and social networks from their early teens, they grew up accustomed to having conversations with more than one person at a time, a common feature of texting and social networking. This ability to talk to more than one person at a time seems to have prepared Millennials for communicating successfully with several team members at once. Multitasking is a skill that they have mastered easily. In addition,

10 the idea of waiting to talk to someone is a strange idea to this generation. Millennials, used to talking to people whenever they need to, don't wait to find a landline phone or to see someone in person in order to communicate. They tend to deal with things as they come up, rather than waiting until later. This can be a valuable quality because team members who get things done quickly help create a more efficient team. Perhaps

15 because of these factors, smart employers are recruiting Millennials to build strong teams in their companies.

2 Read the paragraph again. Underline the reduced relative clauses. Rewrite each one, making it a full relative clause by adding the correct relative pronoun and the correct form of *be*.

Writing Task

1 *Write* Use the paragraph in the Pre-writing Task to help you write about Millennials or any other generation you arc familiar with. You can write about one of these topics or use your own ideas.

- another characteristic of Millennials that makes them good at something
- characteristics of a different generation that make them good at something
- characteristics of a particular generation that makes something challenging for them

2 *Self-Edit* Use the editing tips to improve your paragraph. Make any necessary changes.

1. Did you form reduced relative clauses correctly?
2. Did you use these reduced relative clauses to condense information where appropriate?
3. Did you avoid the mistakes in the Avoid Common Mistakes chart on page 319?

Real Conditionals: Present and Future

Media in the United States

1 | Grammar in the Real World

A Do all the news sources you read (websites, magazines, newspapers, etc.) have similar viewpoints about current topics and issues? Read the article about the news media in the United States. What is the writer's view of the media?

The Influence of Media on Public Opinion

The media[1] provide news from a wide range of sources with a variety of viewpoints. Some sources provide a more balanced look at the issues than others. These more balanced news sources offer a deeper
5 understanding of the issues without the influence of the views of political parties. This unbiased[2] view of the news may appear to align[3] with the values of Americans, but is it, in fact, what Americans really want? Some political analysts claim that many Americans tend
10 to read, watch, and listen to the news media that reflect their own views. **If people surround themselves with media that reflect only their beliefs**, they may not be exposed to opposing ideas. The media, in this case, are not informing people, but reinforcing that their view of the world is right.

President Proposes Solution to Economic Troubles

NATIONAL NEWS
Presidential Policies Cause Economic Troubles

One example of this occurs during an economic crisis. **If people watch certain TV news**
15 **stations,** they will hear mostly positive things about the president's solutions. **If they support the president's policies,** they may also choose to read online news pages with a similar view. These websites likely explain how the crisis was caused by politicians from the opposing party. **If those people read only these websites,** they might be convinced that the crisis was the fault of the opposing party. They might conclude that the president was doing a wonderful
20 job. On the other hand, **if people mostly disagree with the president's policies,** they often

[1]**media:** newspapers, magazines, television, and radio, considered as a group | [2]**unbiased:** not influenced by personal opinion | [3]**align:** agree with and support something or someone

choose to watch news shows that criticize the president. They might also visit websites and read blogs that do not support the president's policies. **When they rely only on these news sources,** they come to a different conclusion. They are convinced that the president is failing.

    If predictions of increased Internet use are correct, people will likely become even more
25 isolated in their beliefs. This is because links in blogs and web pages will connect people with information that supports only their views. How might this affect politics in the future? **If we don't address this issue today,** could the isolation of beliefs become problematic in our political future?

B *Comprehension Check* Answer the questions.

1. How do some political analysts describe the behavior of Americans toward media?
2. What is an example of how media sources reinforce someone's political views?
3. Why might people become even more isolated in their beliefs in the future?

C *Notice* Read the sentences from the article. Which sentence describes a present situation? Which sentence describes a future situation?

1. On the other hand, if people mostly disagree with the president's policies, they often choose to watch news shows that criticize the president.
2. If predictions of increased Internet use are correct, people will likely become even more isolated in their beliefs.

2 Present Real Conditionals

▶ Grammar Presentation

Present real conditionals describe situations that are possible now and their results. They describe general truths, facts, and habits.	*If people share beliefs, they often get along better. I usually believe something when I read it in a good newspaper.*

2.1 Forming Present Real Conditionals

a. Use an *if* clause to describe a possible situation. The *if* clause is the condition. The main clause describes the result. It expresses what happens when the condition exists.

IF CLAUSE (CONDITION) MAIN CLAUSE (RESULT)
***If I like a reporter**, I read her articles.*

Use the simple present in the *if* clause and in the main clause.

***If I have time in the morning**, I <u>read</u> the newspaper.*

2.1 Forming Present Real Conditionals *(continued)*

b. You can use *when* or *whenever* in the *if* clause. The meaning does not change.

When you trust people, *you tend to believe them.* = **If you trust people,** *you tend to believe them.*

c. You can put the *if* clause or the main clause first, but the punctuation is different. If the *if* clause is first, a comma follows it. If the main clause is first, do not use a comma. Usually the *if* clause comes first.

IF CLAUSE   MAIN CLAUSE
If you control the media, *you control public opinion.*

MAIN CLAUSE   IF CLAUSE
You control public opinion **if you control the media.**

d. You can use conditionals in questions. Use question word order only in the main clause.

IF CLAUSE   MAIN CLAUSE
If you see something on the news, <u>do you</u> always <u>believe</u> it?

▸◂ Conditionals: See page A15.

2.2 Using Present Real Conditionals

a. Use present real conditionals to describe:
    Facts and general truths
    Habits and routines

If a website is popular, *people talk about it.*
I always read the news online **if I wake up early.**

b. You can emphasize the result by putting the *if* clause first and using *then* to introduce the main clause. Using *then* is more common in speaking.

If you only read one news website, <u>then</u> you never get the full story.

▶ # Grammar Application

Exercise 2.1 Present Real Conditionals for Habits and Routines

Complete the article about news habits. Use present real conditionals with the verbs in parentheses. Add commas when necessary.

City Voices: The News and You

City Voices talked to several area residents. Here's what they had to say.

"When I __*am*__ (be) in the car, I _____ (listen) to the radio. My husband
   (1)   (2)

_____ (watch) the comedy news shows if he _____ (stay) up
   (3)   (4)
late." – Alexa, 28, office manager.

"If a friend _____ (text) me about something interesting I generally
                (5)

_____ (check) out other websites to find out more information." – Su Ho, 32, engineer.
   (6)

Exercise 2.2 Present Real Conditionals for Facts, General Truths, Habits, and Routines

Complete the interview with a foreign correspondent. Use the conditions and results in the chart.

Condition	Result
1. I hear about a story	I get on the phone
2. I hear about a good story	I try to go beyond the basic facts
3. I feel like I'm getting emotionally involved in a story	I drop it
4. A story is important	Many people talk about it
5. My editor calls and tells me to investigate a story	I move quickly

Careers Magazine

Careers Today, we are talking to our foreign correspondent, Mercedes Rivera. Ms. Rivera, how do you get a story?

Mercedes If _I hear about a story, I get on the phone_ . I make appointments
(1)
to interview people connected with the story.

Careers What makes your reporting special?

Mercedes If _____ . I look
(2)
at all the details to give both sides of the story.

Careers How do you avoid bias?

Mercedes If _____ . I give
(3)
it to another reporter.

Careers What is difficult about your job?

Mercedes There's a certain amount of pressure. _____
(4)
when _____ . I have to work fast in the digital
(4)
age. _____ if _____ .
(5)   (5)

Careers Well, thank you for talking to us today, Ms. Rivera.

Exercise 2.3 Emphasizing the Result in Present Real Conditiona

A Read the tips on how to detect bias in the media. Then rewrite the tips as present real conditionals with the words in parentheses and *probably* (*not*) *be*. Emphasize the result by using *then*.

How to Detect Bias in the Media

To detect bias in the media, be aware of the following conditions. These conditions often indicate bias.

(1) A newspaper, website, or TV station ignores important stories.
(2) A newspaper prints sensational headlines.
(3) A newspaper prints an important story in the back of the newspaper.
(4) A magazine prints an unflattering[1] photo of a politician.
(5) A reporter uses words with negative connotations[2] instead of neutral terms.

[1]**unflattering:** making someone look less attractive or seem worse than they usually do | [2]**connotation:** a feeling or idea that is suggested by a word in addition to its basic meaning

1. (impartial) _If a newspaper, website, or TV station ignores important stories,_
   then it probably isn't impartial.

2. (accurate) _____

_____

3. (balanced) _____

_____

4. (biased) _____

_____

5. (fair) _____

_____

B *Pair Work* Discuss other ways that the media show that they are biased or fair. Write two sentences using *if* clauses and the expressions with *probably* (*not*) *be* in A.

Exercise 2.4 Present Real Conditionals

A *Over to You* Answer the questions with information that is true for you. Write present real conditionals on a separate piece of paper. Use the phrases in the box or your own ideas.

get the news online   pay attention to the news
know a story is accurate   read a newspaper
listen to news on the radio   watch TV news

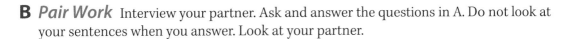

- Do you pay attention to the news?
- How do you get the news?
- How do you know a news story is accurate?

If there's a big story in the news, I watch one of the TV news channels, but I don't pay attention to the news much in general.

B *Pair Work* Interview your partner. Ask and answer the questions in A. Do not look at your sentences when you answer. Look at your partner.

3 Future Real Conditionals

Grammar Presentation

Future real conditionals describe possible situations in the future and the likely results.	**If you don't like a politician**, *you won't like his or her policies.*

3.1 Forming Future Real Conditionals

a. Use the simple present in the *if* clause and a future verb form in the main clause.

If you <u>arrive</u> early tomorrow at the debate, *you <u>will get</u> a good seat.*

b. Use a comma after the *if* clause only when it begins the sentence.

*We will have a more balanced view **if we read a variety of news websites**.*
***If Sandra doesn't agree with a politician's ideas,** she will not vote for him.*

3.2 Using Future Real Conditionals

a. Use future real conditionals to describe: Plans Predictions	***If traditional media don't cover the debate tonight**, I'll read a blog about it.* ***If you read this article**, you won't be disappointed.*
b. Use *even if* when you believe the result will not change. *Even if* means "whether or not."	*Some people will believe the news **even if it isn't true**. (The news may or may not be true. Some people will believe it either way.)*
Use *unless* to state a negative condition more strongly. It often has the same meaning as *if . . . not*.	***Unless a reporter interviews many people**, she won't find out the truth.* *= **If a reporter does not interview many people**, she won't find out the truth.*
c. When an *if* clause has many results, use the *if* clause only once.	***If people believe everything they hear**, they won't know the truth. They will be easily fooled.* NOT *If people believe everything they hear, they won't know the truth. ~~If people believe everything they hear~~, they will be easily fooled.*

▶ Grammar Application

Exercise 3.1 Future Real Conditionals for Predictions

Complete the sentences about being well informed about political viewpoints. Circle the correct verb forms. Add commas when necessary.

1. If a person (studies) / will study history, she understands / (will understand) political issues better.

2. You **are** / **will be** a better critical thinker if you **listen** / **will listen** to opposing viewpoints.

3. You **become** / **will become** a more informed voter if you **understand** / **will understand** the issues.

4. You **make** / **will make** better choices in future elections if you **learn** / **will learn** about the candidates' voting records.

5. If a person **learns** / **will learn** about economics he **makes** / **will make** wiser financial decisions.

6. If people **get** / **will get** the news from several sources they **have** / **will have** a more complete picture of an issue.

Exercise 3.2 Future Real Conditionals for Predictions and Plans

A A newspaper is having financial difficulties. Write future real conditionals with the information in the chart.

Proposals	Predictions and Plans
1. fire 10 reporters	be able to stay in business
2. stop home deliveries	lose money
3. charge for online access	increase revenue
4. not find new advertisers	not make more money
5. put more articles online	attract new readers

1. *If we fire 10 reporters, we'll be able to stay in business.*

2. _____

3. _____

4. _____

5. _____

B Read what members of the staff have to say about the proposals in A. Circle the correct meaning for each opinion.

1. Even if we fire 10 reporters, we won't be able to stay in business.
   a. Firing reporters will help.   b. Firing reporters won't help.

2. Unless we fire 20 reporters, we'll go out of business.
   a. Firing reporters will help.   b. Firing reporters won't help.

3. Unless we charge for online access, we won't increase revenue.
   a. Charging will help.   b. Charging won't help.

4. Even if we stop home deliveries, we'll lose money.
   a. Stopping home deliveries will help.   b. Stopping home deliveries won't help.

5. Even if we find new advertisers, we won't make more money.
   a. Finding new advertisers will help.   b. Finding new advertisers won't help.

6. Unless we put more articles online, we won't attract new readers.
   a. Putting more articles online will help.   b. Putting more articles online won't help.

Exercise 3.3 Future Real Conditionals with More than One Resu

Over to You Complete the sentences about being informed. Write two or more results for the conditions. Don't repeat the *if* clauses for the second or third results. Write sentences that are true for you.

1. If people stop reading newspapers, *newspapers will go out of business. Many reporters will be unemployed.*

2. If people get only one source of news, _____
   _____

3. If you only listen to people you agree with, _____
   _____

4. If you are not an informed voter, _____
   _____

4 Real Conditionals with Modals, Modal-like Expressions, and Imperatives

▶ Grammar Presentation

Modals, modal-like expressions, and imperatives can be used in the main clause of real conditionals.	**If I watch a lot of TV**, I may become more aware of political issues. **If you have finished reading the paper**, put it in the recycling container.

4.1 Forming Real Conditionals with Modals, Modal-like Expressions, and Imperatives

a. In present and future real conditionals with modals and modal-like expressions, use a present form of the verb in the *if* clause. Use a present or future modal or modal-like expression in the main clause.	**If you haven't heard the news yet**, you <u>should read</u> the newspaper. **If you are planning to vote**, you <u>have to register</u>. She <u>might learn</u> more about politics **if she subscribes to that political magazine**.
b. In present and future real conditionals, you can use the imperative in the main clause.	**If you are at home tonight at 7:00 p.m.**, <u>watch</u> the president's speech.

▶▶ Modals and Modal-like Expressions: See page A3.

Exercise 4.1 Real Conditionals with Modals and Modal-like Expressions

Complete the sentences about being an involved citizen. Use the words in parentheses.

1. If people don't vote, *they must not be interested in politics* .
   (be interested in politics / not / must)

2. If you haven't registered to vote yet, _____ .
   (do it today / should)

3. People _____ if they want to become involved in
   (volunteer / ought to)
   their community.

4. People _____ if they enjoy teaching.
   (tutor children / can)

5. If you want to become informed, _____ .
   (watch the news / have to)

6. If people participate in elections, _____ .
   (influence the outcome / might)

7. If you aren't happy, _____ .
   (change things / could)

8. People _____ if they have not already tried to
   (complain / not / should)
   find solutions to community problems.

Exercise 4.2 Real Conditionals with Imperatives

Pair Work Answer the questions about how you think people can be better citizens.
Write real conditionals and share them with a partner. Use *you* in the *if* clause and an
imperative in the main clause. Use the phrases in the box or your own ideas.

be aware of bias in the media	study both sides of an issue
research alternative news sources	volunteer

- What should people do if they want to become better informed?

- What should people do if they want to become better citizens?

If you want to become better informed, research alternative news sources.

Exercise 4.3 Real Conditionals with Modals, Modal-like Expressions, and Imperatives

A 🔊 Listen to an interview about how to be an informed voter. As you listen, complete the chart. Check (✔) *Do* if this is something an informed voter should do. Check (✔) *Don't* if this is something an informed voter should not do.

Action	Do	Don't
1. register early	✓	
2. visit campaign headquarters		
3. visit candidates' websites		
4. rely on campaign ads		
5. pay attention to what media sources say		
6. be influenced by other people's opinions		

B 🔊 Listen to the interview again. As you listen, complete the sentences with the words you hear.

1. If you _aren't registered_ to vote, _register_ early so you don't miss the deadline.

2. If you _____ to be an informed voter, _____ the local campaign headquarters for the candidates of both parties.

3. If you _____ to make the right choice, you _____ also _____ the websites of all the candidates.

4. _____ campaign ads for information about the candidates or the issues if you _____ to be an informed voter.

5. _____ attention to what media sources say about a candidate, either, if you _____ the truth.

6. Finally, _____ other people's opinions influence your vote if you _____ to make good choices.

5 Avoid Common Mistakes ⚠

1. In future real conditionals, use the simple present in the *if* clause.

              has

   If my son ~~will have~~ time, he will buy tickets for the show.

2. Remember that *if* clauses are followed by a comma when they start a sentence.

   If I get the time off work and the weather looks good‸ I will join you.

3. Remember to use *if*, not *when*, to describe possible future conditions.

                        if

   We will cancel the speech ~~when~~ it rains tomorrow.

4. In questions with *if* clauses, remember to use question word order in the main clause.

                       should

   If I don't have a signal, what I ~~should~~ do?

Editing Task

Find and correct the mistakes in the paragraphs about the advantages of a campus blog.

                                                should

    If incoming students want to learn what this college is like, where they ~~should~~ look? If they visit the college website they can learn about sports and campus events. However, incoming freshmen might want a more personal perspective. They may not have the time to attend lectures and other events, or they may want some anonymity. I have decided to
5 start a blog that provides an alternative source of information and help.

    When I want the blog to be successful at helping students, I will need to provide practical suggestions. For example, one concern may be, "If I want to meet people with similar interests, what I can do?" I will tell that person places where he or she can post requests on the school website and how to write his or her requests. I will also include
10 ways to safely respond to queries.

    In addition, if a student will have a problem with a teacher, I will write about it in my blog and provide possible ways to solve it. If people want to add advice, how they can do so? They can share advice by commenting. If professors want to comment, they can, too.

    I will not try to write like a journalist and give a lot of facts. If students will want
15 facts, they can go to the college website. In contrast, I will give them personal advice that will help them with everyday problems. If students want real answers to their problems they should try my blog.

6 Grammar for Writing ✐

Using a Single *If* Clause with Multiple Main Clauses

When writing about present or future real conditions, writers often use one *if* clause with more than one main clause. Additional main clauses can be separate sentences. Read these example paragraphs:

If people stop getting their news from different sources, they will stop hearing different sides of the stories. If they only get their news from one source, they are likely to grow overly confident of their own opinions. If they never hear any other opinions, they may also be less knowledgeable.

If people stop getting their news from different sources, they will stop hearing different sides of the stories. They are likely to grow overly confident of their own opinions. They may also be less knowledgeable.

Pre-writing Task

1 Read the paragraph below. What problem is the writer concerned about? What is the writer's suggestion?

Choosing Movies

It is the weekend, and you want to see a movie. How do you choose which movie to see? If you are like some people, you choose movies based on the actors that are in them. However, if that is how you choose, you probably are not always happy with your movie choice. You probably end up wasting your money sometimes on forgettable movies or
5 even on movies that put you to sleep. Many moviegoers choose movies based on their previews and TV advertisements. However, trusting these sources is another ineffective way to choose movies because previews and ads are expertly created to make even the worst movie look like an award-winning film. You are more likely to be happy with your choices if you read movie reviews before choosing movies. However, even reading
10 movie reviews can cause problems. You might not agree with the reviewer. If you want to minimize your chances of being disappointed with your movie choice, read more than one movie critic's review. Choose your reviewers carefully. Find reviewers with whom you almost always agree. If you use the Internet for finding movie times and locations, use it to read reviews of movies you loved, too. When you find reviewers that like the same movies
15 you like, return to those reviewers' websites when choosing a movie to see. This technique will not guarantee that you will love every movie that you choose from now on, but you probably will not fall asleep at the next movie you see.

2 Read the paragraph again. Underline the *if* clauses that have more than one main clause. <u>Double underline</u> all of the main clauses that relate to the *if* clauses. Circle the *if* clauses that have only one main clause. Choose one *if* clause and rewrite it with another main clause.

Writing Task

1 *Write* Use the paragraph in the Pre-writing Task to help you write about how you use a particular type of media, and recommend this type of media to others. You can write about one of these topics or use your own ideas.

- how you find out about sales
- how you follow politics
- how you learn about new music
- websites that you find useful
- where you get the news

2 *Self-Edit* Use the editing tips to improve your paragraph. Make any necessary changes.

1. Did you use present or future real conditional sentences and questions correctly?
2. Did you use real conditionals with one *if* clause and more than one main clause?
3. Did you avoid the mistakes in the Avoid Common Mistakes chart on page 333?

UNIT 25
Unreal Conditionals: Present, Future, and Past
Natural Disasters

1 | Grammar in the Real World

A Think of some natural disasters in recent history. Were there any positive effects or changes that resulted from the disasters? Read the article about Hurricane Katrina. What is one positive effect of Hurricane Katrina?

Hurricane Katrina

In 2005, Hurricane Katrina devastated New Orleans, Louisiana. The storm killed over 1,800 people and caused over $75 billion in damages. Certainly, Katrina was a catastrophe.¹ **People wish it had**
5 **never happened.** Nonetheless, some say Katrina saved the city's schools from failure. In fact, U.S. Education Secretary, Arne Duncan, said, "I think the best thing that happened to the education system in New Orleans was Hurricane Katrina." Although some
10 people thought Duncan's comment was inappropriate, is it possible that the storm did the city a favor and helped its school system?

If you had been a public school student in New Orleans prior to 2005, you would have had little hope for the future of your education. With low test scores and high dropout rates, the New Orleans School District was already in trouble when the hurricane
15 struck. The storm destroyed almost every school in the city. State legislators realized the hurricane was tragic. They also knew it provided a fresh start to rebuild the city's schools. **If they found a strong school superintendent**, they could hope for real change.

In 2007, Paul Vallas was hired to rescue the poverty stricken and low-performing district. He knew that in order to succeed, he would have to make drastic changes. He
20 hired top teachers and modernized classrooms. Vallas also started several charter schools. Charter schools are independently run public schools. They control their own academics and policies but must show the state how their students have improved. Vallas knew that **if state exam scores improved**, the charter schools would be considered a success.

¹**catastrophe:** a sudden event that causes great suffering or destruction

25 Vallas received national praise for his experiment with charter schools. Student scores on state tests went up every year that he worked for the district. The Sophie B. Wright Charter School is a good example. It was a failing traditional school before the hurricane. **If Katrina hadn't happened**, the school might have been closed down. Instead, it became a successful charter school.

30 As for Duncan's comment about Katrina, **some wish he had used a better choice of words.** A number of educational experts disagree. They say that in the end, New Orleans schools are only successful because of the work that Vallas did to rebuild the school system.

B *Comprehension Check* Answer the questions.

1. Why is Hurricane Katrina considered a catastrophe?
2. What did Paul Vallas do to improve New Orleans's schools?
3. What are charter schools?

C *Notice* Read the sentences from the article. Underline the main clause in each sentence.

1. If they found a strong school superintendent, they could hope for real change.
2. If you had been a public school student in New Orleans prior to 2005, you would have had little hope for the future of your education.
3. Vallas knew that if state exam scores improved, the charter schools would be considered a success.
4. If Katrina hadn't happened, the school might have been closed down.

Is the situation in each main clause real or imaginary?

2 | Present and Future Unreal Conditionals

Grammar Presentation

Present and future unreal conditionals describe imagined situations (situations that are not true).	*If children got better grades on their exams, parents wouldn't be so worried.*

2.1 Forming Present and Future Unreal Conditionals

a. Use the simple past or the past progressive in the *if* clause. Use the modals *could*, *might*, or *would* in the main clause.	*If I studied every day*, *I could pass all my tests.* (But I don't study every day, so I can't pass all my tests.) *Parents wouldn't worry so much about their children's future if their children's grades were improving*. (But the children's grades aren't improving, so their parents are worried.)
b. In formal language, use *were* for the verb *be* for all subjects, including *I*. In informal language, native speakers often use *was* for the subject pronouns *I*, *he*, *she*, and *it*.	*If I were better at math*, *I would become an engineer.* (formal) *If I was better at math*, *I would become an engineer.* (informal)

▸▸ Conditionals: See page A15.

2.2 Using Present and Future Unreal Conditionals

a. The *if* clause describes an imagined condition (something that is not true at the time of speaking or writing). The main clause describes the predicted result or possible outcome.	*If all public schools worked well*, *parents wouldn't choose private schools.* (But some public schools don't work well, so parents choose private schools.)
b. Use *would* in the main clause to express the predicted result.	*If teachers gave students study guides*, *more students would pass their exams.* (Passing is a predicted result.)
Use *could* or *might* in the main clause to express something that is possible or doable.	*If students studied more for exams*, *more of them could/might pass.* (Passing exams is doable.)
c. Use *could* or the past progressive in the *if* clause to describe an imagined possible situation.	*If the city could hire more teachers*, *we would have smaller classes.* (But they can't hire more teachers, so we have large classes.) *We wouldn't feel hopeful if schools weren't improving*. (But schools are improving, so we do feel hopeful.)
d. Use time words to show present or future time.	*We wouldn't have a place to learn if our school closed next year*. *If classes were smaller today*, *students might be more motivated.*
e. Use unreal conditionals with *If I were you* to give advice. Use *I would* in the main clause.	*If I were you*, *I'd study harder.* (My advice is to study harder.) *I wouldn't drop out of school if I were you*. (My advice is to stay in school.)

Grammar Application

Exercise 2.1 Present and Future Unreal Conditionals

Complete the sentences about natural disasters. Use present and future unreal conditionals. If you are writing a main clause, use the modals in parentheses.

1. Their house is damaged, so they have to build a new one.

   If their house weren't damaged, _they wouldn't have to build a new one_ (wouldn't).

2. We don't have flood insurance, so we have to pay for water damage.

   If we had flood insurance, we wouldn't have to pay for water damage.

3. There aren't earthquakes here, so we don't need earthquake insurance.

   If there were earthquakes here, _____ (might).

4. There's a tsunami[1] warning, so they have to leave the beach.

   _____, they wouldn't have to leave the beach.

5. We don't have a first-aid kit, so we aren't prepared for an earthquake.

   If we had a first-aid kit, _____ (would).

6. There's a tornado warning, so José is going into the basement.

   _____, José wouldn't go into the basement.

7. The fire alarm is ringing, so we have to leave the building.

   If the fire alarm weren't ringing, _____ (might not).

8. Everyone is worrying about the storm, so we are leaving.

   _____, we wouldn't be leaving.

[1]**tsunami:** an extremely high wave of water that is caused by an earthquake

Exercise 2.2 Present and Future Unreal Conditionals: Imagined Possibilities

Complete the statements made by earthquake experts. Use present and future unreal conditionals with *could* (*not*) in the *if* clause and *would* (*not*) in the main clause.

Dr. Sarah Green:

1. The government can't repair old bridges. Therefore, people don't feel safe.

   If the government _could repair_ old bridges, people _would feel_ safe.

2. They can't build quake-proof bridges very quickly, so we aren't optimistic.

   If the government _____ quake-proof bridges quickly, we

   _____ optimistic.

Dr. Joe Wu:

3. Certain regions can build quake-proof buildings. Therefore, they don't suffer a lot of damage.

   If certain regions _____

   quake-proof buildings, they _____

   a lot of damage.

Dr. Rafael Rodriguez:

4. Some countries often can't avoid contaminated water after an earthquake. Therefore, people get sick.

   If some countries _____ contaminated water after an

   earthquake, people _____ sick.

5. Engineers aren't able to improve the water systems in all places, so people are not healthy.

   If engineers _____ the water systems in all places, people

   _____ healthy.

Exercise 2.3 Present and Future Unreal Conditionals: Predicted Results

A *Over to You* Answer the questions with information that is true for you. Write your answers on a separate piece of paper. Use the ideas in the box or your own ideas. Write present and future unreal conditionals.

basement	escape	exit	higher ground
emergency services	evacuate	find shelter	take cover

What would you do if:

- you knew a hurricane were coming?
- an earthquake struck?
- you were driving and heard a tornado warning on the radio?
- you were within a half mile of a wildfire?
- you were at the beach and got a tsunami warning?
- you were in a heat wave?

If I knew a hurricane were coming, I would evacuate the area immediately.

B *Group Work* Brainstorm other answers to the questions in A. Share them with another group.

Exercise 2.4 *If I Were You . . .* for Advice

A Complete the conversations. Write sentences that give advice. Use *If I were you* and the ideas in the box. Sometimes more than one answer is possible.

~~build a new one~~	leave immediately	not go to work
get earthquake insurance	leave the building	stay indoors

1. *A* The house was damaged in the hurricane. What should we do?

   B *If I were you, I'd build a new one.*

2. *A* I live in an earthquake zone. What should I do?

   B _____

3. *A* There's a blizzard warning for tomorrow. What should I do?

   B _____

4. *A* Forecasters are predicting a terrible heat wave for tomorrow. What should we do?

   B _____

5. *A* There's a wildfire three blocks from our house. What should we do?

   B _____

6. *A* The fire alarm is ringing. What should we do?

   B _____

B *Pair Work* Take turns asking and answering the questions in A. Use your own ideas in your answers.

3 Past Unreal Conditionals

Grammar Presentation

Past unreal conditionals express situations that were not true in the past. They describe something that was possible but did not happen.	***If I had stayed home from school**, I would have missed the exam.* (But I went to school, so I didn't miss the exam.)

3.1 Forming Past Unreal Conditionals

a. Use the past perfect in the *if* clause. Use *could have, may have, might have,* or *would have* and the past participle of the verb in the main clause.	*If the city **had hired** more teachers, the schools <u>might have improved</u>.* (But the city didn't hire more teachers, and the schools didn't improve.)
b. The *if* clause typically comes before the main clause, but it may also follow the main clause.	*The schools might have improved **if the city had hired more teachers**.*

3.2 Using Past Unreal Conditionals

a. The *if* clause expresses the past unreal condition (a situation that was untrue in the past). The main clause describes an imagined result.	*If the hurricane **had missed our city**, the schools wouldn't have received money from the government.* (But it didn't miss our city, so the schools have received money.)
b. Use *would have* in the main clause to express a predicted result.	*If you **had applied**, you <u>would have gotten</u> the job.* (Getting the job was a predicted result.)
c. Use *could have* or *might have* in the main clause to express something possible or doable.	*I <u>could have / might have passed</u> the test **if I had studied harder**.* (Passing the test was doable.)
d. You can use past unreal conditionals to express regrets or sadness.	*If I **hadn't quit school**, I would have become an engineer.* (But I quit school, and I regret it.)
e. Use *If I had been you* to give advice indirectly. Use *I would (not)* in the main clause. *Had* is often contracted (*'d*).	*If I'd been you, I wouldn't have quit school.*

▶ Grammar Application

Exercise 3.1 Past Unreal Conditionals

Complete the interview with a scientist who studied Mount Vesuvius, a volcano that erupted[1] in 79 CE near Pompeii, Italy. Use past unreal conditionals with the verbs in parentheses.

> *Reporter* Today, I'm talking to Dr. Adam Gannon. Dr. Gannon, we are all fascinated
>
> by Vesuvius, I think, because it practically erased an ancient city.
>
> *Dr. Gannon* That's correct. If Vesuvius <u>*hadn't erupted*</u> (not / erupt), Pompeii
> (1)
> <u>*would not have disappeared*</u> (not / would / disappear).
> (2)

[1]**erupt:** throw out smoke, fire, and melted rocks

Reporter   So, Pompeii _____
(3)
(would / survived) if Vesuvius

_____ (not / explode)?
(4)

Dr. Gannon   Yes, that's correct. On the other hand, if ash

_____ (not / cover) the
(5)

city, it _____ (not / would / be preserved).
(6)

Reporter   The volcano caused other great changes, too, didn't it?

Dr. Gannon   Yes. In fact, it completely changed the direction of a nearby river. The Sarno

_____ (would / stay) in the same place if Vesuvius
(7)

_____ (not / change) the course of the river.
(8)

It was a very powerful eruption.

Reporter   How do we know so much about the eruption of Vesuvius?

Dr. Gannon   We have the writer Pliny the Younger to thank for that. If he and his

uncle _____ (not / be) near Pompeii that day,
(9)

we _____ (not / would / know) much about the
(10)

eruption of Vesuvius. But we still don't know everything.

Reporter   Fascinating. Thank you, Dr. Gannon.

Exercise 3.2 Past Unreal Conditionals: Regret

A *Group Work*   Look at the pictures and discuss these questions in groups: What does
a volcanic eruption look like? What are some of the effects of a volcanic eruption?

Mount St. Helens,
Washington State

landslide

ash cloud

B ◀))) Listen to a man talk about his experience surviving the 1980 Mount St. Helens volcano eruption. Circle *T* if the statement is true. Circle *F* if the statement is false.

1. The speaker and his family were hiking on the mountain the day the volcano erupted.   T   (F)
2. Falling trees hit the speaker and his friends.   T   F
3. The speaker thinks it's possible that many people on the mountain survived.   T   F
4. The speaker's wife wasn't affected by the eruption.   T   F
5. The sideways eruption of Mount St. Helens caused a lot of damage.   T   F
6. Ten years after the eruption, the speaker returned to his campsite.   T   F
7. Scientists didn't learn anything from the eruption.   T   F

C ◀))) Listen again and check your answers.

D Complete the statements about the story. Use the words in parentheses to write past unreal conditionals with possible or predicted results.

1. If we hadn't gone camping that day, we _might have avoided the disaster_
   (**possible:** avoid / the disaster).
2. If we hadn't been in a hole, falling trees _____ (**possible:** hit) us.
3. If people hadn't been on the mountain, they _____ (**predicted:** survive
4. If his wife had been with him, the eruption _____ (**possible:** affect) he
5. If Mount St. Helens hadn't been a sideways explosion, it _____
   (**predicted:** not / do) so much damage.
6. If the speaker and his friends hadn't returned to the mountain, they
   _____ (**predicted:** not / see) the site of the destruction.
7. If the eruption hadn't happened, scientists _____
   (**predicted:** not / learn) how quickly plant and animal life can return.

Wishes About the Present, Future, and Past

Grammar Presentation

Sentences with *wish* express a desire for something to be different, or feelings of sadness or regret.	*I **wish (that)** every child could have a better education.* (Unfortunately, not every child can have a better education.)

4.1 *Wish* in the Present, Future, and Past

a. *Wish* is followed by a *that* clause. Use a past form of the verb in the *that* clause, similar to conditional sentences. The word *that* is often omitted in informal speaking.	*There aren't enough teachers. We **wish that** we could hire more teachers.*
b. Wishes about the present are followed by *that* clauses with verbs in the simple past or past progressive, or the modal *could*.	*I **wish (that)** we had more classrooms.* (We don't have a lot of classrooms.) *I **wish (that)** my son were doing well in school.* (My son is not doing well in school.) *Some people **wish (that)** they could afford to go to college.* (They can't afford to go to college.)
c. Wishes about the future are followed by *that* clauses with *was / were going to* or the modals *could* or *would*.	*I **wish (that)** I were going to have time to meet you tonight.* (I'm not going to have time to meet you.) *She **wishes (that)** she could go to class tonight, but she has to work.* (She can't go to class tonight.) *We **wish (that)** the school would build a parking lot, but it's too costly.* (The school will not build a parking lot.)
d. Wishes about the past are followed by *that* clauses with the verb in the past perfect.	*We **wish (that)** we had had more time to study for the test.* (We didn't have enough time to study.)

Data from the Real World

In academic writing, *wish* followed by a singular subject is more commonly followed by *were* than *was*.	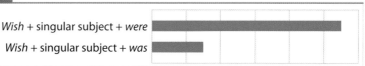 Wish + singular subject + were Wish + singular subject + was

*The president wishes the solution to the problem **were** simpler.* (more common in academic writing)
*The president wishes the solution to the problem **was** simpler.* (less common in academic writing)

▶ Grammar Application

Exercise 4.1 Present and Future Wishes

Complete the sentences about a family's disaster. Write wishes in the present and future. Sometimes more than one answer is possible.

1. There isn't a lot of light. Ben _wishes (that) there was/were more light_ .

2. We don't have enough bottled water. We _____ .

3. The roof is leaking. Mom _____ .

4. We are running out of batteries. Paul _____ .

5. The electricity doesn't work. Dad _____ .

6. The Internet isn't working. Sue _____ .

7. The furniture is going to be ruined. Grandma and Grandpa _____

_____ .

8. We can't go to a hotel. We _____ .

Exercise 4.2 Past Wishes

Read the sentences about some past disasters. Then write sentences about the speakers' wishes. Use past wish forms. Sometimes more than one answer is possible.

1. An architect: The 1906 earthquake destroyed a historic building. There wasn't enough money to rebuild it.

   I wish the earthquake hadn't destroyed the building./I wish there had

   been enough money to rebuild it.

2. A surfer: They closed my favorite beach after the storm. They didn't let people in to clean it up.

   _____

3. A historian: A flood destroyed the ancient city. There were no records of what life was like there.

   _____

4. A student: A hurricane destroyed my high school. We weren't able to attend graduation.

   _____

5 | Avoid Common Mistakes ⚠

1. When forming the present unreal conditional, use the past (not present) form of the verb after *if*.

understood
If I ~~understand~~ my teacher, I would enjoy my class more.

2. Remember to include a subject when forming an *if* clause.

she
She would feel safer if∧ could stay with us during the storm.

3. When forming the past unreal conditional, use the past perfect form in the *if* clause.

had not ruined
If the flood ~~did not ruin~~ his car, he would have arrived home safely.

4. When making past unreal wishes, use the past perfect (not the simple past).

had not moved
I wish I ~~did not move~~ to such a dangerous place.

Editing Task

Find and correct eight more mistakes in the story about Hurricane Ike.

had
    If Hurricane Ike ~~did~~ not come, we would have had an easier time. If the storm missed

us, we would not have lived without electricity for two weeks. We would have been able to

go to work and school. Our trees would look a lot better if had not been destroyed by the

strong winds. For these reasons, some people wish that Hurricane Ike never happened.

5 However, I do not. If the storm did not come to Houston, we would not have learned many

valuable lessons.

    First, we learned about our neighbors. We all came together to help each other

before and after the storm. If I live in a different place, maybe I would not have gotten to

know my neighbors in this way. Second, we learned good emergency survival skills. If we

10 had not learned to board our houses, might have been damaged. If another storm comes

today, my house would be safe.

    Sometimes I wish that my family did not move to this city. However, I do not feel this

way because of the hurricanes. The hurricanes have made our community stronger.

6 Grammar for Writing

Using *If* Clauses to Support Ideas

Unreal conditionals are useful to explain and illustrate a writer's ideas using hypothetical situations. Read these examples:

> *It is still very difficult to predict many earthquakes and volcanic eruptions. If more money had been spent on research before the Northridge earthquake, scientists might have been able to warn people.*

> *Last year's fire moved very slowly. If it had moved faster, firefighters wouldn't have stopped it so quickly.*

Pre-writing Task

1 Read the paragraph below. What should the writer's family have done earlier?

A Family Plan

Every family should have an escape plan in case of a house fire, but California families need escape plans for wildfires as well. My family discovered this last year. A wildfire began several miles away from our house on a Sunday afternoon. By Tuesday, it was very close. We didn't have an escape plan because we were new to California. At
5 the time, we did not know about the dangers of wildfires. If we had lived in California longer, we would have thought about wildfire preparation more carefully. At 7:00 that evening, the police called to tell us that our area was in a warning zone. They told us that we should start getting prepared to leave. My children and I started packing up our belongings. We also thought about where to go. We decided that we would go to a friend's
10 house. We could not have brought our pets if we had gone to the emergency shelter. By 8:30, the wildfire had started moving faster, and we got the call that we had to evacuate. We had not finished packing, but we put the animals in the car and left. Two days later, we were able to return to our home. We were lucky because our house was fine. When we looked around, we realized we had taken silly things and left important things. If our
15 house had burned down, we could have lost many important papers. We decided that we had to make a list of important things immediately in case of another fire. We would not have panicked as much, and we might have packed better, if we had made that list before the fire. Next time, we will be prepared.

2 Read the paragraph again. Underline the past unreal conditionals. <u>Double underline</u> the conditionals that have the main clause first and the *if* clause last. What other modals besides *would* are used in the main clauses?

Writing Task

1 *Write* Use the paragraph in the Pre-writing Task to help you write about a surprising situation that happened to you or to people you know. You can write about one of these topics or use your own ideas.

- a natural disaster
- a power outage
- a time you or someone you know got caught in bad weather

2 *Self-Edit* Use the editing tips to improve your paragraph. Make any necessary changes.

1. Did you use unreal conditionals to support important ideas or to give reasons for why things happened the way they did?
2. Did you use the correct verb forms in the main and *if* clauses?
3. Did you include any conditionals that have the main clause first and the *if* clause last?
4. Did you avoid the mistakes in the Avoid Common Mistakes chart on page 347?

Conjunctions

Globalization of Food

1 | Grammar in the Real World

A Have you ever had fast food in a foreign country? Do you think the food looks and tastes the same everywhere that it is sold? Read the web article about the globalization of fast-food chains. What do fast-food businesses do to their products to make customers happy?

The Globalization of Fast Food

Mochi Ring Donut

Do you want a glazed[1] donut for breakfast? Go to your favorite Dunkin' Donuts in Arizona, New York, **or** almost anywhere in the United States **and** you will find it. That is not surprising since sweet foods are popular with
5 Americans, **but** you might not be able to find that donut in other countries. Instead, in parts of Asia you might find green tea or mango mochi ring donuts. In Korea, they offer kimchi[2] croquettes, donuts filled with pickled[3] vegetables. In Singapore, you would find donuts filled with wasabi[4]
10 cheese **and** seaweed cheese. The wasabi creates a very hot-tasting donut that appeals to people in Singapore. In Thailand, Dunkin' Donuts makes delicious Kai-yong donuts, a combination of glazed donut and shredded chicken that is topped with a
15 spicy Thai chili paste. In Indonesia, they sell donuts filled **not only** with red bean paste **but also** with lychee[5] **and** orange. Thinking globally **but** acting

Kai-yong Donuts

locally has been one of the reasons for Dunkin' Donuts' success in over 32 countries **and** over 10,000 restaurants worldwide.

20   American fast-food chains, like Dunkin' Donuts, seem to be everywhere, **but** these days they are serving **both** food from their U.S. menus **and** food adapted to the tastes **and** customs of other cultures in other countries. McDonald's is another example. In India, there are many people who do not eat meat, **so** McDonald's

[1]**glazed:** covered with a sweet, shiny coating made of sugar │ [2]**kimchi:** a Korean dish of pickled vegetables │
[3]**pickled:** preserved in a liquid containing salt or vinegar │ [4]**wasabi:** a strong-tasting condiment │ [5]**lychee:** a sweet, juicy fruit often found in Southeast Asia and other parts of Asia

in India serves only vegetarian burgers **and** prepares non-vegetarian (chicken and
25 fish) meals in a separate area. McDonald's is one of the largest fast-food restaurants
worldwide. More than one third of its 33,000 restaurants are located outside the
United States. Adapting to local cultures is very important.

The globalization of the fast-food industry is happening with restaurants from
all over the world. Pollo Campero, a fast-food restaurant that began in Guatemala
30 in 1971, started adding stores in **both** Europe **and** Asia after expanding in Central
America. In 2002, it opened its first restaurant in the United States **and** has been
growing ever since. In order to appeal to health-conscious consumers in the United
States, Pollo Campero decided to offer customers a choice: **either** a healthier, grilled
chicken **or** a lightly fried chicken. Grilled **or** fried, the uniquely seasoned chicken has
35 become popular with **both** immigrants from Latin American countries **and** Americans
from other cultural backgrounds.

These days, more and more chain restaurants are selling their food in different
countries. Adapting their products to local preferences is a way to keep customers
happy **and** to keep business booming.[6] It appears to be a strategy for success.

[6]**boom:** grow rapidly, especially economically

B Comprehension Check Answer the questions.

1. What has Dunkin' Donuts done to succeed globally?
2. How has McDonald's changed its menu to attract vegetarians in India?
3. How is the United States affected by the globalization of fast food?

C Notice Find the sentences in the article and complete them. What is the function of the missing words? Circle *a* or *b*.

1. That is not surprising since sweet foods are popular with Americans,

   _____ you might not be able to find that donut in other countries.
   a. to add information
   b. to show a contrast

2. In Indonesia, they sell donuts filled _____ with red bean paste

   _____ with lychee and orange.
   a. to emphasize additional negative information
   b. to emphasize surprising information

3. Adapting their products to local preferences is a way to keep customers happy

   _____ to keep business booming.
   a. to add information
   b. to show a contrast

2 Connecting Words and Phrases with Conjunctions

▶ Grammar Presentation

Conjunctions connect words and phrases. Coordinating conjunctions include *and*, *but*, and *or*.

Correlative conjunctions include *both . . . and*, *neither . . . nor*, *either . . . or*, and *not only . . . but also*.

*I love pizza, hamburgers, **and** hot dogs.*
*I eat **not only** fast food **but also** healthy food.*

2.1 Coordinating Conjunctions

a. Use coordinating conjunctions to link two or more nouns, gerunds, verbs, or adverbs.	*Have you ever eaten pizza with <u>shrimp</u> **or** <u>olives</u>?* (nouns)
Use the same part of speech in linked words or phrases to create parallel structure. This makes speech and writing clearer.	*I've been to fast-food restaurants in <u>Asia</u>, <u>Europe</u>, <u>Africa</u>, **and** <u>North America</u>.* (proper nouns)
*I don't like <u>cooking</u> **or** <u>baking</u>.* (gerunds)
*The meal is <u>unhealthy</u> **but** <u>delicious</u>.* (adjectives)
b. Use *and* to add information.	*There are many vegetarians in India **and** the U.K.*
Use *but* to show a contrast.	*This food is cheap **but** very good.* (*But* contrasts the price of the food and the quality.)
Use *or* to connect related ideas or items in a negative statement or to show alternatives.	*I don't like hamburgers **or** pizza.*
*Do you want to eat at a restaurant **or** at home?*
c. When you connect three or more words or phrases, use a comma between each one.	*I select my food based on taste, nutritional value, **and** price.*
Put the conjunction before the last word or phrase.	*Would you like to have juice, milk, **or** water with your meal?*

2.2 Correlative Conjunctions

a. Correlative conjunctions have two parts. They often emphasize equality between the words or phrases they connect.	***Both** fried foods **and** grilled foods are served here.*
*Fast food is **neither** delicious **nor** healthy.*

2.2 Correlative Conjunctions *(continued)*

b. Use *both . . . and* to add information. When connecting two subjects, use a plural verb.

Both the food ***and*** the atmosphere <u>are</u> wonderful.

Use *either . . . or* to emphasize alternatives. The verb agrees in number with the noun that is closest to it.

Either potatoes ***or*** rice <u>is</u> fine with me. (Use a singular verb with *rice*.)
Either rice ***or*** potatoes <u>are</u> fine with me. (Use a plural verb with *potatoes*.)

Use *not only . . . but also* to emphasize surprising information.
The verb agrees in number with the noun that is closest to it.

Not only two drinks ***but also*** dessert <u>comes</u> with this entree. (Use a singular verb with *dessert*.)
Not only dessert ***but also*** two drinks <u>come</u> with this entree. (Use a plural verb with *drinks*.)

Use *neither . . . nor* to emphasize additional information in negative statements.
The verb agrees in number with the noun that is closest to it.

Neither my parents ***nor*** my brother <u>wants</u> to try eel. (Use a singular verb with *brother*.)
Neither my brother ***nor*** my parents <u>want</u> to try eel. (Use a plural verb with *parents*.)

Grammar Application

Exercise 2.1 Coordinating Conjunctions

Combine the sentences about global food. Use the coordinating conjunctions in parentheses. Sometimes more than one answer is possible.

1. There's a Taco Bell in Iceland. There's a Taco Bell in India. (and)

   There's a Taco Bell in Iceland and in India.

2. Starbucks operates in Asia. It operates in Europe. It operates in Latin America. (and)

   _____

3. The U.S. branch doesn't have vegetarian burgers. It doesn't have lamb burgers. (or)

   _____

4. Would you prefer to try something unusual? Would you prefer to try something familiar? (or)

   _____

5. Vegans don't eat eggs. Vegans don't eat cheese. Vegans don't eat yogurt. (or)

   _____

6. The food is cheap. The food is very healthy. (but)

   _____

7. The coffee is expensive. The coffee is very popular. (but)

   _____

Globalization of Food 353

Exercise 2.2 Correlative Conjunctions

A Read the monthly sales report from Branch #345. Then complete the report to headquarters. Circle the correct correlative conjunctions.

Branch #345 – Shanghai, China – June		
Products		
Frozen Yogurt and Smoothies	**Drinks**	**Snacks**
frozen yogurt: 55% smoothies: 45%	coffee: 50% tea: 43% mineral water: 5% milkshakes: 2%	chips: 59% cookies: 41%

Flavors of Frozen Yogurt and Smoothies		
Western Flavors	chocolate: 3%	
	vanilla: 2%	
Asian Flavors	dragon fruit: 55%	
	lychee: 40%	

Report to Headquarters on Branch #345

This branch offers **both** / **neither** Western **and** / **or** Asian flavors. Asian flavors seem to be
         (1)   (1)
more popular. For example, dragon fruit and lychee are the most popular flavors this month.

Most customers tend to choose **neither** / **either** dragon fruit **nor** / **or** lychee yogurt. Therefore,
          (2)   (2)
please note that **both** / **neither** chocolate **and** / **nor** vanilla is selling well at this branch.
         (3)   (3)

Neither / **Not only** frozen yogurt **nor** / **but also** smoothies are popular at this branch.
    (4)   (4)

Either / **Neither** mineral water **or** / **nor** milkshakes sold well this month. The reason is that
   (5)   (5)
most customers prefer **neither** / **either** coffee **nor** / **or** tea. **Both** / **Neither** coffee **and** / **nor**
        (6)   (6)   (7)   (7)
tea are selling well. It is interesting to note that customers are buying snacks. Surprisingly,

neither / **not only** chips **nor** / **but also** cookies are selling well.
   (8)   (8)

I recommend that we create more locally flavored products to offer at this location.

B *Group Work* In groups, choose a country that you know well. Discuss possible frozen yogurt flavors and types of drinks and snacks that you think would or would not sell well in this country. Then write five sentences about your choices with correlative conjunctions.

Both chocolate and vanilla would sell well in Mexico.

Exercise 2.3 More Correlative Conjunctions

Combine the sentences about the availability of items in a Latin American coffee chain's global locations. Use the correlative conjunctions in parentheses.

1. Milk is available in the United States. Juice is available in the United States. (both . . . and)

   Both milk and juice are available in the United States.

2. Tea is inexpensive in Egypt. Tea is very popular in Egypt. (both . . . and)

3. You can use your own mug at coffee shops in the U.K. You can use a store cup at coffee shops in the U.K. (either . . . or)

4. Donuts are available in the United States. Muffins are available in the United States. (not only . . . but also)

5. Recycling is encouraged in China. Reusing cups is encouraged in China. (not only . . . but also)

6. Generally, forks are not available in Chinese restaurants. Generally, knives are not available in Chinese restaurants. (neither . . . nor)

7. Hot dogs are not typically eaten for lunch in the Dominican Republic. Pizza is not typically eaten for lunch in the Dominican Republic. (neither . . . nor)

3 Connecting Sentences with Coordinating Conjunctions

▶ Grammar Presentation

The coordinating conjunctions *and*, *but*, *or*, *so*, and *yet* can connect independent clauses.	Kevin doesn't eat meat, **but** he eats fish. Jennifer is a vegetarian, **so** we shouldn't put meat in the lasagna.

3.1 Connecting Sentences with *And*, *But*, and *Or*

a. Use a comma before the coordinating conjunction when you connect two complete sentences. The comma implies a pause.

Starbucks opened in 1971**, and** it has become an international success.
The café sold muffins**, but** it did not sell sandwiches.
Consumers liked the food**, so** sales were good.

b. When you connect sentences with the same subject with *and* or *or*, you do not need to repeat the subject. The result is a compound verb. Do not use a comma with compound verbs.

If the modals or the auxiliary verbs are the same, you do not have to repeat the modals or auxiliaries.

CLAUSE, + AND + CLAUSE
We ate at that restaurant last week, **and** we really liked it.
VERB + AND + VERB
We ate at that restaurant last week **and** really liked it.

Karen can ride with us, **or** she can meet us at the restaurant.
Karen can ride with us **or** meet us at the restaurant.
My brother has visited India, **and** he has eaten fast food there.
My brother has visited India **and** eaten fast food there.

c. In some writing, such as in newspapers and magazines, sentences begin with conjunctions like *and* and *but* to emphasize information.
Do not do this in academic writing.

The changes to the menu attracted many new customers. **And** the company's profits rose significantly.

3.1 Connecting Sentences with *And, But,* and *Or* (continued)

d. Use *and* to connect an independent clause that adds information. You can also use *and* to show a sequence of events.

*He is an excellent cook, **and** I love his recipes.*
*This restaurant changed its chef, **and** now it is very popular.*

Use *but* to introduce contrasting or surprising information.

*This is supposed to be a good Mexican restaurant, **but** my Mexican friends don't like it.*

Use *or* to introduce a choice or alternative. It is often used in questions or statements with modals of possibility.

*We could have seafood, **or** we could make pasta.*
*Could you prepare the meal, **or** should I ask Sam to prepare it?*

3.2 Connecting Sentences with *So* and *Yet*

a. Use *so* to connect a cause and its result.

| CAUSE | RESULT |

*Henry doesn't like pizza, **so** we ordered pasta.*
*That spice is rare in my country, **so** I substitute a different one.*

Use *yet* to connect contrasting ideas or surprising information. *Yet* sometimes expresses a stronger contrast than *but*.

*Cathy doesn't eat clams, **yet** she eats oysters.*
*The restaurant serves wonderful food, **yet** it is known more for its music.*

b. Use a comma to combine sentences with *so* and *yet*. Do not use a compound verb.

*Mary is a vegetarian, **so** she eats tofu.*
NOT *Mary is a vegetarian so eats tofu.*

▶ Grammar Application

Exercise 3.1 Connecting Sentences with *And, But, Or*

Complete the sentences about a European supermarket chain that opened stores in the United States. Circle the correct conjunctions. Add commas when necessary.

1. FoodCo opened 100 stores in the United States in 2008, **and** / **but** the managers expected to have great success in certain areas.

2. First, they studied the new market **but** / **and** they even sent anthropologists to study U.S. eating and shopping habits.

3. They opened stores in wealthy neighborhoods **or** / **and** they also opened some in low-income neighborhoods.

4. The trend in the United States is toward "big box" stores[1] **and** / **but** FoodCo decided to open small, convenience-type stores.

[1] **"big box" store:** a very large store that sells almost everything, including food

5. Convenience stores in the United States usually do not sell fresh produce **but / or** FoodCo has changed the definition of *convenience store* with its new stores.

6. FoodCo has positioned itself as a healthy convenience store **and / or** it provides high-quality groceries and produce at reasonable prices.

7. Customers can use FoodCo's shops to pick up last-minute items **but / or** they can do their weekly shopping there.

8. Now shoppers in low-income neighborhoods have a choice. They can buy junk food at a convenience store **but / or** they can buy healthy products at a FoodCo shop.

Exercise 3.2 Connecting Sentences with *So* and *Yet*

Complete the article about Chinese-American dishes. Use *so* or *yet*. Add commas when necessary.

Many Chinese restaurants serve dishes that are not authentic. Chinese restaurant owners wanted to be successful in foreign countries _‚ SO_ they adapted
(1)
dishes to local tastes. Here are some examples: Fortune cookies are popular desserts in many Chinese restaurants _____ they were never popular in China. In fact, the
(2)
cookies were actually invented in Japan and then introduced to the United States by an immigrant in the early 1900s (although some people dispute this and say that a Chinese immigrant invented them first). General Tso's Chicken is another example. No one is absolutely certain of its origin _____ it appears on many U.S. Chinese
(3)
restaurant menus. It's fried chicken with a sweet sauce. Fried chicken is a traditional American dish _____ a clever Chinese restaurant owner probably invented it to
(4)
appeal to American tastes for sweet sauces. Chop suey is another Chinese-American invention. There are many legends about its creation _____ no one really knows
(5)
for sure how it came about. In one story, a Chinese-American dishwasher created the dish from leftover bits of meat and vegetables. The man received part of his pay in food _____ he took what he could find at
(6)
the end of the day. Customers asked about the delicious-smelling creation _____ the restaurant manager put it on the menu.
(7)
Some of these dishes may seem inauthentic _____ they have
(8)
been extremely popular in the United States since the 1900s.

Exercise 3.3 Combining Sentences

Combine the sentences about the localization of food. Use the conjunctions in parentheses. Omit the subject and use a compound verb when possible. Add commas when necessary.

1. You can travel to many countries. You can still find dishes from home. (and)

   You can travel to many countries and still find dishes from home.

2. I have eaten tacos in China. I have ordered kimchi in France. (and)

   _____

3. You might get an authentic dish abroad. You might find a local version of it. (or)

   _____

4. I often find international dishes abroad. They are usually adapted to local tastes. (but)

   _____

5. Beef isn't eaten in some countries. A fast-food chain might sell lamb burgers. (so)

   _____

6. I travel constantly. I never miss food from home. (yet)

   _____

Exercise 3.4 Using So and Yet

Over to You   On a separate piece of paper, complete the answers about local food tastes. Write sentences that are true for you. Discuss your ideas with a partner.

1. How do supermarkets in your neighborhood address local tastes?

   Supermarkets in my neighborhood want to address local tastes, so

   they have an imported-food section .

2. How might an international food company adapt a product to local tastes?

   People in _____ like _____ , so _____ .
         (name a country)   (food or taste)

3. What inauthentic ethnic dishes are sometimes very popular?

   _____ is inauthentic, yet _____ .
   (name of dish)

4 Reducing Sentences with Similar Clauses

▶ Grammar Presentation

When you connect sentences that have similar clauses, you can often reduce the words in the second clause.	*Shrimp is one of my favorite foods. Chicken is one of my favorite foods.* *Shrimp is one of my favorite foods, **and** chicken is, **too**.*

4.1 Reducing Sentences

a. In sentences with *be* as the main verb, use the *be* verb in the reduced clause.	*Their Chinese food <u>isn't</u> very good, **but** their Thai food <u>is</u>.*
b. For other verb forms with auxiliaries, you can reduce the verb form in the reduced clause.	*My brother <u>didn't eat</u> fast food in college, **and** I <u>didn't</u>, **either**.*
For the present progressive or past progressive, keep the form of *be* and omit verb + *-ing*.	*The price of beef <u>was rising</u> last month, **but** the price of chicken <u>wasn't</u>.*
For simple verb forms, use *do/does* (*not*) or *did* (*not*).	*I <u>don't like</u> this restaurant, **and** Lisa <u>doesn't</u>, **either**.* *We <u>went</u> out to eat, **and so** <u>did</u> Victor.*
For the present progressive or past perfect, use *have/has* or *had* and omit the past participle.	*The cost of eating out <u>has risen</u>, **and** the cost of cooking at home <u>has</u>, **too**.*
For modals or future forms, use the modal or future form by itself.	*Jason <u>can join</u> us for lunch, **and** Liz <u>can</u>, **too**.* *I <u>won't eat</u> fried food, **and** Greg <u>won't</u>, **either**.*
c. Use *and . . . too* or *and so* to combine two affirmative sentences. Use:	AFFIRM. SENT. + AFFIRM. SENT. *I ate there yesterday. She ate there yesterday.*
• *and* + subject + auxiliary + *too*	AND + SUBJ. + AUX. + TOO *I ate there yesterday, **and** <u>she did</u>, **too**.*
• *and so* + auxiliary + subject Note that the order of the auxiliary and subject are reversed in *and so* reduced clauses. We usually use a comma before *too*.	AND SO + AUX. + SUBJ. *I ate there yesterday, **and so** <u>did she</u>.*

4.1 Reducing Sentences *(continued)*

d. Use *and . . . not*, *either* or *and neither* to combine two negative sentences. Use:

- *and* + subject + auxiliary + *not, either*

- *and neither* + auxiliary + subject

NEG. SENT. + NEG. SENT.
I don't have any coffee. Kim doesn't have any coffee.

AND + SUBJ. + AUX. + *NOT, EITHER*
*I don't have any coffee, **and** Kim doesn't, **either**.*

AND NEITHER + AUX. + SUBJ.
*I don't have any coffee, **and neither** does Kim.*

e. Use *but* to combine an affirmative and a negative sentence.

AFFIRM. SENT. + NEG. SENT.
The beef is dry. The chicken isn't dry.

AFFIRM. CLAUSE + *BUT* + NEG. CLAUSE
*The beef is dry, **but** the chicken isn't.*

NEG. CLAUSE + *BUT* + AFFIRM. CLAUSE
*The chicken isn't dry, **but** the beef is.*

f. You can also use *too, so, either*, and *neither* in separate sentences in speaking and less formal writing.

Use *too* and *so* for two affirmative sentences. Use *either* and *neither* for two negative sentences.

*Japanese food is delicious. Korean food is, **too**.*
*Japanese food is delicious. **So** is Korean food.*
*The coffee isn't warm. The tea isn't, **either**.*
*The coffee isn't warm. **Neither** is the tea.*

Exercise 4.1 Reducing Sentences with Similar Clauses

Combine the sentences about food localization in India. Use coordinating conjunctions. If there are two lines, write the sentence in two different ways.

1. Americans like fast food. Indians like fast food.

   Americans like fast food, and Indians do, too.
   Americans like fast food, and so do Indians.

2. Some U.S. food companies are successful in India. Some U.S. food companies aren't successful in India.

   _____

3. Beef isn't popular in India. Pork isn't popular in India.

   _____

   _____

4. McDonald's adapts its menu to local tastes. Pizza Hut adapts its menu to local tastes.

   _____

   _____

5. Pizza Hut doesn't serve meat in some regions. McDonald's doesn't serve meat in some regions.

   _____

   _____

Exercise 4.2 Reducing Verb Forms

A *Group Work* Match the words with pictures of food. Tell the group which foods you have eaten raw.

<u>b</u> 1. eel

_____ 2. jellyfish

_____ 3. sea urchin

_____ 4. seaweed

_____ 5. tuna

a

b

c

d

e

B 🔊 Listen to the interview with the chef of a restaurant. Circle *T* if the statement is true. Circle *F* if the statement is false.

1. The chef is talking about Asian dishes that he serves at his restaurant.	(T)	F
2. All the dishes he offers are popular with his customers.	T	F
3. The chef has adapted some dishes to local tastes.	T	F
4. The chef does not plan to make any changes to his menu.	T	F

C 🔊 Listen again. Rewrite the statements to match what the chef says. Use reduced forms.

1. Raw fish is getting more popular. Seaweed salad is getting more popular.

    Raw fish is getting more popular, *and so is seaweed salad* .

2. Tuna has been selling well. Eel hasn't been selling well.

    Tuna has been selling well, _____ .

3. Jellyfish didn't sell well last month. Sea urchin didn't sell well last month.

    Jellyfish didn't sell well last month, _____ .

4. Spicy noodles have sold well. Cold noodles have sold well.

    Spicy noodles have sold well, _____ .

5. This restaurant can't get customers interested in Thai dishes. Our other restaurants can't get customers interested.

    This restaurant can't get customers interested in Thai dishes,

    _____ .

6. We'll probably stop offering Thai dishes. The other branches will probably stop offering Thai dishes.

   We'll probably stop offering Thai dishes, _____ .

7. We won't serve that. Most other Asian restaurants won't serve that.

   We won't serve that, _____ .

8. The ice cream has been selling well. The cake has been selling well, too.

   The ice cream has been selling well, _____ .

Avoid Common Mistakes ⚠

1. Use *or* to connect ideas in a negative sentence.
   There were no nuts in the vegetarian ~~and~~ *or* the meat dishes.

2. Use *both*, not *either*, when joining ideas with *and*.
   They use ~~either~~ *both* butter and oil for cooking.

3. Use *either*, not *too*, after a negative verb.
   They do not eat pork, and we don't, ~~too~~ *either*.

4. Do not use a comma when a conjunction joins two phrases.
   Most local people love durian fruit~~,~~ but dislike the smell.

Editing Task

Find and correct eight more mistakes in the paragraphs about food.

Intercultural Dinners

My roommate and I come from different cultures, so ~~either~~ *both* our eating habits and food preferences differ. Fortunately, we have some food preferences in common. I do not eat junk food, and he does not, too. There are no cookies and other desserts in our house. Instead, we have either fresh fruits and nuts for snacks.

5 However, we have some differences. I eat either rice and pasta every day. My roommate, however, thinks meals with rice, and dishes with pasta will make him gain weight, so he does not want to eat them often. Likewise, I do not like to eat a lot of meat and dairy products because I believe they are not healthy. Fortunately, I do not complain about his tastes, and he does not complain about mine, too. When we cook, we try to

10 make food that represents either his culture and mine.

6 Grammar for Writing ✎

Using Coordinating and Correlative Conjunctions to Join Words and Clauses

The coordinating conjunctions *and*, *but*, and *or* and the correlative conjunctions *both . . . and*, *neither . . . nor*, *either . . . or*, and *not only . . . but also* are used in writing to add information or to show a sequence of events, a contrast, or alternatives.

When you connect words or phrases with these conjunctions, be sure to use the same part of speech for the words that you connect. This is called parallel structure. Read these examples:

                         NOUN   NOUN

My neighborhood has several Japanese restaurants but no Chinese restaurants.

            GERUND   GERUND

I enjoy not only eating Mexican food but also cooking it.

Pre-writing Task

1 Read the paragraph below. What is one difference between Mexican and Tex-Mex food?

Tex-Mex or Mexican?

Mexican food can be found in most parts of the United States, but Americans will probably be very surprised on their first trip to Mexico. U.S. visitors to Mexico are unlikely to find many of the foods they usually order in their favorite Mexican restaurants. For example, they will find neither nachos nor chimichangas, which are foods commonly

5 found in typical Mexican restaurants in the United States. That's because these dishes are either American foods that were influenced by Mexican foods or Mexican dishes that were combined with American dishes. A common U.S. variation of Mexican food is the addition of sour cream and cheese to many dishes. Mexicans sometimes use a little bit of something similar to sour cream or sprinkle some cheese on their dishes, but they do not

10 use much. Many of these Mexican-influenced American dishes originated in Texas near the Mexican border and then spread throughout the United States. This is where the term "Tex-Mex" came from.

2 Read the paragraph again. Underline the uses of *but*. Double underline the correlative conjunctions. Circle the remaining uses of *and* and *or*.

Writing Task

1 *Write* Use the paragraph in the Pre-writing Task to help you write a paragraph about variations of ethnic foods. You can write about one of these topics or use your own ideas.

- the influence of foreign foods in your culture
- popular ethnic foods in your country

2 *Self-Edit* Use the editing tips to improve your paragraph. Make any necessary changes.

1. Did you use coordinating conjunctions and correlative conjunctions to add information, show a contrast, show a sequence of events, or show alternatives?
2. Did you use the conjunctions to link parallel structures?
3. Did you avoid the mistakes in the Avoid Common Mistakes chart on page 363?

Adverb Clauses and Phrases

Consumerism

1 | Grammar in the Real World

A What are some normal behaviors that can become problems under certain circumstances? Read the web article about shopping addiction. When is shopping an addiction?

Shopping Addiction:
When Spending Hurts

Some people have closets filled with new clothes that they do not wear. Others have desks covered with electronics that they never use. **Even though these people**
5 **do not need more clothes or electronics,** they keep buying them. They cannot help themselves. **Although many people like to shop,** some people shop too much. If someone is unable to control spending, he or she may be a shopping addict, or "shopaholic." **Because shopping may be seen as an amusing addiction,** society does
10 not always consider it a serious problem. As a result, many people do not recognize they have a problem that needs treatment. However, if this addiction is not treated, it can ruin a person's life.

Shopping can activate[1] chemicals in the brain associated with pleasure, so some people get a natural "high"[2] while shopping. Also,
15 some people shop **because it makes them feel in control**. This often happens **when they face difficulties in their personal or professional lives**. These feelings could be signs of shopping addiction. **While it may appear to some that many more women than men are affected by this addiction**, current statistics show that this is not true. The percentage of
20 men addicted to shopping is about the same as the percentage of women (around 5 percent).

[1]**activate:** cause something to start | [2]**high:** a feeling of being excited or full of energy

Like most addictions, a shopping addiction can cause serious problems. First of all, it is difficult for addicts. **Even though shopaholics enjoy the excitement**, they often feel depressed or guilty after a shopping trip. 25 **Spending more money than they have**, many shopaholics have financial problems. **As they spend**, they may lie to their families about their spending habits. These lies are almost always hurtful and can even destroy the family.

Fortunately, shopping addiction can be treated. **In order to change** 30 **their behavior**, shopping addicts must admit that they have a problem and then seek help. In addition, shopping addicts should always take a friend along **when they need to** buy something. Most shopping addicts only overspend **when they shop alone**.

While shopping is usually a harmless activity, an addiction 35 to shopping can cause financial and personal problems. Therefore, people should understand the signs of a shopping addiction **so that they can get help**. Shopping should be a constructive activity, not a destructive one.

B *Comprehension Check* Answer the questions.

1. Why aren't shopping addictions considered a serious problem by most people?
2. What problems can a shopping addiction lead to?
3. What are two ways in which shopaholics can treat their problem?

C *Notice* Find the sentences in the article and complete them. Then circle the meaning of the words.

1. _____ these people do not need more clothes or electronics, they keep buying them.
   a. The words introduce contrasting ideas.   b. The words give a reason.

2. _____ shopping may be seen as an amusing addiction, society does not always consider it a serious problem.
   a. The word introduces contrasting ideas.   b. The word gives a reason.

3. _____ shopaholics enjoy the excitement, they often feel depressed or guilty after a shopping trip.
   a. The words introduce contrasting ideas.   b. The words give a reason.

2 | Subordinators and Adverb Clauses

▶ Grammar Presentation

Adverb clauses show a relationship between ideas in two clauses. They begin with subordinators, such as *although* and *because*.	***Although she enjoys wearing new clothes,*** *she doesn't enjoy shopping.* *Eric doesn't go shopping often* ***because he doesn't like to spend money.***

2.1 Forming Adverb Clauses

a. An adverb clause has a subject and a verb, but it is a dependent clause. It is not a complete sentence.	MAIN CLAUSE DEPENDENT CLAUSE *She shops* ***because it makes her feel good.***
b. In general, use a comma when an adverb clause begins the sentence.	***Although I sometimes buy things I don't need,*** *I'm not a shopping addict.*

2.2 Using Adverb Clauses

a. Use *because* and *since* to give reasons. *Because* is more common.	***Because shopping is necessary,*** *shopping addicts aren't easily recognized.* *Treatment is important for shopping addicts* <u>***since it is very difficult to overcome this problem on one's own***</u>.
b. Use *although, even though,* and *though* to show a contrasting idea or something unexpected. *Although* is a little more formal. Use a comma with adverb clauses that include these subordinators, whether they begin or end the sentence.	<u>***Even though***</u> ***shopping addicts enjoy shopping,*** *they feel depressed afterward.* *She spends a lot on clothing,* <u>***though she doesn't make much money***</u>.
c. Use *while* to show contrasting ideas. Use a comma whether the adverb clause begins or ends the sentence.	*Shopping addicts buy things they don't need,* <u>***while nonaddicts tend to buy mostly things they need***</u>.
d. You can use *as, since, when,* and *while* in adverb clauses to express time relationships.	*It has been six weeks* <u>***since he went shopping***</u>. <u>***While she was at the mall,***</u> *she bought many useless things.*

Grammar Application

Exercise 2.1 Adverb Clauses

Combine the sentences about shopping addiction. Use the subordinators in parentheses. Add commas when necessary. Sometimes more than one answer is possible.

1. We are surrounded by advertising messages. It is often difficult to avoid shopping. (since)

   Since we are surrounded by advertising
   messages, it is often difficult to
   avoid shopping.

2. Many people feel that it is patriotic to shop. Some politicians say that it is good for the economy. (because)

   _____

   _____

3. We may not need items. We sometimes want what others have. (even though)

   _____

   _____

4. Shopping addiction seems to be a recent problem. It has almost certainly existed for centuries. (although)

   _____

   _____

5. Addicts may shop to escape negative feelings. Normal people shop to buy things they need. (while)

   _____

   _____

6. Normal shoppers use the items they buy. Compulsive shoppers often do not use them. (while)

   _____

   _____

Exercise 2.2 More Adverb Clauses

A Complete the interview with a shopping addict. Rewrite each pair of sentences as one sentence. Use one of the subordinators in parentheses.

Jane So, Claire, how did you know you were a shopping addict?

Claire I saw a show on TV. I realized I was an addict. (when / since)

    1. *When I saw a show on TV, I realized I was an addict.*

Jane I understand that you're getting help.

Claire Yes. My insurance pays for it. I was able to sign up for therapy. (because / although)

    2. _____

Jane Is your therapy helping?

Claire Definitely. I've only been in therapy a short time. I'm feeling better already. (although / when)

    3. _____

Jane How are things different now?

Claire I only buy what I really need. I'm spending much less money. (since / although)

    4. _____

Jane Describe a recent shopping trip.

Claire I was at the mall yesterday. I only went to one store. (even though / since)

    5. _____

    I had a list. I only bought things I truly needed. (since / while)

    6. _____

Jane Good for you! Thank you for sharing your story with us.

B 🔊 Listen to the interview and check your answers.

Exercise 2.3 Using Adverb Clauses

Group Work What are some ways to avoid bad shopping habits? Write five sentences using adverb clauses. Use the ideas in the unit and your own ideas. Decide as a group which two ideas are the most effective and give reasons.

You should take a friend with you when you shop.

Reducing Adverb Clauses

▶ Grammar Presentation

Sometimes you can reduce adverb clauses to *-ing* forms. The subject of the main clause must be the same as the subject of the adverb clause.	***While he was shopping***, *he bought things he didn't need.* ***While shopping***, *he bought things he didn't need.*

3.1 Reducing Adverb Clauses

In many cases, you can reduce adverb clauses. Omit the subject, and use the verb + *-ing*.	***While he was shopping***, *he bought a jacket.* ***While shopping***, *he bought a jacket.*

3.2 Reducing Clauses That Give Reasons

You can reduce clauses that give reasons when the verb is in the simple past, present perfect, or past perfect.	
For the simple past, omit the subordinator and the subject, and use the verb + *-ing*.	***Because he was cautious***, *he didn't spend much money.* ***Being cautious***, *he didn't spend much money.*
For the present perfect and past perfect, change *have* to *having*. The *-ing* forms usually begin the sentences.	***Since she has gotten help***, *she no longer shops so often.* ***Having gotten help***, *she no longer shops so often.*

3.3 Reducing Time Clauses

a. You can reduce a time clause when the verb is in the present progressive or past progressive. Omit the subject and the form of *be*.	*You can save money **while you <u>are going</u> to college**.* *You can save money **while going to college**.* ***While he was <u>shopping</u>***, *he bought a jacket.* ***While shopping***, *he bought a jacket*
b. You can also reduce a time clause with a verb in the simple present or simple past. Omit the subject, and use the verb + *-ing*.	*She started shopping at malls **before she <u>realized</u> that shopping was addictive**.* *She started shopping at malls **before realizing that shopping was addictive**.*

▶ Grammar Application

Exercise 3.1 Reducing Clauses That Give Reasons

Complete the sentences about Mike and Eric, two hoarders.[1] Rewrite the reason clauses in parentheses as reduced clauses.

1. _Buying new things all the time_ , Mike filled his apartment with useless items.
   (because he bought new things all the time)

2. _____ , he took action.
   (because he understood that he had a problem)

3. _____ , he had no savings.
   (because he had spent so much money on clothes)

4. _____ , Eric is now able to keep his apartmer
   (since he has received treatment)
   much cleaner.

5. _____ , he no longer feels anxious.
   (because he has worked with a therapist)

6. _____ , he no longer hoards useless items.
   (since he has gotten help)

[1]**hoarder:** a person who collects large supplies of things, usually more than he or she needs

Exercise 3.2 Reducing Time Clauses

Complete the sentences about a compulsive spender. Rewrite the time clauses in parentheses as reduced clauses.

1. _While shopping online_ , Amy was ecstatic.
   (while she was shopping online)

2. _____ , she was in an altered state.
   (while she was spending money)

3. Amy had spent over $30,000 _____ .
   (before she got treatment)

4. _____ , Amy decided to join Debtors
   (before she spent more money)
   Anonymous (DA).[1]

5. _____ , Amy learned how to budget.
   (after she joined DA)

6. She also got help with her credit _____ .
   (after she started DA)

7. Amy has changed her behavior _____ .
   (since she received treatment)

[1]**Debtors Anonymous (DA):** an organization that helps compulsive spenders

Subordinators to Express Purpose

Grammar Presentation

Some subordinators can express a purpose.	He got help for his shopping addiction **so that** he could feel better. (= He got help for the purpose of feeling better.)

4.1 Using Subordinators to Express Purpose

a. Use *so* or *so that* to show a reason or purpose. Clauses with *so that* usually come after the main clause.

*People go to psychologists **so that** they can talk about their problems.*

*I keep track of my money **so** I don't spend too much.*

b. You can also show a reason or purpose with *in order to* or *to* when the subject of the main clause and the adverb clause are the same. Do not repeat the subject.

*Shopping addicts buy things they don't need **to** feel good.* (= Shopping addicts buy things they don't need so that they feel good.)

*Shopping addicts may get help **in order to** stop shopping.* (= Shopping addicts may get help so that they stop shopping.)

Grammar Application

Exercise 4.1 Using Subordinators to Express Purpose

A Complete the sentences from the book *Consumer World*. Put the subordinators in parentheses in the right place in the sentences.

1. Psychologists have shown that we actually need very little *in order to* feel happy. (in order to)

2. Some people buy things feel good about themselves. (to)

3. Some people acquire things they have a sense of who they are. (so that)

4. It's also possible that people acquire things feel secure. (in order to)

5. They buy a lot feel that they are financially secure. (in order to)

6. They buy a lot they are prepared for any emergency. (so that)

7. Find out how little you really need, think about what you would do if you had to move. (to)

8. I think that have true peace of mind, you should have as little as possible. (in order to)

B *Group Work* Discuss the questions with your group. Use *in order to*, *so*, *so that*, and *to* in your discussion.

- Does owning things make people happy?
- What are some of the problems that owning things can cause?
- What do people have to do to be truly happy?
- What are some ways to live with less?

A *In order to be truly happy, you should focus on people, not things.*
B *I agree, but to have a happy life, you need some possessions.*

C Write sentences about your five best ideas in B. Use subordinators to express purpose.

In order to be truly happy, you should focus on people, not things.
Pretend you are moving so you can decide what to get rid of.

5 Avoid Common Mistakes ⚠

1. Remember that *even though* is two words, not one.

I bought a computer bag ~~eventhough~~ *even though* I do not own a computer.

2. Use *even though*, not *even*, to create an adverb clause.

~~Even~~ *Even though* it was late, the store was open.

3. Do not start a new sentence with *because*, *whereas*, or *although* when the clause refers to the previous sentence.

I returned the camera to the ~~store. Because~~ *store because* I did not really need it.

4. Remember to use the verb + *-ing* in reduced clauses after words like *after*, *before*, *while*, and *when*.

When ~~watch~~ *watching* ads on TV, some people feel a strong urge to buy the products.

Editing Task

Find and correct eight more mistakes in the paragraphs about addictions.

After ~~look~~ *looking* at research, we see clearly that alcohol and drug addictions are serious physical conditions. Psychologists are now considering adding shopping to the list. Eventhough these experts say that shopping is as addictive as drugs, I disagree that it should be considered a serious addiction.

5   People who argue that shopping is addictive have good reasons. While shop, many people get a good feeling. They like spending money even they may not need to buy anything. However, after go home, they feel regret. They have spent money on something they did not want or need. Because buying something makes them feel a sense of power.

10   However, after examine the situation of over-shopping closely, one can see that many people are victims of advertising. Even they may not plan to buy something, a powerful advertisement can change their mind. If people did not watch so much TV, they would not feel the urge to shop as strongly. In this way, shopping addiction differs from drug and alcohol addictions, which create a chemical change in the body that is 15 very difficult to resist.

Eventhough shopping too much is a serious problem, it should not be considered an addiction. If advertisements disappeared, society would not have this problem called shopping addiction.

6 | Grammar for Writing ✒

Using Adverb Clauses to Give More Information About Main Clauses

Adverb clauses give more information about main clauses. Writers often use them to show contrasting ideas, reasons, or purposes. However, the main clause always contains the most important information. Read these examples:

Since having more than one credit card often leads to debt, financial advisers often advise people to cut up all but one credit card.

Some people are able to effectively use only one credit card _even though they have many_.

Recovering shopaholics should not carry credit cards with them _so that they don't overspend_.

A credit card feels like an infinite amount of money, _while a wallet full of cash does not_.

Pre-writing Task

1 Read the paragraph below. Why don't you need money for the kind of shopping that the writer describes?

Shopping for Free

Although shopping usually requires money, it has not always, and it does not have to now. In the past, instead of paying for things that they needed with money, people swapped skills and homemade items so that they could "buy" the things they wanted or needed. For example, a baker might trade freshly baked bread for coal or wood for
5 the bakery oven. This was called bartering, and it used to be done between neighbors and friends. The Internet has helped bring back this form of shopping, but this time with a modern twist. Since the Internet is worldwide, it is no longer necessary to find someone in your community to barter with. Now, you can barter with people all over the world. Bartering on the Internet not only saves people money but also solves the
10 problem of how to get rid of unwanted things without creating more garbage. Instead of throwing things away, you can find homes for the things you no longer want or need. Because there are so many websites that make this an easy thing to do, more and more people are participating. Some websites require a token membership fee of a dollar or two, while others simply require that you have something to give away before you can
15 "buy" something for yourself. Anyone can do this, provided that they can afford postage

to send the things they are giving away. After you have made a bartering agreement with someone, all you have to do is sit back and wait for the things you have ordered to arrive. Internet bartering sites have made shopping both easy and painless, and they could even be helpful for shopaholics.

2 Read the paragraph again. Underline the subordinators and the adverb clauses that follow. Notice that in each sentence, the most important information is in the main clause. <u>Double underline</u> the subordinators that show contrasting ideas. Put a check (✔) over the subordinators that signal reason or cause and effect. Put an ✗ over the subordinator that expresses purpose.

Writing Task

1 *Write* Use the paragraph in the Pre-writing Task to help you write about some aspect of consumerism. You can write about one of these topics or use your own ideas.

- garage sales
- shopping on the Internet
- shopping on TV
- shopping at thrift stores
- using what you have instead of buying more

2 *Self-Edit* Use the editing tips to improve your paragraph. Make any necessary changes.

1. Did you use adverb clauses with subordinators to modify main clauses?
2. Did you put the most important information in the main clause?
3. Did you use the correct subordinators to show cause-and-effect relationships, express purpose, show reasons, or show contrasting or opposite ideas?
4. Did you avoid the mistakes in the Avoid Common Mistakes chart on page 374?

1 Grammar in the Real World

A How are video games today different from the games of 5 or 10 years ago? Read the web article about a kind of animation technology that is being used in games today. How has it changed the look of video games?

Motion Capture Technology

Computer animation was first introduced in the late 1970s; **however**, today's animation is much more realistic than it was then. While the first animated video game characters moved in only two
5 directions, today's animated game heroes can jump, kick, and spin. The use of sensors[1] to record these movements is called motion capture, or "mocap."

Because of the realism that mocap gives its animated figures, a common use for mocap is in
10 video games. Video game creators use real people to help create their characters. With sports video games, for example, famous athletes are used **instead of** actors. **Consequently,** the games can feature each athlete's unique moves. How does it work? **First**, the athlete puts on a tight suit that has special markers[2] all over it. **Next**, he or she performs a sequence of actions. Video cameras record these
15 movements using the markers. **Finally**, digital information is collected from the markers and the video. This information is used to create the movements of the video character.

Another common use of mocap is in movies. *Avatar*, an epic fantasy adventure movie, used mocap to create its human-like characters. It also featured a computer-generated 3D world. **Despite** *Avatar*'s success, not all movie studios want to use mocap. **Besides**
20 **being** very expensive, mocap cannot copy every motion. **As a result**, studios must add other forms of animation.

[1]**sensor:** a device that discovers and reacts to changes in such things as movement, heat, and light | [2]**marker:** a small, reflective dot that is taped to a figure

> In addition to these uses, motion capture technology is used in medicine. For instance, doctors have patients in mocap suits walk on treadmills. The mocap information helps doctors diagnose problems such as weak bones. Furthermore,
> 25 mocap can be used in training for jobs such as firefighting. New firefighters can use mocap games to practice moving through virtual[3] house fires. Instead of taking risks in a real setting, they can practice in a virtual reality.
>
> Despite the expense, mocap technology is becoming more popular in many different areas. Due to its success so far, who knows what it will be used
> 30 for next?
>
> [3]virtual: created by a computer

B Comprehension Check Answer the questions.

1. What is "mocap"?
2. In what areas is mocap used?
3. Why isn't mocap used more often in movies and video games?

C Notice Match the words in bold with their meaning.

1. **Because of** the realism that mocap gives its animated figures, a common use for mocap is in video games. _____

2. **Furthermore**, mocap can be used in training for jobs such as firefighting. _____

3. **Despite** the expense, mocap technology is becoming more popular in many different areas. _____

a. introduces additional information

b. introduces a reason

c. introduces contrasting information

2 | Connecting Information with Prepositions and Prepositional Phrases

Grammar Presentation

Some prepositions and prepositional phrases can connect information to an independent clause. Like subordinators, these prepositions can be used to add information, give reasons, show contrasts, present alternatives, or give exceptions.

Video games look realistic today *because of* improvements in computer animation.
Despite the popularity of animation, most people prefer to watch live-action movies.

2.1 Using Prepositions and Prepositional Phrases to Connect Ideas

a. One-word prepositions, such as *besides* and *despite*, and multi-word prepositions, such as *as well as, because of, in addition to,* and *in spite of,* are followed by nouns, noun phrases, or gerunds.	**Besides** <u>being</u> very expensive, animated movies can take a long time to produce. Some animated movies are also popular with adults **in spite of** <u>their appeal</u> to kids.
b. Prepositional phrases, like adverb clauses, can come before or after the main clause. Use a comma when the prepositional phrase comes first.	Video games usually use athletes **instead of actors**. **Instead of actors,** video games usually use athletes.

2.2 Meanings of Prepositions Used to Connect Ideas

a. Use *as well as, besides,* and *in addition to* to emphasize another idea.	I enjoy animated movies **as well as** live-action movies. This TV has 3D technology **in addition** to high definition. **Besides** being a talented director, he is an excellent actor.
b. Use *as a result of, because of,* and *due to* to give reasons.	**Because of** the high cost of tickets, many people don't go to the movies. **As a result of** voters' opinions, the director was nominated for an Academy Award. The movie's appeal is **due to** its special effects.
c. Use *instead of* to give alternatives.	Let's see a drama **instead of** a comedy. **Instead of** going out, they watched TV at home.
d. Use *except* or *except for* to give exceptions. When the main clause is a negative statement, you can also use *besides* to mean "except for."	This composer wrote the music for all the Alien Adventures movies **except** the first one. **Except for** their parents, the audience was mostly children. **Besides** the parents of the children, there weren't any adults in the audience.
e. Use *despite* and *in spite of* to show contrasting ideas.	**Despite** being made for children, this movie is enjoyed by adults. **In spite of** its short length, the movie was very powerful.

Grammar Application

Exercise 2.1 Prepositional Phrases to Connect Ideas

Complete the paragraphs about one use of motion capture technology. Use the words in the box. Sometimes more than one answer is possible.

as well as   because of   due to   in addition to   instead of   ~~in spite of~~

In spite of the high cost of mocap, its use is expanding. For example, Ford
  (1)
Motor Company, a car manufacturer, is using mocap technology to create digital

humans.[1] _____ their human-like behavior, digital humans are used
              (2)
to study people's behavior in cars. _____ studying driver behavior,
                                          (3)
engineers are also studying ways to make passengers feel more comfortable. For example,

_____ using a real human, the company uses a short digital female to test
       (4)
a short driver's ability to reach the gas pedal.

   Motion capture technology helps the company improve worker safety

_____ driver safety. _____ the technology's ability to replicate
       (5)   (6)
workers' movements, the company has reduced the number of assembly line accidents.

[1]**digital human:** an electronic representation of a person

Exercise 2.2 More Prepositional Phrases to Connect Ideas

Complete the sentences about using mocap technology to help athletes recover from injuries and improve their speed. Circle the correct prepositions.

1. (**In addition to**)/ **Because of** filmmakers, physical therapists are using motion capture technology to help injured athletes.

2. **As a result of** / **Instead of** an injury, athletes could lose their careers.

3. An athlete's career could be destroyed **because of** / **instead of** injuries.

4. Analyzing an injury without motion capture technology is not always accurate, **due to** / **besides** being time-consuming.

5. With motion capture technology, therapists accurately see the problem **in spite of** / **instead of** guessing where the problem is.

6. The success of motion capture technology with Olympic athletes is **in spite of** / **due to** its ability to analyze the athletes' movements at high speeds.

7. **Except for** / **Despite** the success of motion capture technology with athletes, it cannot replace the hours of practice that athletes need to succeed.

Exercise 2.3 Using Prepositional Phrases to Connect Ideas

A Combine the ideas about the use of technology in health care. Use the prepositions in parentheses and the underlined words to create prepositional phrases.

1. Some hospitals are not using <u>paper medical records</u>. They are using electronic medical records. (instead of)

   Instead of paper medical records, some hospitals are using electronic records.

2. Everyone has <u>quick access to your records</u>. Doctors can share information with each other more easily. (Due to)

   _____

3. There are <u>many advantages to electronic records</u>. Some doctors still have serious concerns. (in spite of)

   _____

4. There should be <u>accurate information in the records</u>. The information could contain data input errors. (instead of)

   _____

5. There will be <u>a lot of security</u>. Hackers could still steal information from hospitals. (despite)

   _____

B *Group Work* Choose an area that could change because of technology. Use one of the ideas below or your own idea. As a group, write statements that explain the technology, its effects, and the possible advantages and disadvantages of using it. Use prepositional phrases.

- high speed trains
- online learning
- use of cell phones instead of money to purchase products

3 | Connecting Information with Transition Words

▶ Grammar Presentation

Transition words are words or phrases that connect ideas between sentences. They are frequently used in academic writing and formal situations.	*It's important not to judge a movie's quality by whether it is animated or not.* **Furthermore,** *you should not assume that a movie with human actors is superior to an animated movie.*

3.1 Using Transition Words

a. Transition words join the ideas in two sentences.

*Movie stars often do the voices in animated movies. **However**, their fans don't always recognize them.*

Coordinating conjunctions (*but*, etc.), subordinators (*although*, etc.), and prepositions (*in spite of*, etc.) combine two different sentences into one new sentence.

*Music in movies is very important for setting the tone, **but** most people don't pay attention to it.*
***Although** animated movies sometimes win the best picture award, they also have their own category.*
***In spite of** having a lot of famous actors, the movie did not get very good reviews.*

b. Most transition words occur at the beginning of the second sentence and are followed by a comma. You can also use a semicolon between the two sentences that you combine.

*The studio executives choose a script. **After that**, they select a director.*
*She is a very talented artist**; moreover**, her use of color is exceptional.*

Many – but not all – transition words can go in the middle of the sentence or at the end. When the transition word comes at the end, it is preceded by a comma.

*Most people**, however**, associate animation with movies.*
*Most people associate animation with movies**, however**.*

c. The short transition words *so*, *then*, and *also* are often used without a comma. *So* is used at the beginning of a sentence only in informal writing.

*My daughter enjoys animated movies a lot. **So** we take her to them pretty often. **Then** she usually wants to stop for a snack on the way home. I am **also** usually hungry after a long movie.*

Use more formal transition words with the same meanings in academic writing: *afterward, in addition, therefore.*

*Children often enjoy animated movies. **Therefore**, their parents often take them to the movies. **Afterward**, it is not unusual to stop for something to eat. **In addition**, parents often buy a book or souvenir connected to the movie for their children.*

3.2 Meanings of Transition Words

a. To show a sequence or the order of events or ideas, use *first, second, then, next, after that*, and *finally*.

*How do animators capture an athlete's movement? **First**, the athlete puts on a special suit. **Then** the athlete performs the action. **Next**, the computer collects digital information.*

b. To summarize ideas, use *in conclusion, to conclude*, and *to summarize*.

***In conclusion**, technological innovations will change many fields, including animation.*

c. To give additional information, use *also, furthermore, in addition*, and *moreover*.

*Animation is used in movies, video games, and other entertainment industries. **In addition**, it is used in sports medicine.*

3.2 Meanings of Transition Words *(continued)*

d. To give alternatives, use *instead*.	*I had expected the movie to be boring. **Instead**, I thought it was quite entertaining.*
e. To give contrasting ideas, use *on the other hand* and *in contrast*.	*The story was not very original. **On the other hand**, the animation was impressive.*
f. To give a result, use *as a result, consequently, therefore*, and *thus*.	*The game was designed with animation. **Therefore**, the characters were very lifelike.*
g. To give examples, use *for example* or *for instance*.	*Many animated movies are very popular. **For example**, Kung Fu Panda and Shrek were huge box office hits.*

Data from the Real World

The most common transition words in writing are:	The most common transition words in conversation are:
however, so, then, therefore, thus	*anyway, so, then, though*

▶ Grammar Application

Exercise 3.1 Transition Words to Show Sequence

A *Pair Work* Look at the steps involved in computer game design. Can you put them in the correct order? Make guesses with your partner and try to number the steps in order from 1 to 6.

_____ a. Make a prototype (a model or "first draft") of the game and test it.

_____ b. Work with the marketing team to get the game ready to sell.

__1__ c. Decide on the theme and environment of the game.

_____ d. Do research on the theme.

_____ e. Figure out the goal of the game and the rules.

_____ f. Make any necessary changes to the game.

B 🔊 Now listen to a game designer describing her job. Were your answers correct?

C ◀))) Listen again and complete the sentences. Use the sequence words in the box. Add commas when necessary.

after that   finally   ~~first~~   next   second   then

1. _____*First,*_____ I decide on an overall concept for a game.
2. _____ I figure out the goal of the game and the rules.
3. _____ I do research on the theme.
4. _____ I use software to make a prototype of the game.
5. _____ I go back to the computer and make any necessary changes.
6. _____ I work with the marketing people.

Exercise 3.2 Transition Words for Academic Writing

Complete the paragraph about the differences between computer animation and traditional animation. Circle the correct transition words.

Computer-generated animation (CGA) is very popular today.
The spectacular effects of CGA in big-budget movies impress many people.
Therefore /(However), in my opinion, CGA is not as pleasant to look at as
‾‾‾‾‾‾‾‾‾‾‾(1)
traditional animation (TA). **First / Afterward**, CGA does not require the
‾‾‾‾‾‾‾‾‾‾‾‾(2)
same skill as TA. Traditional animators draw by hand, and the resulting
images look complex and rich in style. **Instead / To summarize**,
‾‾‾‾‾‾‾‾‾‾‾‾(3)
computer animators use software to produce images. These images often
have a cold, hard look to them. **To conclude / Furthermore**, with CGA,
‾‾‾‾‾‾‾‾‾‾‾‾(4)
objects are often overly bright. This adds to the unnaturalness of their
appearance. **In contrast / Thus**, the images from TA are often soft
‾‾‾‾‾‾‾‾‾‾(5)
and appear more natural. **In conclusion / Moreover**, TA produces
‾‾‾‾‾‾‾‾‾‾‾‾(6)
better-looking images that have more style as well as a lifelike appearance;
on the other hand / therefore, it is better than CGA.
‾‾‾‾‾‾‾‾‾‾‾(7)

Computer-Generated Animation

Traditional Animation

Exercise 3.3 Using Transition Words

A Look at the brainstorming notes a student made for a paragraph comparing two movies. Use the words to write sentences to summarize the ideas. Use the notes to help you.

War of the Aliens	The Magical Forest
excellent computer graphics	poor animation
dull plot[1]	interesting story
unappealing characters	likeable characters
bad dialog	good dialog

[1]**plot:** story

1. excellent computer graphics / in contrast / poor animation

   War of the Aliens had excellent computer graphics. In contrast,
   The Magical Forest had poor animation.

2. excellent computer graphics / however / dull plot

   _____

3. furthermore / unappealing characters

   _____

4. on the other hand / interesting story

   _____

5. in addition / likeable characters

   _____

6. moreover / good dialog

   _____

7. in contrast / bad dialog

   _____

8. in conclusion / a better movie than

   _____

B *Over to You* Think of two movies you have seen that have animation or special effects. Which one was better? Why? Write four to six sentences comparing the two movies. Use transitions to add ideas and show contrasts.

Cowboys in Space *was very popular. On the other hand,* Cowboys in Space II *didn't do very well.*

Avoid Common Mistakes ⚠️

1. **The prepositional expressions *as well as, in spite of, despite*, and *in addition to* are followed by a noun phrase or a gerund, not a subject + verb.**

   the high costs
   Despite ~~the costs are high~~, 3D TVs are becoming very popular.

   using
   The filmmakers used mocap in addition to ~~they used~~ digital technology.

2. **Use *on the other hand*, not *in the other hand*, when contrasting points of view.**

   on
   The movie industry has many career opportunities; ~~in~~ the other hand, it is very competitive.

Editing Task

Find and correct four more mistakes in the paragraph about the filmmaking industry.

the slow economy
Filmmaking is a durable industry. Despite ~~the economy is slow~~, the movie industry is doing well. People always seem to find money for entertainment. As a result, movie production companies often hire people because it takes many professionals to create a movie. In addition to they hire actors and directors, they hire tens of thousands of other

5 professionals that are not well known – for example, grips (people who set up and tear down the sets), production assistants, and camera operators. The jobs can be exciting and challenging; in the other hand, some can be low paying. As with most other careers, it is necessary to work hard and be ambitious to succeed. The work can also be especially tough for production crews – for example, camera operators, production

10 assistants, and makeup artists – who work up to 18 hours a day. Despite they have long hours, these jobs can be difficult to find because there is a lot of competition for them. In general, moviemaking is seen as a glamorous profession, and some people want to be a part of that glamour more than anything else. Movies often require celebrities and artists; in the other hand, they also rely on many people with other skills. It is a growing

15 industry, too. The Bureau of Labor Statistics states that employment opportunities for people in the filmmaking industry will increase 14 percent between 2008 and 2018. In short, this industry is competitive, but young people should pursue it if they have an interest in movies.

5 | Grammar for Writing ✎

Using Prepositions and Transition Words to Support an Argument

Writers often need to argue their opinions in persuasive writing. Good arguments in academic writing have logic that is easy for the reader to follow. Prepositions and transition words help to clarify the steps in the writer's logic as they link ideas together in meaningful relationships. Read this example paragraph:

> *In the future, I think all special effects will be computer-generated. <u>First,</u> audiences seem to prefer the effects from computer-generated animation. <u>Second,</u> computer-generated effects are cheaper <u>due to</u> their not requiring real life models of the sets. <u>Also,</u> it's safer to use them than to use actors and stuntmen. <u>Therefore,</u> movies made with this technology are likely to make more money.*

Pre-writing Task

1 Read the paragraph below. What is the writer's opinion about 3D technology?

Is 3D Technology Here to Stay?

Movies that are in 3D can be a lot of fun and are becoming much more common. However, the technology should not be used too much because it is not good for all types of movies. First, 3D technology can be good for adventure, science fiction, and animated movies. However, it does not seem to work well for serious dramas and art
5 films, where the plot and the characters are very important. Instead of getting involved in the plot and the characters, people tend to watch the special effects of the 3D technology when they watch a 3D movie. As a result, the plot and characters fade in importance. Thus, the 3D technology distracts the audience from the more important elements of the movie. Second, many people cannot watch 3D movies for health
10 reasons. Some people cannot physically see 3D technology because of an eye problem. There are others who get headaches or feel nauseated when they watch 3D movies. Third, tickets for 3D movies are more expensive than tickets for regular movies. If more movies are made with 3D technology, people who do not want to spend a lot of money may have fewer movie choices. As a result, people may go out to the movies less often. If
15 moviemakers start making more 3D movies, they will be making movies that entertain only rather than enrich, which will be a terrible loss for the art of moviemaking. In conclusion, I hope that 3D technology is used primarily for animated or science-fiction movies, and not for all types of movies.

2 Read the paragraph again. Circle the prepositions and transition words that are used to link ideas. Underline the prepositions and transition words that begin sentences. Notice how they link to the information in the previous sentences.

Writing Task

1 *Write* Use the paragraph in the Pre-writing Task to help you write about your opinion of some aspect of technology in entertainment. You can write about one of these topics or use your own ideas.

- 3D technology on TVs
- HD TV
- satellite radio
- video gaming
- video streaming on TV
- watching TV shows on the computer

2 *Self-Edit* Use the editing tips to improve your paragraph. Make any necessary changes.

1. Did you use prepositions, prepositional phrases, or transition words to show the relationships among ideas?
2. Did you add prepositions, prepositional phrases, or transition words to clarify the logic in your paragraph?
3. Did you avoid the mistakes in the Avoid Common Mistakes chart on page 387?

Appendices

1. Irregular Verbs

Base Form	Simple Past	Past Participle	Base Form	Simple Past	Past Participle
be	was/were	been	hide	hid	hidden
become	became	become	hit	hit	hit
begin	began	begun	hold	held	held
bite	bit	bitten	hurt	hurt	hurt
blow	blew	blown	keep	kept	kept
break	broke	broken	know	knew	known
bring	brought	brought	leave	left	left
build	built	built	lose	lost	lost
buy	bought	bought	make	made	made
catch	caught	caught	meet	met	met
choose	chose	chosen	pay	paid	paid
come	came	come	put	put	put
cost	cost	cost	read	read	read
cut	cut	cut	ride	rode	ridden
do	did	done	run	ran	run
draw	drew	drawn	say	said	said
drink	drank	drunk	see	saw	seen
drive	drove	driven	sell	sold	sold
eat	ate	eaten	send	sent	sent
fall	fell	fallen	set	set	set
feed	fed	fed	shake	shook	shaken
feel	felt	felt	show	showed	shown
fight	fought	fought	shut	shut	shut
find	found	found	sing	sang	sung
fly	flew	flown	sit	sat	sat
forget	forgot	forgotten	sleep	slept	slept
forgive	forgave	forgiven	speak	spoke	spoken
get	got	gotten	spend	spent	spent
give	gave	given	stand	stood	stood
go	went	gone	steal	stole	stolen
grow	grew	grown	swim	swam	swum
have	had	had	take	took	taken
hear	heard	heard	teach	taught	taught

Base Form	Simple Past	Past Participle	Base Form	Simple Past	Past Participle
tell	told	told	wake	woke	woken
think	thought	thought	wear	wore	worn
throw	threw	thrown	win	won	won
understand	understood	understood	write	wrote	written

. Stative (Non-Action) Verbs

Stative verbs do not describe actions. They describe states or situations. Stative verbs are not usually used in the progressive. Some are occasionally used in the present progressive, but often with a different meaning.

Research shows that the 25 most common stative verbs in spoken and written English are:

agree	dislike	hope	love	see
believe	expect	hurt	need	seem
care (about)	hate	know	notice	think
cost	have	like	own	understand
disagree	hear	look like	prefer	want

Other stative verbs:

appear	deserve	mean	smell
be	feel	owe	sound
belong	forgive	recognize	taste
concern	look	remember	weigh
contain	matter		

Stative verbs that also have action meanings:

be	have	look	taste
expect	hear	see	think
feel	hope	smell	weigh

Using the present progressive form of these verbs changes the meaning to an action.
*Can you **see** the red car?   (= use your eyes to be aware of something)*
*I'm **seeing** an old friend tomorrow.   (= meeting someone)*
*I **think** you're right.   (= believe)*
*Dina **is thinking** of taking a vacation soon.   (= considering)*
*I **have** two sisters.   (= be related to)*
*We're **having** eggs for breakfast. (= eating)*
*He **is** in his first year of college.   (= exist)*
*She **is being** difficult.   (= act)*

3. Modals and Modal-like Expressions

Modals are helper verbs. Most modals have multiple meanings.

Function	Modal or Modal-like Expression	Time	Example
Advice less strong	*could* *might (not)*	present, future	He **could** do some puzzles to improve his memory. You **might** try some tips on improving your memory.
stronger	*ought to* *should (not)*	present, future	We **ought to** take a memory class next month. Greg **should** improve his memory.
	had better (not)	present, future	You**'d better** pay attention now.
Past Advice, Regret, or Criticism	*ought to have* *should (not)* *have*	past	She **ought to have** tried harder to improve her memory. You **should have** made an effort to improve your memory. He **shouldn't have** taken that difficult class.
Permission	*can (not)* *may (not)*	present, future	You **can** register for the class next week. You **may not** register after the first class.
	could (not)	past	You **could** ask questions during the lecture yesterday, but you **could not** leave the room.
formal →	*be (not) allowed to* *be (not) permitted to*	past, present, future	He **was not allowed to** talk during the test, but he **was allowed to** use his books. Students **will not be permitted to** refer to notes during examinations.
Necessity / Obligation	*have to* *need to* *be required to* *be supposed to*	past, present, future	I **have to** study tonight. She **needs to** quit her stressful job. You **won't be required to** take a test. He **is supposed to** tell you his decision tomorrow.
	must (not)	present, future	You **must** have experience for this job.
Obligation not to / Prohibition	*must not* *be not supposed to*	present, future	You **must not** talk during the exam. Students **are not supposed to** take their books into the exam room.

A3

Modals and Modal-like Expressions *(continued)*

Function	Modal or Modal-like Expression	Time	Example
Lack of Necessity / Choices or Options	*not have to* *not need to* *be not required to*	past, present, future	You **didn't have to** bring your notes. You **don't need to** study tonight. You **are not required to** bring your books.
Ability	*can (not)*	present, future	We **can** meet the professor at noon tomorrow.
	could (not)	past	I **could** understand the lecture, but I **could not** remember it.
	be (not) able to	past, present, future	She **wasn't able to** see very well from her seat.
	could have	past	I **could have** done well on that memory test.
	could not have	past	I **couldn't have** taken the test yesterday. I was in another state!
Probability	*can't* *could (not)* *(not) have to* *must (not)*	present	Hackers **can't** be interested in my data. He **could** be online now. She **has to** be at work right now. He **must not** be worried about data security.
	may (not) *might (not)* *ought to* *should (not)*	present, future	Your computer **may** be at risk of hacking. That software **might not** be good enough. That password **ought to** be strong enough. It **shouldn't** be difficult to find good software.
	could *will (not)*	future	The company **could** start using cloud computing next month. My sister **will** probably get a new computer soon.
	can't have *could (not) have* *may (not) have* *might (not) have* *must (not) have*	past	I **can't have** entered the wrong password! The expert **could not have** given you good advice. The company **may have** been careless with security. I **might have** written the wrong password down. Someone **must have** stolen all the passwords.

4. Noncount Nouns and Measurement Words to Make Noncount Nouns Countable

Category of noncount noun	Noun Examples	Measurement Words and Expressions
Abstract concepts	courage, luck, space, time	a bit of, a kind of *You had **a bit of** luck, didn't you?*
Activities and sports	dancing, exercise, swimming, tennis, yoga	a game of, a session of *They played **two games of** tennis.*
Diseases and health conditions	arthritis, cancer, depression, diabetes, obesity	a kind of, a type of *She has **a type of** diabetes called Type 2.*
Elements and gases	gold, hydrogen, oxygen, silver	a bar of, a container of, a piece of, a tank of *We have **tanks of** oxygen in the storage room*
Foods	beef, broccoli, cheese, rice	a bottle of, a box of, a bunch of, a can of, a grain of, a head of, a loaf of, a package of, a piece of, a pinch of, a serving of, a slice of, a wedge of *I'll take **a serving of** rice and beef.*
Liquids	coffee, gasoline, oil, tea	a bottle of, a cup of, a gallon of, a glass of, a quart of *I would like **a cup of** tea.*
Natural phenomena	electricity, rain, sun, thunder	a bolt of, a drop of, a ray of *There hasn't been **a drop of** rain for three months.*
Particles	pepper, salt, sand, sugar	a grain of, a pinch of *My food needs **a pinch of** salt.*
Subjects and areas of work	construction, economics, genetics, geology, medicine, nursing	an area of, a branch of, a field of, a type of *There are a lot of specialty areas in **the field o** medicine.*
Miscellaneous	clothing, equipment, furniture, news	an article of, a piece of *I need **a piece of** furniture to go in that empty corner.*

Order of Adjectives Before Nouns

When you use two (or more) adjectives before a noun, use the order in the chart below.

Opinion	Size	Quality	Age	Shape	Color	Origin	Material	Nouns as Adjectives
beautiful	big	cold	ancient	oval	black	American	cotton	computer
comfortable	fat	free	antique	rectangular	blue	Canadian	glass	evening
delicious	huge	heavy	new	round	gold	Chinese	gold	government
expensive	large	hot	old	square	green	European	leather	rose
interesting	long	safe	young	triangular	orange	Japanese	metal	safety
nice	short				purple	Mexican	paper	software
pretty	small				red	Peruvian	plastic	summer
rare	tall				silver	Thai	silk	training
reasonable	thin				yellow		silver	
shocking	wide				white		stone	
special							wooden	
ugly							woolen	
unique								

Examples:

*That was a **delicious green Canadian** apple!* (*opinion before color before origin*)
*I saw the **shocking government** report on nutrition.* (*opinion before noun as adjective*)
*Wei got a **small oval glass** table.* (*size before shape before material*)

Verbs That Can Be Used Reflexively

allow oneself	challenge oneself	hurt oneself	remind oneself
amuse oneself	congratulate oneself	imagine oneself	see oneself
ask oneself	cut oneself	introduce oneself	take care of
be hard on oneself	dry oneself	keep oneself (busy)	talk to oneself
be oneself	enjoy oneself	kill oneself	teach oneself
be pleased with oneself	feel sorry for oneself	look after oneself	tell oneself
be proud of oneself	forgive oneself	look at oneself	treat oneself
behave oneself	get oneself	prepare oneself	
believe in oneself	give oneself	pride oneself on	
blame oneself	help oneself	push oneself	

7. Verbs Followed by Gerunds Only

admit	keep (= *continue*)
avoid	mind (= *object to*)
consider	miss
delay	postpone
defend	practice
deny	propose
discuss	quit
enjoy	recall (= *remember*)
finish	risk
imagine	suggest
involve	understand

8. Verbs Followed by Infinitives Only

afford	help	pretend
agree	hesitate	promise
arrange	hope	refuse
ask	hurry	request
attempt	intend	seem
choose	learn	struggle
consent	manage	tend (= *be likely*)
decide	need	threaten
demand	neglect	volunteer
deserve	offer	wait
expect	pay	want
fail	plan	wish
forget	prepare	would like

9. Verbs Followed by Gerunds or Infinitives

begin	like	regret*
continue	love	start
forget*	prefer	stop*
get	remember*	try*
hate		

*These verbs can be followed by a gerund or an infinitive, with a difference in meaning.

0. Expressions with Gerunds

Use a gerund after certain fixed verb expressions.	
Verb expressions spend time / spend money waste time / waste money have trouble / have difficulty / have a difficult time	*I **spent time helping** in the library.* *Don't **waste time complaining**.* *She **had trouble finishing** her degree.*

Use a gerund after certain fixed noun + preposition expressions.	
Noun + preposition expressions an excuse for in favor of an interest in a reason for	*I have **an excuse for not doing** my homework.* *Who is **in favor of not admitting** him?* *He has **an interest in getting** a scholarship.* *He has **a reason for choosing** this school.*

1. Verbs + Objects + Infinitives

advise	force	remind	ask*
allow	get	request	choose*
cause	hire	require	expect*
challenge	invite	teach	help*
convince	order	tell	need*
enable	permit	urge	pay*
encourage	persuade	warn	promise*
forbid			want*
			wish*

* These verbs can be followed by an object + infinitive or an infinitive only, with a difference in meaning.

Examples: *My boss **advised me to go** back to school.* *They **urged the advertisers not to surprise** people.* *My department **chose* Sally to create** the new ads.* *My department **chose* to create** the new ads.*

12. *Be* + Adjectives + Infinitives

be afraid	be delighted	be encouraged	be lucky	be sad
be amazed	be depressed	be excited	be necessary	be shocked
be angry	be determined	be fortunate	be pleased	be sorry
be anxious	be difficult	be fun	be proud	be surprised
be ashamed	be easy	be happy	be ready	be upset
be curious	be embarrassed	be likely	be relieved	be willing

13. Verbs + Prepositions

Verb + *about*	Verb + *by*	Verb + *of*	Verb + *to*
ask about	be affected by	be afraid of	admit to
care about	be raised by	approve of	belong to
complain about	Verb + *for*	be aware of	confess to
be excited about	apologize for	consist of	listen to
find out about	apply for	dream of	look forward to
forget about	ask for	be guilty of	refer to
hear about	care for	hear of	talk to
know about	look for	know of	be used to
learn about	pay for	take care of	Verb + *with*
read about	be responsible for	think of	agree with
see about	wait for	be warned of	argue with
talk about	Verb + *from*	Verb + *on*	bother with
think about	graduate from	concentrate on	deal with
worry about	Verb + *in*	count on	start with
be worried about	believe in	decide on	work with
Verb + *against*	find in	depend on	
advise against	include in	insist on	
decide against	be interested in	keep on	
Verb + *at*	involve in	plan on	
look at	result in	rely on	
smile at	show in		
be successful at	succeed in		
	use in		

4. Adjectives + Prepositions

Adjective + *about*	Adjective + *by*	Adjective + *in*	Adjective + *to*
concerned about	amazed by	high in	accustomed to
excited about	bored by	interested in	due to
happy about	surprised by	low in	similar to
nervous about	Adjective + *for*	Adjective + *of*	Adjective + *with*
pleased about	bad for	accused of	bored with
sad about	good for	afraid of	content with
sorry about	ready for	ashamed of	familiar with
surprised about	responsible for	aware of	good with
upset about	Adjective + *from*	capable of	satisfied with
worried about	different from	careful of	wrong with
Adjective + *at*	safe from	full of	
amazed at	separate from	guilty of	
angry at		sick of	
bad at		tired of	
good at		warned of	
successful at			
surprised at			

5. Verbs and Fixed Expressions that Introduce Indirect Questions

Do you have any idea…?	I'd like to know…	I don't know…
Can you tell me…?	I wonder / I'm wondering…	I'm not sure…
Do you know…?	I want to understand…	I can't imagine…
Do you remember…?	Let's find out…	We don't understand…
Could you explain…?	Let's ask…	It doesn't say…
Would you show me…?	We need to know…	I can't believe…

16. Tense Shifting in Indirect Speech

Direct Speech	Indirect (Reported) Speech
simple present She said, "The boss **is** angry."	**simple past** She **said** (that) the boss **was** angry.
present progressive He said, "She **is enjoying** the work."	**past progressive** He **said** (that) she **was enjoying** the work.
simple past They said, "The store **closed** last year."	**past perfect** They **said** (that) the store **had closed** last year.
present perfect The manager said, "The group **has done** good work."	**past perfect** The manager **said** (that) the group **had done** good work.
will He said, "The department **will add** three new managers."	**would** He **said** (that) the department **would add** three new managers.
be going to She said, "They **are going to hire** more people soon."	**be going to (past form)** She **said** (that) they **were going to hire** more people soon.
can The teacher said, "The students **can work** harder."	**could** The teacher **said** (that) the students **could work** harder.
may Their manager said, "Money **may not be** very important to them."	**might** Their manager **said** (that) money **might not be** very important to them.

* Note: *should, might, ought to,* and *could* do not change forms.

17. Reporting Verbs

Questions	Statements				Commands and Requests	
ask	admit	convince	notify	show	advise	request
inquire	announce	exclaim	observe	state	ask	say
question	assert	explain	promise	suggest	command	tell
	assure	find	remark	swear	demand	urge
	claim	indicate	remind	yell	order	warn
	comment	inform	reply			
	complain	mention	report			
	confess	note	shout			

8. Passive Forms

	Active	Passive
present progressive	*People are speaking English at the meeting.*	*English is being spoken at the meeting.*
simple present	*People speak English at the meeting.*	*English is spoken at the meeting.*
simple past	*People spoke English at the meeting.*	*English was spoken at the meeting.*
past progressive	*People were speaking English at the meeting.*	*English was being spoken at the meeting.*
present perfect	*People have spoken English at the meeting.*	*English has been spoken at the meeting.*
past perfect	*People had been speaking English at the meeting.*	*English had been spoken at the meeting.*
simple future	*People will speak English at the meeting.*	*English will be spoken at the meeting.*
future perfect	*People will have spoken English at the meeting.*	*English will have been spoken at the meeting.*
***be going to* (future)**	*People are going to speak English at the meeting.*	*English is going to be spoken at the meeting.*
Questions	*Do people speak English at the meeting?* *Did people speak English at the meeting?* *Have people spoken English at the meeting?*	*Is English spoken at the meeting?* *Was English spoken at the meeting?* *Has English been spoken at the meeting?*

19. Relative Clauses

	Identifying	Nonidentifying
Subject Relative Clauses	Many people **who/that support the environment** recycle.	My sister, **who lives in Maine**, loves being outside.
	Electricity **that/which saves energy** is a good thing.	People power, **which is a way to create energy**, is popular.
	They are the scientists **whose research has won awards**.	Brad Pitt, **whose movies are well known**, gives a lot of money to environmental causes.
Object Relative Clauses	Detectives are people **(who/whom/that) I respect tremendously**.	The character Sherlock Holmes, who/**whom Arthur Conan Doyle created**, was a fictional detective.
	Evidence **(which/that) criminals leave at the crime scene** is called forensic evidence.	Evidence from criminals, **which we call forensic evidence**, can help police solve cases.
	The person **whose car the thieves stole** was a friend of mine.	Arthur Conan Doyle, **whose medical clinic not many patients attended**, had time to write his stories.
Object Relative Clauses as Objects of Prepositions	There's the police officer (**that/who/whom) I spoke to**. (informal) There's the police officer **to whom I spoke**. (formal)	There's Officer Smith, **who/whom I spoke to yesterday**. (informal) There's Officer Smith, **to whom I spoke yesterday**. (formal)
	Police found evidence from the crime scene under the chair **(that/which) I was sitting on**. (informal) Police found evidence from the crime scene under the chair **on which I was sitting**. (formal)	The door, **which I entered through**, had been broken during the robbery. (informal) The door, **through which I entered**, had been broken during the robbery. (formal)

Relative Clauses *(continued)*

	Identifying	Nonidentifying
Relative Clauses with *Where* and *in Which*	*It's a city **where you can find Wi-Fi almost everywhere**.* *It's a city **in which you can find Wi-Fi almost everywhere**.*	*The city of Atlanta, **where my sister lives**, is very large.* *The city of Atlanta, **in which my sister lives**, is very large.*
Relative Clauses with *When* and *During Which*	*Night is a time **when many students study for exams**.* *Night is a time **during which many students study for exams**.*	*Joe prefers to study at night, **when his children are asleep**.* *Joe prefers to study at night, **during which his children are asleep**.*
Participle Phrases	*Students **concerned with the environment** should get involved in environmental groups on campus.*	*Millennials, **raised in the era of technology, cell phones, and the Internet**, understand technology very well.*
	*The expert **giving tomorrow's talk on Millennials** is very well known.*	*The movie Twilight, **starring Millennials**, is based on a book by Gen Xer Stephenie Meyer.*
Prepositional Phrases	*The computers **in our classroom** are fast.* *Young workers **low in self-esteem** are unusual.*	
Appositives		*Jan Smith, **the president of Myco**, will be speaking at noon today.* *Jan Smith (**the president of Myco**) will be speaking at noon today.* (formal writing)

20. Conditionals

Situation	Tense	*If* clause	Main clause	Example
Real Conditionals	present	simple present	simple present	*If a website **is** popular, people **talk** about it.*
	future	simple present	future	*If you only **listen** to one station, you **will hear** only one opinion.*
Unreal Conditionals	present	simple past or past progressive	*would, could, might* + base form of verb	*If I **studied** every day, I **would pass** all my tests.* *If I **weren't dreaming** all day, I **would pass** all my tests.*
	future	simple past	*would, could, might* + base form of verb	*If our school **closed** next year, we **wouldn't have** a place to learn.*
	past	past perfect	*would have, could have, might have* + past participle	*If the city **had hired** more teachers, the schools **might have improved**.*

Situation	Tense	*that* clause		Example
Wishes	present	simple past, past progressive, *could*		*I wish (that) schools **were improving**.*
	future	*were going to, would, could*		*I wish (that) the teachers **were going to** give us a party.*
	past	past perfect		*I **wish** (that) I **had studied** more.*

1. Academic Word List (AWL) Words and Definitions

The meanings of the words are those used in this book. ([U1] = Unit 1)

Academic Word	Definition
academics (n) [U25]	the subjects that you study in high school or college
access (n) [U5] [U6]	the opportunity or ability to use something
access (v) [U8]	get information, especially when using a computer
accurate (adj) [U22]	correct and without any mistakes
adapt (v) [U2] [U26]	change something so that it is suitable for a different use or situation
adequately (adv) [U20]	good enough but not very good
adult (n) [U4] [U8] [U9]	someone (or something such as a plant or animal) grown to full size and strength
affect (v) [U5] [U10] [U14] [U15] [U17] [U19] [U20] [U24] [U27]	have an influence on someone or something
aid (n) [U12]	help or support, especially in the form of food, money, or medical supplies
aid (v) [U9]	help or support
alter (v) [U20]	change a characteristic, often slightly; cause something to happen
alternative (adj) [U21]	available as another choice
alternative (n) [U18]	something that is different, especially from what is usual; a choice
analyst (n) [U24]	someone who studies or examines something in detail, such as finances, computer systems, or the economy
analyze (v) [U22]	study something in a systematic and careful way
appreciation (n) [U17]	being grateful for something
approach (n) [U2] [U15]	a method or way of doing something
approximately (adv) [U19]	almost exact
area (n) [U19] [U26] [U28]	a particular part of a country, city, town, etc.
attitude (n) [U1] [U15]	the way you feel about something or someone, or a particular feeling or opinion
author (n) [U7] [U9] [U17]	a writer of a book, article, etc.; a person whose main job is writing books
automatically (adv) [U22]	done in a manner as a natural reaction or without thinking
available (adj) [U14] [U18]	ready to use or obtain
aware (adj) [U8] [U21]	knowing that something exists; having knowledge or experience of a particular thing
beneficial (adj) [U10] [U20]	tending to help; having a good effect
benefit (n) [U11] [U20]	a helpful service given to employees in addition to pay; a helpful or good effect

Academic Word	Definition
challenge (n) [U8]	something needing great mental or physical effort in order to be done successfully
challenge (v) [U7]	test someone's ability or determination
challenging (adj) [U23]	difficult in a way that tests your ability or determination
chemical (n) [U20] [U27]	any basic substance that is used in or produced by a reaction involving changes to atoms or molecules
cite (v) [U20]	mention something as an example or proof of something else
civil rights (n) [U3]	the rights of every person in a society, including equality under law
classic (adj) [U10]	having a traditional style that is always fashionable
colleague (n) [U23]	one member of a group of people who work together
communication (n) [U5]	the exchange of messages or information
complex (adj) [U8] [U17]	having many, but connected, parts making it difficult to understand
computer (n) [U5] [U6] [U8] [U9] [U22] [U23] [U28]	an electronic device that can store, organize, and change large amounts of information quickly
computing (n) [U6]	the use of computers to complete a task; the study or use of computers
concentrate (v) [U7] [U12]	direct your attention and thought to an activity or subject
conclude (v) [U24]	cause something to end; end
conclusion (n) [U24]	a decision made after a lot of consideration
consequently (adv) [U16] [U28]	as a result; therefore
consist of (v) [U12] [U20]	be made up or formed of various specific things
constant (adj) [U5]	not changing
constantly (adv) [U1]	nearly continuously or very frequently
consumer (n) [U13] [U26]	a person who buys goods or services for their own use
contact (v) [U4]	have communication with a person or with a group or organization
contribute (v) [U3] [U10]	help by providing money or support, especially when other people or conditions are also helping
controversial (adj) [U4]	causing or likely to cause disagreement
convert (v) [U21]	change the character, appearance, or operation of something
convince (v) [U13] [U15] [U24]	cause someone to believe something or to do something
corporation (n) [U3]	a large company
create (v) [U1] [U2] [U7] [U15] [U17] [U20] [U21] [U26] [U28]	cause something to exist, or to make something new or imaginative
creation (n) [U16] [U19]	something that is made
creative (adj) [U13] [U18]	producing or using original and unusual ideas
creatively (adv) [U18]	done in a new or imaginative way

Academic Word	Definition
creator (n) [U28]	a person who creates something
crucial (adj) [U7] [U10]	extremely important because many other things depend on it
cultural (adj) [U15] [U19] [U26]	relating to the way of life of a country or a group of people
culture (n) [U2] [U14] [U19] [U26]	the way of life of a particular people, especially shown in their ordinary behavior and habits, their attitudes toward each other, and their moral and religious beliefs
data (n) [U6]	information collected for use
debate (n) [U4] [U20]	a discussion or argument about a subject
demonstrate (v) [U1]	show how to do something; explain
depressed (adj) [U27]	unhappy and without hope
design (v) [U18] [U20]	make or draw plans for something
despite (prep) [U28]	used to say that something happened or is true, although something else makes this seem not probable
device (n) [U5] [U6] [U8]	a piece of equipment that is used for a particular purpose
distribution (n) [U20]	the division of something among several or many people, or the spreading of something over an area
dominant (adj) [U4]	more important, strong, or noticeable
dominate (v) [U19]	control a place or person, want to be in charge, or be the most important person or thing
dramatically (adv) [U10]	suddenly or noticeably
economic (adj) [U14] [U21] [U24]	connected to the economy of a country
eliminate (v) [U6]	remove or take away
energy (n) [U9] [U21]	the power to do work and activity
environment (n) [U4] [U10] [U13] [U17] [U20] [U21]	the conditions that you live or work in, and the way that they influence how you feel or how effectively you can work; the air, water, and land in or on which people, animals, and plants live
error (n) [U23]	a mistake, especially in a way that can be discovered as wrong
ethnic (adj) [U3]	relating to a particular race of people who share a system of accepted beliefs and morals
evidence (n) [U16] [U22]	something that helps to prove that something is or is not true
expert (n) [U6] [U7] [U9] [U18] [U19] [U22] [U23] [U25]	a person with a high level of knowledge or skill about a particular subject
external (adj) [U17]	relating to the outside part of something
facility (n) [U11]	a place where a particular activity happens
file (n) [U6]	a collection of information in a computer stored as one unit with one name
final (adj) [U7]	last

Academic Word	Definition
finally (adv) [U4] [U12] [U16] [U18] [U20] [U28]	at the end, or after some delay
financial (adj) [U11] [U12] [U16] [U27]	relating to money
flexible (adj) [U18]	able to change or be changed easily according to the situation
focus (v) [U11] [U17] [U21]	direct attention toward someone or something
found (v) [U3]	start an organization, especially by providing money
foundation (n) [U3]	an organization that provides financial support for activities and groups
furthermore (adv) [U6] [U15] [U28]	also and more importantly
generate (v) [U6] [U21]	produce
generation (n) [U23]	all the people within a society or family of about the same age
global (adj) [U2] [U3] [U19] [U20]	relating to the whole world
globalization (n) [U26]	the increase of business around the world, especially by big companies operating in many countries
globally (adv) [U26]	pertaining to the whole world
goal (n) [U3] [U4]	an aim or purpose, something you want to achieve
grade (n) [U17]	the measure of the quality of a student's schoolwork
grant (n) [U12]	money that a university, government, or organization gives to someone for a purpose, such as to do research or study
guarantee (v) [U8]	promise that a particular thing will happen
identical (adj) [U4]	exactly the same
identify (v) [U22]	recognize or be able to name someone or something; prove who or what someone or something is
identity (n) [U19]	who a person is, or the qualities of a person, thing, or group that make them different from others
image (n) [U2] [U7] [U22]	an idea, especially a mental picture, of what something or someone is
immigrant (n) [U26]	a person who has come into a foreign country in order to live there
impact (n) [U4] [U10]	the strong effect or influence that something has on a situation or person
implicit (adj) [U1]	suggested but not communicated directly
inappropriate (adj) [U2] [U25]	unsuitable, especially for the particular time, place, or situation
inconclusive (adj) [U22]	not leading to a definite result or decision; uncertain
individual (n) [U4] [U18]	a person, especially when considered separately and not as part of a group
individualism (n) [U15]	the quality or state of being different from other people

Academic Word	Definition
innovation (n) [U11]	something new or different
institute (n) [U9] [U11]	an organization where people do a particular kind of scientific, educational, or social work
internal (adj) [U17]	happening inside a person, group, organization, place, or country
investigate (v) [U1] [U4] [U22]	try to discover all the facts about something
investigation (n) [U22]	the search for facts
investigator (n) [U22]	a person who examines the particulars of an event in an attempt to learn the facts
isolated (adj) [U24]	separated from other things
issue (n) [U11] [U12] [U14] [U20] [U24]	a subject or problem that people are thinking and talking about
job (n) [U11] [U12] [U14] [U19] [U23] [U24] [U28]	the regular work that a person does to earn money
legislator (n) [U25]	a member of an elected group of people who has the power to make or change laws
link (n) [U9] [U24]	a connection; a word or image on a website that can take you to another document or website
link (v) [U20]	make a connection
locate (v) [U26]	put or establish something in a particular place
location (n) [U6]	a place or position
maintain (v) [U7]	make a situation or activity continue in the same way
maintenance (n) [U23]	the work that is done to keep something in good condition
major (adj) [U2] [U9] [U21]	more important, bigger, or more serious than others of the same type
media (n) [U24]	newspapers, magazines, television, and radio considered as a group
mental (adj) [U7]	relating to the mind, or involving the process of thinking
method (n) [U18] [U22]	a way of doing something
minority (n) [U3]	a part of a group that is less than half of the whole group, often much less
modify (v) [U20]	change something in order to improve it
motivate (v) [U17]	cause someone to behave in a certain way, or to make someone want to do something well; give a reason for doing something
motivation (n) [U17]	enthusiasm to do something
negative (adj) [U23]	not happy, hopeful, or approving
nondominant (adj) [U7]	not as important, strong, or noticeable
nonetheless (adv) [U6] [U25]	despite what has just been said or referred to
occupy (v) [U4]	fill or use

Academic Word	Definition
occur (v) [U8] [U22] [U23] [U24]	happen
option (n) [U12]	a choice
participant (n) [U18]	a person who becomes involved in an activity
percent (adv) [U11] [U14] [U21] [U27]	for or out of every 100
physical (adj) [U9]	relating to the body
plus (conj) [U12]	added to
policy (n) [U24] [U25]	a set of ideas or a plan of what to do in particular situations that has been agreed on by a government or group of people
portion (n) [U9]	the amount of food served to, or suitable for, a person
pose (v) [U6]	cause a problem or difficulty
positive (adj) [U13] [U15] [U17] [U23] [U24]	happy or hopeful
potential (adj) [U20]	possible but not yet achieved
predict (v) [U5] [U16]	say that an event will happen in the future
prediction (n) [U24]	events or actions that may happen in the future
principle (n) [U3]	a rule or belief which influences your behavior and is based on what you think is right
prior (adv) [U25]	existing or happening before something else
priority (n) [U7]	something that is considered more important than other matters
process (n) [U1] [U18]	a series of actions or events performed to make something or achieve a particular result, or a series of changes that happens naturally
professional (adj) [U18] [U21] [U27]	relating to the workplace; engaging in as a career; relating to a skilled type of work
project (n) [U7] [U16]	a piece of planned work or activity that is completed over a period of time and intended to achieve a particular aim
psychologist (n) [U1] [U17]	someone who studies the mind and emotions and their relationship to behavior
range (n) [U24]	the level to which something is limited, or the area within which something operates
react (v) [U1] [U13]	feel or act in a way because of something else
refined (adj) [U9]	made more pure by removing unwanted material
relaxed (adj) [U10]	comfortable and informal
relaxing (adj) [U10]	feeling happy and comfortable because nothing is worrying you
reliable (adj) [U6]	to be trusted or believe
relocate (v) [U14]	move to a new place
rely (v) [U24]	need or trust someone or something
require (v) [U18]	need something, or to make something necessary

Academic Word	Definition
research (n) [U1] [U2] [U4] [U5] [U10] [U14] [U15] [U16] [U17]	the detailed study of a subject or an object in order to discover information or achieve a new understanding of it
research (v) [U1]	study a subject in order to discover information
researcher (n) [U3] [U4] [U5] [U15] [U17]	a person who studies something to learn detailed information about it
reveal (v) [U1]	allow something to be seen that had been hidden or secret
role (n) [U4]	the duty or use that someone or something usually has or is expected to have
route (n) [U7]	the roads or paths you follow to get from one place to another place
schedule (n) [U16]	a list of planned activities or things to be done at or during a particular time
secure (adj) [U6]	safe
seek (v) [U27]	search for something
sequence (n) [U28]	a series of related events or things that have a particular order
series (n) [U2]	several things or events or the same type that come one after the other
similar (adj) [U2] [U3] [U4] [U24]	looking or being almost the same, although not exactly
similarity (n) [U4]	when two things or people are almost the same
similarly (adv) [U10]	in almost the same way
site (n) [U6] [U11] [U13] [U24]	a place where something is, was, or will be; a place on the Internet with one or more pages of information about a subject
source (n) [U21] [U24]	origin or beginning of something
specific (adj) [U20]	relating to one thing and not others; particular
specifically (adv) [U1]	for a particular reason or purpose
strategy (n) [U11] [U13] [U26]	a plan for achieving something or reaching a goal
stress (n) [U11]	a feeling of worry caused by a difficult situation
style (n) [U10] [U13]	a way of doing something that is typical to a person, group, place, or time
sum (n) [U6]	an amount of money
survey (n) [U6]	a set of questions to find out people's habits or beliefs about something
survive (v) [U15]	continue to live, especially after a dangerous situation
team (n) [U12] [U22] [U23]	a group of people who work together, either in a sport or in order to achieve something
technique (n) [U7] [U18] [U22]	a specific way of doing a skillful activity
technological (adj) [U8]	relating to or involving technology

Academic Word	Definition
technology (n) [U5] [U6] [U20] [U21] [U22] [U23] [U28]	the method for using scientific discoveries for practical purposes, especially in industry
tradition (n) [U15]	a custom or way of behaving that has continued for a long time in a group of people or a society
traditional (adj) [U13] [U18] [U22] [U25]	established for a long time, or part of a behavior and beliefs that have been established
traditionally (adv) [U15]	relating to or involving tradition
transfer (v) [U12]	move someone or something from one place to another
trend (n) [U9]	the direction of changes or developments
unbiased (adj) [U24]	not influenced by personal opinion
unique (adj) [U28]	different from everyone and everything
uniquely (adv) [U26]	in a manner that is unusual or special
variation (n) [U18]	a change in quality, amount, or level
varying (adj) [U10]	different
version (n) [U18]	a form of something that differs slightly from other forms of the same thing
virtual (adj) [U28]	created by a computer
visualization (n) [U7]	an image in your mind of someone or something
visualize (v) [U7]	create a picture in your mind of someone or something
voluntary (adj) [U11]	done or given because you want to and not because you have been forced to

2. Pronunciation Table International Phonetic Alphabet (IPA)

Vowels	
Key Words	**International Phonetic Alphabet**
cake, mail, pay	/eɪ/
pan, bat, hand	/æ/
tea, feet, key	/iː/
ten, well, red	/e/
ice, pie, night	/aɪ/
is, fish, will	/ɪ/
cone, road, know	/oʊ/
top, rock, stop	/ɑ/
blue, school, new, cube, few	/uː/
cup, us, love	/ʌ/
house, our, cow	/aʊ/
saw, talk, applause	/ɔː/
boy, coin, join	/ɔɪ/
put, book, woman	/ʊ/
alone, open, pencil, atom, ketchup	/ə/

Consonants

Key Words	International Phonetic Alphabet
bid, jo**b**	/b/
do, fee**d**	/d/
food, sa**f**e	/f/
go, do**g**	/g/
home, be**h**ind	/h/
kiss, ba**ck**	/k/
load, poo**l**	/l/
man, plu**m**	/m/
need, ope**n**	/n/
pen, ho**p**e	/p/
road, ca**r**d	/r/
see, re**c**ent	/s/
show, na**ti**on	/ʃ/
team, mee**t**	/t/
choose, wa**tch**	/tʃ/
think, bo**th**	/θ/
this, fa**th**er	/ð/
visit, sa**v**e	/v/
watch, a**w**ay	/w/
yes, on**i**on	/j/
zoo, the**s**e	/z/
bei**g**e, mea**s**ure	/ʒ/
jump, bri**dg**e	/dʒ/

Glossary of Grammar Terms

action verb a verb that describes an action.
> I **eat** breakfast every day.
> They **ran** in the 5K race.

active sentence a sentence that focuses on the doer and the action.
> **Jorge played** basketball yesterday.

adjective a word that describes or modifies a noun.
> That's a **beautiful** hat.

adjective clause *see* **relative clause**

adverb a word that describes or modifies a verb, another adverb, or an adjective. Adverbs often end in -ly.
> Please walk **faster** but **carefully**.

adverb clause a clause that shows how ideas are connected. Adverb clauses begin with subordinators such as *because, since, although,* and *even though.*
> **Although it is not a holiday**, workers have the day off.

adverb of degree an adverb that makes other adverbs or adjectives stronger or weaker.
> The test was **extremely** difficult. They are **really** busy today.

adverb of frequency an adverb such as *always, often, sometimes, never,* and *usually* that describes how often something happens.
> She **always** arrives at work on time.

adverb of manner an adverb that describes how an action happens.
> He has **suddenly** left the room.

adverb of time an adverb that describes when something happens.
> She'll get up **later**.

agent the noun or pronoun performing the action of the verb in a sentence.
> **People** spoke English at the meeting.

appositive a reduced form of a nonidentifying relative clause. Appositives are formed by removing the relative pronoun and the verb *be,* leaving only a noun phrase.
> Jan Smith, **an expert on Millennials**, will be speaking at noon today.

article the words *a/an* and *the.* An article introduces or identifies a noun.
> I bought **a** new MP3 player. **The** price was reasonable.

auxiliary verb (also called **helping verb**) a verb that is used before a main verb in a sentence. *Do, have, be,* and *will* can act as auxiliary verbs.
> **Does** he want to go to the library later? **Have** you received the package? **Will** he arrive soon?

base form of the verb the form of a verb without any endings (-s or -ed) or *to.*
> **come**   **go**   **take**

clause a group of words that has a subject and a verb. There are two types of clauses: **main clauses** and **dependent clauses** (*see* **dependent clause**). A sentence can have more than one clause.

MAIN CLAUSE   DEPENDENT CLAUSE   MAIN CLAUSE

I woke up when I heard the noise. It was scary.

common noun a word for a person, place, or thing. A common noun is not capitalized.

mother   *building*   *fruit*

comparative the form of an adjective or adverb that shows how two people, places, or things are different.

*My daughter is **older than** my son.* (adjective)

*She does her work **more quickly** than he does.* (adverb)

conditional a sentence that describes a possible situation and the result of that situation. It can be a real or unreal condition / result about the present, past, or future.

If a website is popular, people talk about it. (present real conditional)

If I had studied harder, I would have passed that course. (past unreal conditional)

conjunction a word such as *and, but, so, or,* and *yet* that connects single words, phrases, or clauses.

*We finished all our work, **so** we left early.*

Some more conjunctions are *after, as, because, if, and when.*

consonant a sound represented in writing by these letters of the alphabet: ***b, c, d, f, g, h, j, k, l, m, n, p, q, r, s, t, v, w, x, y,*** and ***z.***

count noun a person, place, or thing you can count. Count nouns have a plural form.

*There are three **banks** on Oak Street.*

definite article *the* is the definite article. Use *the* with a person, place, or thing that is familiar to you and your listener. Use *the* when the noun is unique – there is only one (*the sun, the moon, the Internet*). Also use *the* before a singular noun used to represent a whole class or category.

The *movie we saw last week was very good.*

The *Earth is round.*

The *male robin is more colorful than **the** female.*

dependent clause a clause that cannot stand alone. A dependent clause is not a complete sentence, but it still has a subject and verb. Some kinds of dependent clauses are adverb clauses, relative clauses, and time clauses.

After we return from the trip, *I'm going to need to relax.*

determiner a word that comes before a noun to limit its meaning in some way. Some common determiners are *some, a little, a lot, a few, this, that, these, those, his, a, an, the, much,* and *many.*

These *computers have **a lot** of parts.*

*Please give me **my** book.*

direct object the person or thing that receives the action of the verb.

*The teacher gave the students **a test**.*

direct question a type of direct speech (see **direct speech**) that repeats a person's question.

The president asked, ***"Who were your best employees last month?"***

direct speech (also called **quoted speech**) repeats people's exact words. A direct speech statement consists of a reporting clause and the exact words of a person inside quotation marks.

The manager said, ***"Workers need to use creativity."***

factual conditional *see* **present real conditional**

formal a style of writing or speech used when you don't know the other person very well or where it's not appropriate to show familiarity, such as in business, a job interview, speaking to a stranger, or speaking to an older person who you respect.

Good evening. I'd like to speak with Ms. Smith. Is she available?

future a verb form that describes a time that hasn't come yet. It is expressed in English by *will*, *be going to*, and present tense.

*I'****ll meet*** *you tomorrow.*

*I'****m going to visit*** *my uncle and aunt next weekend.*

My bus ***leaves*** *at 10:00 tomorrow.*

*I'****m meeting*** *Joe on Friday.*

future real conditional describes a possible situation in the future and the likely result. The *if* clause uses the simple present. The main clause uses a future form of the verb.

If *you only* ***listen*** *to one station, you* ***will hear*** *only one opinion.*

future unreal conditional describes an imaginary situation in the future. The *if* clause uses the simple past. The main clause uses the modals *would*, *could*, or *might*.

If *teachers* ***prepared*** *students better for exams, more students* ***would pass***.

gerund the *-ing* form of a verb that is used as a noun. It can be the subject or object of a sentence or the object of a preposition.

We suggested ***waiting*** *and* ***going*** *another day.*

Salsa ***dancing*** *is a lot of fun.*

I look forward to ***meeting*** *you.*

habitual past a verb form that describes repeated past actions, habits, and conditions using *used to* or *would*.

Before we had the Internet, we ***used to*** *go to the library a lot.*

Before there was refrigeration, people ***would*** *use ice to keep food cool.*

helping verb *see* **auxiliary verb**

if **clause** the condition clause in a conditional. It describes the possible situation, which can be either real or unreal.

If it rains tomorrow, *I'll stay home.*

imperative a type of clause that tells people to do something. It gives instructions, directions to a place, and advice. The verb is in the base form.

Listen *to the conversation.*

Don't open *your books.*

Turn *right at the bank and then* ***go*** *straight.*

indefinite article *a/an* are the indefinite articles. Use *a/an* with a singular person, place, or thing when you and your listener are not familiar with it, or when the specific name of it is not important. Use *a* with consonant sounds. Use *an* with vowel sounds.

*She's going to see **a** doctor today.*

*I had **an** egg for breakfast.*

indefinite pronoun a pronoun used when the noun is unknown or not important. There is an indefinite pronoun for people, for places, and for things. Some examples are *somebody, anyone, nobody, somewhere, anywhere, nothing, everything,* etc. Use singular verb forms when the indefinite pronoun is the subject of the sentence.

Everybody *is going to be there. There is **nowhere** I'd rather work.*

indirect object the person or thing that receives the direct object.

*The teacher gave **the students** a test.*

indirect question (also called **reported question**) tells what other people have asked or asks a question using a statement. There are two kinds of indirect questions: *Yes/No* and information questions. Indirect questions follow the *subject-verb* word order of a statement.

*Mia **asked whether** we **would begin** Creative Problem Solving soon.*

*The president asked **who** my best employees **were** last month.*

indirect speech (also called **reported speech**) tells what someone says in another person's words. An indirect speech statement consists of a reporting verb (see **reporting verb**) such as *say* in the main clause, followed by a *that* clause. *That* is optional and is often omitted in speaking.

*He **said** (that) she **was enjoying** the work.*

infinitive *to* + the base form of a verb.

*I need **to get** home early tonight.*

infinitive of purpose *in order* + infinitive expresses a purpose. It answers the question *why.* If the meaning is clear, it is not necessary to use *in order.*

*People are fighting **(in order) to change** unfair laws.*

informal is a style of speaking to friends, family, and children.

Hey, there. Nice to see you again.

information question (also called **Wh- question**) begins with a *wh*-word (*who, what, when, where, which, why, how, how much*). To answer this type of question, you need to provide information rather than answer *yes* or *no.*

inseparable phrasal verb a phrasal verb that cannot be separated. The verb and its particle always stay together.

*My car **broke down** yesterday.*

intransitive verb a verb that does not need an object. It is often followed by an expression of time, place, or manner. It cannot be used in the passive.

*The flight **arrived** at 5.30 p.m.*

irregular adjective an adjective that does not change its form in the usual way. For example, you do not make the comparative form by adding *-er.*

good → *better*

irregular adverb an adverb that does not change its form in the usual way. For example, you do not make the comparative form by adding *-ly*.

badly → *worse*

irregular verb a verb that does not change its form in the usual way. For example, it does not form the simple past with *-d* or *-ed*. It has its own special form.

go → *went*   *ride* → *rode*   *hit* → *hit*

main clause (also called **independent clause**) a clause that can be used alone as a complete sentence. In a conditional, the main clause describes the result when the condition exists.

After I get back from my trip, ***I'm going to relax****.*

If I hear about a good story, ***I move quickly to get there and report it****.*

main verb a verb that functions alone in a clause and can have an auxiliary verb.

They ***had*** *a meeting last week.*

They have ***had*** *many meetings this month.*

measurement word a word or phrase that shows the amount of something. Measurement words can be singular or plural. They can be used to make noncount nouns countable.

I bought ***a box*** *of cereal, and Sonia bought* ***five pounds*** *of apples.*

modal a verb such as *can*, *could*, *have to*, *may*, *might*, *must*, *should*, *will*, and *would*. It modifies the main verb to show such things as ability, permission, possibility, advice, obligation, necessity, or lack of necessity.

It ***might*** *rain later today.*

You ***should*** *study harder if you want to pass this course.*

non-action verb *see* **stative verb**

noncount noun refers to ideas and things that you cannot count. Noncount nouns use a singular verb and do not have a plural form.

Do you download ***music****?*

noun a word for a person, place, or thing. There are common nouns and proper nouns. (*see* **common nouns, proper nouns**)

COMMON NOUN	PROPER NOUN
I stayed in a ***hotel*** *on my trip to New York.*	*I stayed in the* ***Pennsylvania Hotel****.*

object a noun or pronoun that usually follows the verb and receives the action.

I sent ***the flowers****. I sent* ***them*** *to* ***you****.*

object pronoun replaces a noun in the object position.

Sara loves exercise classes. She takes ***them*** *three times a week.*

participle phrase a reduced form of an identifying relative clause. Participle phrases are formed by removing the relative pronoun and the verb *be*. Participle phrases can be used when the verb in the relative clause is in the form verb + *-ing* (present participle) or the past participle form.

He is the person ***using the Internet too much at work****.*

particle a small word like *down*, *in*, *off*, *on*, *out*, or *up*. These words (which can also be prepositions) are used with verbs to form **two-word verbs** or **phrasal verbs**. The meaning of a phrasal verb often has a different meaning from the meaning of the individual words in it.

passive sentence a sentence that focuses on the action or on the person or thing receiving the action. The object is in the subject position.

*English **was spoken** at the meeting.*

past participle a verb form that can be regular (base form + *-ed*) or irregular. It is used to form perfect tenses and the passive. It can also be an adjective.

*I've **studied** English for five years.*
*The **frightened** child cried.*

past progressive a verb form that describes events or situations in progress at a time in the past. The emphasis is on the action.

*They **were watching** TV when I arrived.*

past unreal conditional describes a situation that was not true in the past. Past unreal conditionals describe something that was possible but did not happen. The *if* clause uses the past perfect. The main clause uses the modals *would have*, *could have*, or *might have* and the past participle form of the verb.

*If we **hadn't had** a hurricane, the schools **wouldn't have closed**.*

phrasal verb (also called **two-word verb**) consists of a verb + a particle. There are two kinds of phrasal verbs: separable and inseparable. (*see* **particle, inseparable phrasal verbs, separable phrasal verbs**)

      VERB + PARTICLE

*They **came back** from vacation today.* (inseparable)
*Please **put** your cell phone **away**.* (separable)

phrase a group of words about an idea that is not a complete sentence. It does not have a main verb.

  across the street   ***in the morning***

plural noun a noun that refers to more than one person, place, or thing.

  students   ***women***   ***roads***

possessive adjective *see* **possessive determiner.**

possessive determiner (also called **possessive adjective**) a determiner that shows possession (*my*, *your*, *his*, *her*, *its*, *our*, and *their*).

possessive pronoun replaces a possessive determiner + singular or plural noun. The possessive pronoun agrees with the noun that it replaces.

*My exercise class is at night. **Hers** is on the weekend.* (hers = her exercise class)

preposition a word such as *to*, *at*, *for*, *with*, *below*, *in*, *on*, *next to*, or *above* that goes before a noun or pronoun to show location, time, direction, or a close relationship between two people or things. A preposition may go before a gerund as well.

*I'm **in** the supermarket **next to** our favorite restaurant.*
*The idea **of** love has inspired many poets.*
*I'm interested **in** taking a psychology course.*

prepositional phrase a reduced form of an identifying relative clause. Prepositional phrases are formed by removing the relative pronoun and the verb *be,* leaving only a prepositional phrase.

*The computers **in our classroom** are fast.*

present perfect a verb form that describes past events or situations that are still important in the present and actions that happened once or repeatedly at an indefinite time before now.

*Lately scientists **have discovered** medicines in the Amazon.*

*I**'ve been** to the Amazon twice.*

present perfect progressive a verb form that describes something that started in the past, usually continues in the present, and may continue in the future.

*He **hasn't been working** since last May.*

present progressive a verb form that describes an action or situation that is in progress now or around the present time. It is also used to indicate a fixed arrangement in the future.

*What **are** you **doing** right now?*

*I**'m leaving** for Spain next week.*

present real conditional (also called **factual conditional**) describes a situation that is possible now and its result. Present real conditionals describe general truths, facts, and habits. The *if* clause and the main clause use the simple present.

***If** you **control** the media, you **control** public opinion.*

present unreal conditional describes an imaginary situation in the present. The *if* clause uses the simple past or past progressive. The main clause uses the modals *would, could,* or *might.*

***If** I **studied** every day, I **could pass** all my tests.*

pronoun a word that replaces a noun or noun phrase. Some examples are *I, we, him, hers, it.* (*see* **object pronoun, subject pronoun, relative pronoun, possessive pronoun, reciprocal pronoun, reflexive pronoun**.)

proper noun a noun that is the name of a particular person, place, or thing. It is capitalized.

Central Park** in **New York City

punctuation mark a symbol used in writing such as a period (.), a comma (,), a question mark (?), or an exclamation point (!).

quantifier a word or phrase that shows an amount of something. In addition to measurements words, some other quantifiers are *much, many, some, any, a lot, plenty, enough,* etc.

*We have **three bottles** of juice and **plenty of** snacks.*

quoted speech *see* **direct speech**

reciprocal pronoun a pronoun (*each other, one another*) that shows that two or more people give *and* receive the same action or have the same relationship.

*Mari and I have the same challenges. We help **each other**. (I help Mari, and Mari helps me.)*

reflexive pronoun a pronoun (*myself, yourself, himself, herself, ourselves, yourselves, themselves*) that shows that the object of the sentence is the same as the subject.

*I taught **myself** to speak Japanese.*

regular verb a verb that changes its form in the usual way.

live → live**s**

wash → wash**ed**

relative clause (also called **adjective clause**) defines, describes, identifies, or gives more information about a noun. It begins with a relative pronoun such as *who, that, which, whose*, or *whom*. Like all clauses, a relative clause has both a subject and a verb. It can describe the subject or the object of a sentence.

*People **who have sleep problems** can join the study.* (subject relative clause)

*There are many diseases **that viruses cause**.* (object relative clause)

relative pronoun a pronoun (*who, which, that, whose, whom*) that connects a noun phrase to a relative clause

*People **who** have sleep problems can join the study.*

*There are many diseases **that** viruses cause.*

reported question *see* **indirect question**

reported speech *see* **indirect speech**

reporting verb a verb used to introduce direct speech or indirect speech. *Say* is the most common reporting verb. Other such verbs include *admit, announce, complain, confess, exclaim, explain, mention, remark, reply, report, state*, and *swear*, and *tell*.

*The president **said**, "We will change our system of rewarding employees."*

*The president **stated** that they would change their system of rewarding employees.*

result clause *see* **main clause**

sentence a complete thought or idea that has a subject and a main verb. In writing, it begins with a capital letter and has a punctuation mark at the end (. ? !). In an imperative sentence, the subject (*you*) is not usually stated.

This sentence is a complete thought.

Open your books.

separable phrasal verb a phrasal verb that can be separated. This means that an object can go before or after the particle.

***Write down** your expenses.*

***Write** your expenses **down**.*

simple past a verb form that describes completed actions or events that happened at a definite time in the past.

*They **grew up** in Washington, D.C.*

*They **attended** Howard University and **graduated** in 2004.*

simple present a verb form that describes things that regularly happen such as habits and routines (usual and regular activities). It also describes facts and general truths.

*I **play** games online every night.* (routine)

*The average person **spends** 13 hours a week online.* (fact)

singular noun a noun that refers to only one person, place, or thing.

*He is my best **friend**.*

statement a sentence that gives information.

Today is Thursday.

stative verb (also called **non-action verb**) describes a state or situation, not an action. It is usually in the simple form.

*I **remember** your friend.*

subject the person, place, or thing that performs the action of a verb.

***People** use new words and expressions every day.*

subject pronoun replaces a noun in the subject position.

***Sara and I** are friends. **We** work at the same company.*

subordinator a conjunction that connects a dependent clause and an independent clause. Some common subordinators include *although, because, even though, in order to, since,* and *so that.*

***Although** many people like to shop, some people shop too much.*

superlative the form of an adjective or adverb that compares one person, place, or thing to others in a group.

*This storm was **the most dangerous** one of the season. (adjective)*

*That group worked **most effectively** after the disaster. (adverb)*

syllable a group of letters that has one vowel sound and that you say as a single unit.

There is one syllable in the word lunch *and two syllables in the word* breakfast. (*Break* is one syllable and *fast* is another syllable.)

tag question consists of a verb and pronoun added to the end of a statement. Tag questions confirm information or ask for agreement. The tag changes the statement into a question.

*They don't live in Chicago, **do they?***   *Geography is interesting, **isn't it?***

tense the form of a verb that shows past or present time.

*They **worked** yesterday. (simple past)*

*They **work** every day. (simple present)*

third-person singular refers to *he, she,* and *it* or a singular noun. In the simple present, the third-person singular form ends in *-s* or *-es.*

***It looks** warm and sunny today. **He washes** the laundry on Saturdays.*

time clause a phrase that shows the order of events and begins with a time word such as *before, after, when, while,* or *as soon as.*

***Before** there were freezers, people needed ice to make frozen desserts.*

time expression a phrase that functions as an adverb of time. It tells when something happens, happened, or will happen.

*I graduated **in 2010**. She's going to visit her aunt and uncle **next summer**.*

transitive verb a verb that has an object. The object completes the meaning of the verb.

*She **wears** perfume.*

two-word verb *see* **phrasal verb**

verb a word that describes an action or a state.

*Alex **wears** jeans and a T-shirt to school. Alex **is** a student.*

vowel a sound represented in writing by these letters of the alphabet: ***a, e, i, o,*** and ***u***.

Wh- **question** *see* **information question**

***Yes/No* question** begins with a form of *be* or an auxiliary verb. You can answer such a question with *yes* or *no*.

*"**Are** they going to the movies?" "**No**, they're not."*

*"**Can** you give me some help?" "**Yes**, I can."*

/an, 121, 137–138

ction meanings of verbs, 8

ctive sentences vs. passive
   sentences, 256–257, 269

djectives
   and, 130
   be, A9
   commas, 130
   infinitives, 185, 189
   modifying nouns, 130
   order before nouns, A6
   precise, 134
   prepositions, A10

dverbs / adverb clauses and
   phrases (see also time clauses),
   366–368
   giving more information about
      main clauses, 376
   past perfect, 52–53
   present perfect, 32, 37
   present progressive, 4–5
   reducing, 371
   showing degrees of certainty,
      67
   simple past, 17, 20, 37, 53
   simple present, 4, 12
   subordinators, 368, 371, 373

few (of), 121, 141, 142

fter
   future events, 78
   -ing forms of the verb, 374
   past perfect, 53
   simple past, 20

gent in passive sentences, 256,
   263

great deal of, 141

little (of), 141

l (of), 141, 142, 148

lot (of), 141, 142, 147

lready, 32, 37, 83

so, 383, 384

although, 368, 374, 383

and, 130, 352, 356–357, 363, 364
   and . . . either, 361
   and neither, 361
   and . . . not, 361
   and so . . . , 360
   and . . . too, 360

another, 155–156, 162

anybody / anyone, 158, 161, 284

anything, 158

anywhere, 158

appositives, 315, 319, A14
   commas, 315

articles
   definite, 137, 138
   indefinite, 137–138
   omission of, 138

as, 368

as a result (of), 380, 384

as soon as, 20, 78

as well as, 380, 387

auxiliary verbs (see also modals
   and modal-like expressions)
   conjunctions, 356, 360, 361
   negative questions, 192, 199
   reducing sentences, 360, 361
   tag questions, 194, 199

be
   followed by adjectives and
      infinitives, A9
   future, 96
   irregular forms, A1
   passive sentences, 256–257,
      265, 270, 276, 279
   reducing sentences, 360
   relative clauses, 314, 315, 319,
      320
   simple present, 64
   stative verb, 8, 40, A2
   tag questions, 194
   time clauses, 371

be able to, 100–101, 104, A4

be allowed to, 96, 103, A3

because (of), 368, 374, 380

before
   future action, 83
   past perfect, 48, 53
   reduced clauses, 374
   simple past, 20
   time clauses, 78
   time of an event, 88

be going to, 62–63, 67–68, A15
   future events, 78
   future progressive, 70
   indirect speech, A11
   ongoing events, 79
   passive forms, A12
   vs. will, 67–68

be permitted to, A3

be required to, 96, 97, A3, A4

besides, 380

be supposed to, 96, 97, 103, A3

both, 363
   both . . . and, 352, 353, 364

but, 352, 356–357, 361, 364, 383

by
   after adjective, A10
   after verb, A9
   future action, 83
   introducing an agent in passive
      sentences, 256
   past perfect, 48
   reflexive pronouns, 152
   time of an event, 88

by the time, 53, 88

can / cannot / can't (see also could)
   indirect speech, A11
   modals, 96, 100–101, 104, 107,
      108, 113, 114, 118, A3, A4

can't have, 114, A4

certainly, 67, 70

clauses (*see* object relative clauses; relative clauses; subject relative clauses)

commas
  adjectives, 130
  adverb clauses, 368
  appositives, 315
  conjunctions, 356, 357, 363
  direct speech, 230
  identifying object relative clauses, 305
  identifying subject relative clauses, 284
  if clauses, 324, 327, 333
  nonidentifying object relative clauses, 301
  nonidentifying subject relative clauses, 288
  prepositional phrases, 380
  that clauses, 213
  time clauses, 20, 79
  too, 360
  transition words, 383

conditionals, real / unreal (*see* real conditionals; unreal conditionals)

conjunctions, 350–352
  auxiliary verbs, 356, 360, 361
  commas, 356, 357, 363
  coordinating, 352, 364, 383
  correlative, 352–353, 364
  modals, 356
  parallel structure, 364
  reducing sentences, 360–361

consequently, 384

coordinating conjunctions, 352, 364, 383

correlative conjunctions, 352–353, 364

could / could not / couldn't (*see also can*)
  conditionals, 338, A15
  direct speech, 234
  indirect speech, 234, A11
  modals, 92, 96, 104, 107, 108, 110, 111, 113, 114, 118, A3, A4

wishes, 345

could have / could not have / couldn't have
  conditionals, 342, A15
  modals, 101, 114

count nouns (*see also* nouns), 121
  definite articles, 137–138
  indefinite articles, 137–138
  quantifiers, 141–142

definite articles, 137, 138

definitely, 67, 70

despite, 380, 387

determiners
  show possession, 142
  usage, 121, 122

did not have to, 103

didn't use to, 24

direct questions, 223

direct speech, 228–230, 241

due to, 380

each other, 156

either
  reducing sentences, 361
  vs. *whether*, 225

even, 374
  even though, 368, 374

even if, 328

ever, 32

everybody / everyone, 148, 158, 161

everything, 158

everywhere, 158

few (of), 141

for
  after adjective, A10
  after verb, A9
  present perfect, 32, 33

for example, 384

for instance, 384

furthermore, 384

future, 62
  modals, A3–A4
  passive forms, A12

time clauses, 76–77, 78–79

future perfect, 76–77, 83–84
  passive forms, A12
  vs. future perfect progressive, 83, 88

future perfect progressive, 76, 83–84
  prepositions, 83
  time clauses, 83
  vs. future perfect, 83, 88

future progressive, 62, 70
  vs. *will*, 74

gerunds (*see also* -ing form of the verb), 164–166, 169–170, 173, 175–176
  after verbs, A7
  common fixed expressions, 17[?]
  expressions with, A8
  nouns + *of*, 173, 176
  object of preposition, 169, 175[?]
  object of sentence, 166
  passive sentences, 276
  prepositions, 175, 380, 387
  subject of sentence, 166, 175
  subject-verb agreement, 166, 175
  vs. infinitives, 183–184
  vs. present progressive, 166

get, passive sentences, 273–274, A1

had better (not), 92, A3

had to, 97

has / have (*see also* future perfect; past perfect; present perfect)
  forms, A1
  stative verb, 8, 40, A2

has / have to, 96, 97, 107, 108, A3, A4

however, 384

how long
  habitual action, 39
  present perfect progressive, 4[0]

how much / how many, 40, 217

identifying object relative clause[s] (*see also* object relative clause[s] relative clauses)

object of preposition, 303
vs. nonidentifying object
relative clauses, 300

entifying subject relative
clauses (*see also* relative
clauses; subject relative
clauses), 283–284, 297–298
commas, 284, 305
subject-verb agreement, 284
vs. nonidentifying subject
relative clauses, 287–288

clauses
commas, 324, 327, 333
conditionals, A15
future real conditionals,
327–328, 333, 334
future unreal conditionals,
337–338
indirect questions, 245–246,
251
noun clauses, 220–221, 223,
226
past perfect, 347
past progressive, 338
past unreal conditionals,
341–342, 347, 348
present real conditionals,
323–324, 333, 334
present unreal conditionals,
337–338, 347
questions, 324, 333
real conditions with modals
and modal-like expressions,
330
. . . not, in real conditions, 328

mperatives
future real conditions, 330
indirect, 248–249, 251
present real conditions, 330

after adjective, A10
after verb, A9
present perfect, 33

addition (to), 380, 383, 384, 387
contrast, 384
definite articles, 137–138

indefinite pronouns, 158
indirect imperatives
infinitives, 248, 251
requests and advice, 248–249
indirect questions, 223, 244,
245–246, 252, A10
indirect speech, 228–229, 233–
234
reporting verbs, 242
tense shifting, 233–234, A11
without tense shifting, 236
infinitives, 178–179
after adjectives, 185, 189, A9
after nouns, 185
after verbs, 179–180, 189, A7
after verbs + objects, 180, A8
indirect imperatives, 248, 251
negative, 188
not with *if*, 221
passive sentences, 276–277
reduced noun clauses, 218
vs. gerunds, 183–184
with *whether*, 221
information questions, 245
-ing form of the verb (*see also*
gerunds), 2
adverb clauses, 371
future progressive, 70, 76, 79,
83, 87, 88
modals and modal-like
expressions, 117
past perfect progressive, 46,
56, 59
present perfect progressive,
30–31, 39–40, 42, 43
present progressive, 3, 4–5, 8,
13, 14, 16, 18, 20, 21, 27, 63
reduced clauses, 374
relative clauses, 314
used as a noun, 165
in order to, 373
in spite of, 380, 383, 387
instead (of), 380, 384
intransitive verbs, 260–261
irregular verbs, A1–A2
just, 32

likely, 67, 70, 110
little (of), 141, 148
many (of), 121, 141, 148
may (not)
indirect speech, A11
modals, 96, 107, 108, 110, 111,
113, 114, 118, A3, A4
may (not) have, 114, A4
maybe, 67
measurement words, 126, A5
might (not)
indirect speech, 234, A11
modals, 92, 107, 108, 110, 111,
113, 114, A3, A4
real conditionals, A15
unreal conditionals, 338, A15
might (not) have, 114, 342, A4, A15
might (not) want to, 92
modals and modal-like
expressions (*see also* auxiliary
verbs), 90–91, 92–93, 106,
A3–A4
conjunctions, 356
expressing ability, 100–101,
104
expressing advice and regret,
92–93, 103, 104
expressing future probability,
110–111
expressing past probability,
113–114
expressing permission,
necessity, and obligations,
96–97
expressing present probability,
107–108
expressing probability, 106,
107–108, 110–111
future time, A3
indirect imperatives, 248
negative questions, 192
past participles, 113
past time, A3
present time, A3
progressive verbs, 111
real conditions, 330

tag questions, 194
  unreal conditionals, 338
  wishes, 345
modifying nouns, 120, 130
moreover, 384
most (of), 142
most likely, 63
must (not)
  future probability, 117
  modals, 96, 97, 107, 108, 113,
    114, A3, A4
must (not) have, 114, A4
need (to)
  modals, 96, 97, A3
  stative verb, 8, A2
negative infinitives, 188
negative questions, 190–192
  answering, 192, 199
neither, 361
  neither . . . nor, 352, 353, 364
never, 32
nobody, 148, 158
non-action verbs (*see also* stative
  verbs), 8, A2
noncount nouns (*see also* nouns),
  120–123, A5
  definite articles, 137–138
  quantifiers, 141–142
  singular vs. plural, 133
  used as count nouns, 126
none of / no, 141, 142, 148
nonidentifying object relative
  clauses (*see also* object relative
  clauses; relative clauses),
  300–301
  commas, 301
  vs. identifying object relative
    clauses, 300
nonidentifying subject relative
  clauses (*see also* relative
  clauses; subject relative
  clauses), 287–288
  commas, 288
  vs. identifying subject relative
    clauses, 287–288

no one, 148, 158, 161
not a lot of, 141, 142
not any (of), 141, 142, 148
nothing, 158
not many (of), 141, 148
not much (of), 141
not only . . . but also, 352, 353, 364
not . . . until, 78
not yet, 32
noun clauses, 216–217
  if / whether, 220–221, 223, 225,
    226
  wh- words, 217–218, 225, 226
nouns (*see also* count nouns;
  noncount nouns), 120
  count, 121, 137–138
  infinitives, 185
  irregular plurals, 122
  modifying, 120, 130
  noncount, 121, 122–123, 126,
    137–138, A5
  plural forms only, 122
  precise, 134
  same singular and plural forms,
    122
  singular vs. plural, 121
nowhere, 158
object pronouns vs. reflexive
  pronouns, 152
object relative clauses (*see also*
  identifying object relative
  clauses; nonidentifying object
  relative clauses; relative
  clauses), 296–297
  background information, 306
  condense information, 306
  objects of prepositions,
    302–303
objects
  in passive sentences, 260–261,
    266
  of prepositions in object
    relative clauses, 302–303
  used with infinitives, 180, A8

once
  future, 88
  simple past, 20
  time clauses, 78
one, 162
one another, 156, 162
on the other hand, 384, 387
or, 352, 356–357, 364
  or not, 220
other(s), 155–156, 161
ought (not) to, 92, 107, 108, 110,
  111, 234, A3, A4
ought to have, 92, A3
participles, past (*see* past
  participles)
passive, 254–256, 263, 266, ,
  268–269
  agent, 256, 263
  be, 270, 276, 279
  be going to, 269–270, A12
  by + agent, 256
  common verbs, 257, 261
  future perfect, A12
  gerunds, 276
  get, 273–274
  infinitives, 276–277
  intransitive verbs, 260–261
  modals, 269–270
  objects, 260–261, 266
  past forms, 256–257
  past participles, 256–257, 261,
    265, 270, 273, 276, 279
  past perfect, 257, A12
  past progressive, 257, A12
  present forms, 256, 257
  present perfect, 256, 257, A12
  present progressive, 256, 257,
    A12
  questions, A12
  relative clauses, 314
  simple future, A12
  simple past, 257, A12
  simple present, 256, 257, A12
  transitive verbs, 260–261
  vs. active sentences, 256–257,
    269, A12

st
modals, A3
that clauses, 207–208
unreal conditionals, 341–342
vs. present forms of verbs, 28

st participles
conditionals, A15
irregulars, A1–A2
modals and modal-like
    expressions, 92–93, 101, 103,
    113
passive sentences, 256–257,
    261, 265, 270, 273, 276, 279
reducing sentences, 360
relative clauses, 314

st perfect, 46–48
background information, 48,
    59, 60
common verbs, 49
completed actions, 59
conditionals, A15
passive sentences, 257, A12
reducing adverb clauses, 371
reducing sentences, 360
time clauses, 52–53
vs. simple past, 48

st perfect progressive, 46, 56
background information,
    56, 59

st progressive, 16–18
background activities, 18
conditionals, A15
describing an ongoing action,
    21
if clauses, 338
indirect speech, A11
passive sentences, 257, A12
reducing sentences, 360
reducing time clauses, 371
stative verbs, 18
time clauses, 20, 21
two actions in the same clause,
    21
vs. simple past, 18

rhaps, 67

rmitted to, 96

personal pronouns vs. reciprocal
    pronouns, 156
possession with determiners, 142
prepositions and prepositional
    expressions, 378–380, 383
after adjectives, A10
after verbs, A9
commas, 380
future perfect progressive, 83
past perfect, 48
relative clauses, 315, A13–A14
supporting an argument, 388
present (*see also* simple present),
    322–323
if clauses, 323–324, 333, 334
imperatives, 330
modals, A3
that clauses, 207
vs. past forms of verbs, 28
present perfect, 30–33
adverbs, 32, 37
completed actions, 40, 42
habitual actions, 39
indirect speech, A11
passive sentences, 256, 257,
    A12
reducing adverb clauses, 371
reducing sentences, 360
stative verbs, 40
time clauses/expressions, 32,
    78
vs. present perfect progressive,
    39–40, 42, 43
vs. simple past, 36–37, 43
present perfect progressive,
    30–31
habitual actions, 39
ongoing actions, 40, 42
vs. present perfect, 39–40, 42,
    43
vs. simple past, 43
present progressive, 2, 4–5, 62–63
adverbs, 4–5
expressing ongoing events, 79
indirect speech, A11
passive sentences, 256, 257,
    A12

reducing sentences, 360
reducing time clauses, 371
relative clauses, 314
stative verbs, 8, A2
vs. gerunds, 166
vs. simple present, 3–4
probability with modals and
    modal-like expressions, 106,
    107–108, 110–111
probably, 63, 67, 70, 110
pronouns, 150, 162
avoiding repetition, 162
emphasis, 162
hedging, 148
indefinite, 158, 161
other/another, 155–156
reciprocal, 156, 162
reflexive, 151–152, 161
relative, 283–284, 297–298,
    301, 302–303, 314–315
punctuation (*see* commas;
    quotation marks; semicolons)
quantifiers, 141
absolute, 148
count nouns, 141–142
hedging, 148
noncount nouns, 141–142
use/non-use of *of*, 142
questions
direct, 223
indirect, 223, 244, 245–246,
    252, A10
information, 245
negative, 190–191
passive forms, A12
tag, 190–191
yes/no, 245, 251
quite a few (of), 141, 148
quotation marks
in direct speech, 230, 241
real conditionals
future, 327–328, 330, 333, 334
modals, 330
present, 323–324, 330, 334
recently, 32

reciprocal pronouns, 156, 162
 vs. personal pronouns, 156
reduced relative clauses (*see also*
 relative clauses)
 appositives, 315
 clarification, 320
 participle phrases, 314
 prepositional phrases, 315
reducing adverb clauses, 371
reducing sentences, 360–361
reducing time clauses, 371
reflexive pronouns, 151–152
 by, 152
 common verbs, 152
 imperative, 152
 position, 152
 vs. object pronouns, 152
relative clauses (*see also*
 identifying object relative
 clauses; identifying subject
 relative clauses; nonidentifying
 object relative clauses;
 nonidentifying subject relative
 clauses; object relative clauses;
 reduced relative clauses;
 subject relative clauses),
 308–309
 identifying vs. nonidentifying,
 A13–A14
 present participles in, 314
 reduced, 314–315, 320
 when, 310
 where, 310, 311
relative pronouns, 283–284,
 297–298, 301–303, 314–315
 object relative clauses,
 297–298, 301, 302–303
 omission of, 314–315
 reduced relative clauses,
 314–315
 subject relative clauses,
 283–284
 verb agreement, 284
reporting verbs, 236, 238, 242,
 A11
say, 233, 238, 242, 248, A1

semicolons, 383
should (not), *shouldn't*
 indirect imperatives, 248
 modals, 92, 93, 107–108,
 110–111, 248, A3, A4
 probability, 107–108, 110–111,
 A3, A4
should (not) have, *shouldn't have*,
 92, 93, A3
simple past, 16–18
 adverbs, 17, 20, 37
 completed past actions, 24,
 25, 36
 conditionals, A15
 indirect speech, A11
 irregular verbs, A1–A2
 passive sentences, 257
 reducing adverb clauses, 371
 reducing time clauses, 371
 stative verbs, 18
 time clauses, 20–21, 53
 vs. past perfect, 48
 vs. past progressive, 18
 vs. present perfect, 36–37, 43
 vs. present perfect progressive,
 43
simple present (*see also* present),
 2, 4, 12, 64
 adverbs, 4, 12
 conditionals, A15
 expressing an action that
 interrupts another action, 79
 if clauses, 323, 327
 indirect speech, A11
 passive sentences, 256, 257,
 A12
 reducing time clauses, 371
 special meanings, 12
 stative verbs, 8
 time clauses, 78, 83
 vs. present progressive, 3–4
 writing about present time
 situations, 14
since, 32, 33, 368
so, 356, 357, 361, 373, 383, 384
 so that, 373
so far, 32

some (of), 121, 141, 142
somebody / someone, 158, 284
something, 158, 284
somewhere, 158
speech, direct (*see* direct speech)
speech, indirect (*see* indirect
 speech)
stative verbs, 8, A2
 future perfect, 84
 future perfect progressive, 84
 present perfect, 40
 simple past vs. past
 progressive, 18
still, 32
subject relative clauses (*see also*
 identifying subject relative
 clauses; nonidentifying subje
 relative clauses; relative
 clauses), 282–283, 293
 avoiding repetition, 293
 whose, 290–291
subject-verb agreement
 gerunds, 166
 identifying subject relative
 clauses, 284
 present perfect, 42
subordinators, 379
 adverb clauses, 368
 combining sentences, 383
 expressing purpose, 373
 reducing adverb clauses, 371
tag questions, 190–191, 194–19
 affirmative vs. negative, 195
 answering, 195
tell, 251, A1
 indirect imperatives, 248–249
 infinitives, 248
 passive, 261
 reporting verb, 238, 242
that, 284, 287, 293, 298, 301, 303
 305, A13–A14
 identifying object relative
 clauses, 298, 303, A13
 identifying subject relative
 clauses, 284, A13

nonidentifying object relative clauses, 301, 303, A13
nonidentifying subject relative clauses, 287, A13
reduced relative clauses, 314
that clauses, 202–204, 207–208, 214
  after adjectives, 210
  after nouns, 210–211
  commas, 213
  indirect speech, 233
  past verbs, 207–208
  present verbs, 207
  wishes, A15
wishes, 305
e, 121, 122, 137–138
en, 324, 383, 384
erefore, 383, 384
se, 121
s, 121
ose, 121
ough, 368
us, 384
e clauses / expressions / phrases / words (*see also* adverbs)
  commas, 20, 79
  future, 78–79
  future perfect progressive, 83
  past perfect, 52–53
  past progressive, 21
  present perfect, 32, 78
  reducing, 371
  simple past, 17, 20–21, 53
  simple present, 78, 83
  unreal conditionals, 338

after adjective, A10
after verb, A9
expressing purpose, 373
preposition vs. infinitive, 188
o, 360, 361, 363
ansition words, 378–379, 382–384
  commas, 383
  common phrases, 383–384

semicolons, 383
supporting an argument, 388
transitive verbs, 260–261
unless, in real conditions, 328
unreal conditionals, 336–337 A15
  future, 337–338
  modals, 338
  present, 337–338
until
  past perfect, 48, 53
  simple past, 20
  time clauses, 78
use / used to, 24, 27
verbs
  followed by gerunds, A7
  followed by infinitives, 179–180, 189, A7, A8
  followed by objects, A8
  followed by prepositions, A9
  intransitive, 260–261
  irregular, A1–A2
  non-action, 8, A2
  reflexive, A6
  reporting, 236, 238, 242, A11
  stative, 8, A2
  transitive, 260–261
want
  followed by infinitives, 180, 188, 277, A7
  followed by objects, 180, 188, A7
  stative verb, 8, A2
was / were able to (*see also can; could*), 101
wh- words
  indirect questions, 245
  noun clauses, 217–218, 226
what, 217–218, 305
  noun clauses, 217–218
when, 218
  adverb clauses, 368
  expressing ongoing events, 79
  future real conditionals, 333
  if clauses, 324
  noun clauses, 218
  past perfect, 53

  past progressive, 21
  reduced adverb clauses, 374
  relative clauses, 310, 311, 318, A14
  simple past, 20, 21
  simple present, 79
  time clauses, 78
  vs. *while* in the past, 21
whenever, *if* clauses, 324
where
  noun clauses, 218
  relative clauses, 310, 311, 319, A14
whereas, 374
whether
  noun clauses, 220–221, 226
  vs. *either*, 225
which
  noun clauses, 218
  object relative clauses, 298, 301, 303, A13
  reduced relative clauses, 314
  relative clauses, 310, 311
  subject relative clauses, 284, 287, A13
while
  adverb clauses, 368
  expressing ongoing events, 79
  past progressive, 21
  reduced adverb clauses, 374
  simple present, 79
  vs. *when* in the past, 21
who / whom
  noun clauses, 218
  object relative clauses, 298, 301, 302–303, A13
  reduced relative clauses, 314
  subject relative clauses, 284, 287, A13
who's, vs. *whose*, 293
whose
  object relative clauses, 298, 301, A13
  subject relative clauses, 290–291, A13
  vs. *who's*, 293

will (not) / won't
  expressing ongoing events, 79
  future, 67, 78
  future perfect, 87
  future progressive, 70
  indirect speech, A11
  modals, 96, A4
  predictions and expectations, 67
  probability, 110
  quick decisions, 68

requests, offers, and promises, 67
  vs. *be going to*, 67–68
  vs. future progressive, 74
wishes, 345, A15
would
  conditionals, 338, A15
  describing past events, 24, 25, 27
  expressing wishes, 345, A15

tense shifting in indirect speech, A11
would have, 342, A15
yes / *no* questions, 245, 251
yet
  coordinating conjunctions, 356, 357
  present perfect, 32, 36
  simple past, 36

Art Credits

Illustration
Shelton Leong: 62, 116, 164, 346; **Maria Rabinky:** 261; **Monika Roe:** 6, 90, 193, 308, 309; **Rob Schuster:** 139, 225, 322

Photography